XML: A PRIMER

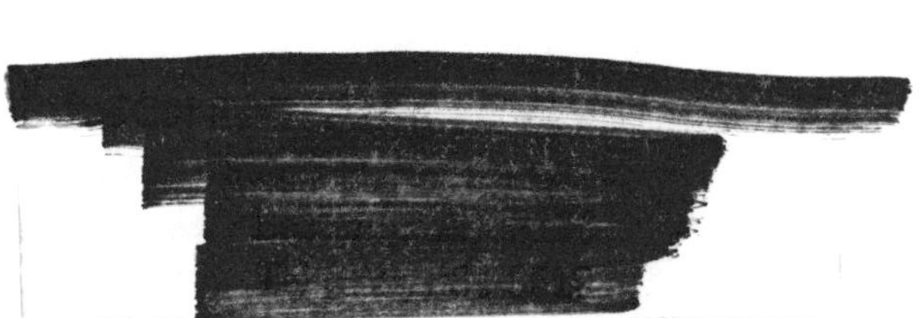

XML: A PRIMER

SIMON ST. LAURENT

MIS:Press
An imprint of IDG Books Worldwide
An International Data Group Company
919 E. Hillsdale Blvd.
Suite 400
Foster City, CA 94404
www.idgbooks.com
www.mispress.com

Printed in the United States of America

First Edition—1998

Library of Congress Cataloging-in-Publication Data

St. Laurent, Simon.
XML: a primer / Simon St. Laurent.
p. cm.
ISBN 1-55828-592-X
1. XML (Document markup language) I. Title.
QA76.76.H94S72 1997
005.7'2--dc21 97-45820
CIP

For sales inquiries and special prices for bulk quantities, please contact our Sales department at 415-655-3200 or write to the address above.

10 9 8 7 6 5 4 3 2 1

Associate Publisher: *Paul Farrell*

Editor: *Ann Lush*
Technical Editor: *Steven Champeon*
Managing Editor: *Shari Chappell*

Production Editor: *Kitty May*
Copy Edit Manager: *Karen Tongish*
Copy Editor: *Sara Black*

For Tracey, who makes my world sparkle.

ACKNOWLEDGMENTS

I'd like to thank my technical editor, Steven Champeon, for helping me sort out the sordid details of SGML, HTML, and XML, making this book far clearer as well as more accurate. He was a much-needed partner in a number of battles. Tracey Cranston read the opening chapters to make sure they stayed intelligible, kept me excited about XML, and made the process far smoother by smiling at me regularly. Ann Lush, my editor, got me excited about XML in the first place, got the proposal through a number of obstacles, and helped keep me sane throughout the process. I'd also like to thank Sara Black for making my prose clearer and Kitty May for presenting it so well. My mother helped keep the writing moving with regular shipments of cookies, for which I'm very grateful.

CONTENTS IN BRIEF

CONTENTS

INTRODUCTION

XML, to a certain extent, is HTML (Hypertext Markup Language) done right. XML (eXtensible Markup Language) offers a unique combination of flexibility, simplicity, and readability by both humans and machines. HTML developers who have spent years cursing the strange formatting quirks of HTML and the extreme difficulty of converting anything *from* HTML are in for a treat. XML gives developers the ability to create and manipulate their own tags and works smoothly with Cascading Style Sheets to allow developers to create pages that are as elegantly presented as they are structured. Programmers can build simple parsers to read XML data (or, better, reuse parsers built by others), making it an excellent format for interchanging data.

If you're an HTML developer who's interested in XML you're in the right place. This book attempts to explain XML in terms that any reasonably experienced HTML developer can understand. Although some of the concepts may be difficult, XML itself is really quite approachable. Unlike the Standard Generalized Markup Language (SGML), its behemoth predecessor, XML uses a reasonably concise syntax that can provide developers with an enormous amount of power—without the learning curve associated with SGML. Although XML is, in a sense, SGML-lite, I've done my best to avoid describing XML from an SGML perspective.

Because much of the best literature (and experience) available on creating document type definitions and using marked-up documents has come from the SGML community, I've pointed out some of the many differences between SGML and XML. If you don't know or care about SGML, you can safely ignore all such information. Still, it won't hurt to learn a bit about SGML, if you have the time and interest.

I have great hopes for XML. XML seems to me the best tool for accomplishing great things with markup, a significant improvement on both HTML and SGML. It has more flexibility than HTML, without the mind-numbing complexity of SGML. XML holds out the promise of markup that both humans and machines can interpret, making it easy for developers to debug their documents and for programmers to build systems around them. Although the "paperless office" has been just over the horizon for the last 20 years, XML, in combination with ubiquitous networking, may finally provide the tools needed to make it a reality. (Don't hold your breath, though; old habits die very slowly.) The simplicity of XML makes it useful for small projects, whereas its clear structures make it useful for larger projects. XML can be massaged, manipulated, processed, fragmented, and rebuilt far more easily than previous formats.

Unfortunately, at press time, there aren't many tools available that work with XML. This book has been written around some of the few tools available—Tim Bray's Lark, Microsoft's MSXML, Norbert Mikula's NXP, and Peter Murray-Rust's Jumbo, all of which deserve praise as bold pioneers. James Clark's NSGMLSU (part of his SP package) deserves honorable mention as a powerful parser, albeit one from the more staid world of SGML. The two leading browsers, Microsoft's Internet Explorer and Netscape Communicator, offer feeble support for XML and no support, respectively. Nonetheless, both companies have made public commitments to providing support and hopefully will make good on those commitments in reasonably short order.

This book definitely focuses on hand-coding XML. Although I certainly hope that hand-coding will be quickly replaced by rapidly evolving tools, hand-coded XML will be around for a short while at least. It took a while for the HTML toolset to grow, and undoubtedly XML will have its growing pains as well. Even though many SGML tools are available and can be applied to XML development, their price ranges and target market seem to stay well above the broader audience for XML. With time, prices will fall, and tools will become more powerful, just as they have in every other area of computing.

This book is a primer and not a complete guide to all things XML. The document type definitions need applications built around them for them to be useful, and most of the tools presented can give only a basic idea of XML's potential. I fully expect that "graduates" of this book will be eager to move on to the next great thing. With any luck, those graduates (and people who have read other books as well) will spread the word about XML, building an XML community as rich and varied as the HTML community is now.

CHAPTER 1

Let Data Be Data

XML promises to transform the basic structure of the Web, moving beyond HTML and replacing it with a stronger, more extensible architecture. It promises to return the Web to content-based structures instead of the format-based structures imposed by designers frustrated by the immaturity of Web design tools. It may also free the Web from the tyranny of browser developers by ending their monopoly on element development and implementation.

The World Wide Web Consortium (W3C) has moved ahead of the commercial browser developers with a very promising new approach to markup. XML, the eXtensible Markup Language, makes it possible for developers to create their own mutually interoperable dialects of markup languages, including but not limited to HTML. This could bring about a cease-fire in the browser wars between Netscape and Microsoft as added features shift to a component model from browser code. More immediately, it allows developers to create markup structures based on logical content rather than formatting. That will make it easier for humans and computers to search for specific content-based information on pages instead of just searching the entire text of a page. XML, in concert with Cascading Style Sheets (CSS), should allow developers to create beautiful pages that are easily managed.

The WYSIWYG Disaster

The first word processor I used was a very simple text editor. I thought it was really amazing how the screen could move around my cursor point to make my 40-column screen display most of an 80-column page, but for the most part it was only good for doing homework and writing other similarly boring documents that I printed out on my lovely dot-matrix printer. After working with computers for a few years, programming them and cursing them, I gave up and bought an electric typewriter. It let me do some pretty fancy things, like underline text without having to enter bizarre escape codes. There wasn't a good way to type boldface text, but I didn't have to worry about wasting acres of paper because of a typo in code. The typewriter gave me what-you-see-is-what-you-get (WYSIWYG) in a classical ink-on-paper kind of way.

I stuck with my typewriter for a couple of years, until I discovered the Macintosh. I'd hated the Mac when it first came out, because every magazine I got covered an expensive machine I didn't own. It didn't even have a decent programming package. But when I encountered the Mac again about four years later, I was thrilled. It was actually fun to write papers, because I could toggle all the style information, write in multiple columns, and even use 72-point type once in a while. It didn't look very good on my Imagewriter, but it was pretty amazing compared to my old dot-matrix computer text. I turned in papers with headlines, bibliographies that used proper italics, multiple columns, and even a picture or two. Writing wasn't just about spewing out sentences anymore. I could create headlines, subheads, tables, footnotes, and use all kinds of other formatting to give even a short paper a set of structures that made it look smart. Using styles made it even easier: apply a set of formatting tools once, then call it up as a named set. It seemed like magic.

Ten years later I still format my documents with headings and subheads. Fortunately, I'm not as concerned about footnotes, but I've developed a new problem: it's hard to reuse my old documents. When I was writing papers for a grade it didn't matter very much—I wrote the paper, turned it in, and never thought about it again. Now I spend my days working with piles of information written years ago by people thousands of miles away, and converting the files into the same word processing format is the least of my worries. Instead of editing material, I frequently find myself spending hours reformatting it, and not because I love doing so. A whole generation that grew up abusing tabs and spaces has created documents that can't be cut and pasted into other documents because everything breaks. Line breaks come out totally wrong, text gets shoved to the left or right, tables collapse, and even simple things like spacing cause problems. The same magic formatting that made it so easy to create documents that looked exactly the way they should is now creating massive problems.

There are other, more subtle problems as well. All those years when I thought I was creating headlines and subheads, I wasn't really. I was creating text that was formatted like a headline. I might even have called the style "headline", but to the computer it was just another collection of letters with no intrinsic meaning. WYSIWYG changed people, too. People who probably shouldn't have been allowed to graduate from a fifth-grade art class started using 30 fonts on a page. After the novelty wore off, many of them adopted a more conservative approach to formatting but always with the declared intention of making their documents look precisely the way they wanted them. Designers became accustomed to specifying placement to thousandths of an inch—as though anyone can see differences measured in such a small increment.

Before WYSIWYG, documents were undoubtedly ugly, but they had a few other virtues that went unnoticed. There were moves afoot to create document management and document markup systems that would allow computers to efficiently manage large libraries of documents. Plain text, dull though it may be, is much easier to manage than the output of the average word processor or desktop publishing program. These document management tools were also very new in the early days of WYSIWYG, and they didn't become affordable or readily available until long after users had become accustomed to systems based on paper-based media. The final printout of a document always remained the final goal of most of the design programs on the market.

The HTML Explosion

When the World Wide Web first received widespread attention in 1994, a small army of amateur and professional designers set out to create the most exciting pages they could. Many left quickly, disappointed by the dearth of HTML formatting tools. The strange differences between browsers made it difficult to predict what any page would look like, and corporate users demanded a level of control over their electronic documents that was similar to the control they had over paper documents. For a while, these complaints nearly throttled HTML development. Like many Internet technologies before it, HTML was spread by enthusiasts who were building pages for fun, not for hire. It was simple enough to learn in a day or two, and it offered a whole new reading and authoring experience. The momentum generated by these early enthusiasts and the press coverage they received gave HTML the potential to become the next big thing.

For the Web to become an economically viable marketplace, however, it had to change. Designers and customers wanted to be able to create pages that looked exactly the way they wanted them, and they wanted to have a level of control comparable to that provided by the average desktop publishing system. The Web still isn't at that level for the average user, but the tools have become a lot more convenient. Web design has become a specialty of designers and communications specialists the world over, making it possible for companies and individuals to post complex if not always visually pleasing sites.

Tables were a huge step forward. They made it possible to create documents that bore some resemblance to the traditional grid systems used in many print designs. Continuing improvements in image map technology made it easy for frustrated designers to create their own point-and-click interfaces when HTML just couldn't produce what they needed. Frames and pop-up windows let developers focus on elements instead of having to rebuild entire screens of information every time they wanted to change something.

The <FONT> tag made it possible to specify text presentation much more precisely than structure-based formatting had allowed. The escalating competition between Microsoft and Netscape added all kinds of tools to the palette as the companies fought for market share and mind share. Netscape created <BLINK>, and Microsoft countered with <MARQUEE>. Both companies created extensions to the elements and the attributes of HTML, frustrating the W3C and confusing developers. Worse still, neither company implemented tags in exactly the same way. Spacing varied, colors could change, and carefully aligned elements would scatter across the page.

At the same time, the number of pages on the Web was exploding. Sites routinely grew to include 10,000 pages or more, organized loosely in hierarchical schemes concocted by developers who knew little about hypertext and less about organization. Many sites were organized according to chaotic directory structures built by developers who were used to the structures of FTP archives and gopher sites, the predecessors of the Web. Large sites presented difficulties to the managers who had to keep up with them and the users who attempted to read them. Navigating hypertext was a strange art form all its own, a blend of organizational skill, memory, good design, and sheer luck. Search engines arrived to help users find their way, but it quickly became clear that librarians could never keep up with the explosive growth of this new medium.

Automated tools appeared as crawlers, and robots began searching the enormous swamp of Web documents. Some merely indexed titles, whereas more sophisticated ones began to index the entire contents of a page. AltaVista, a search engine created by Digital to demonstrate and promote its Alpha processor, brought a brute force approach to the Web, applying multiple processors that shared gigabytes of memory and enormous bandwidth to indexing the Web. Although AltaVista and the other search engines can and do provide a service, they work on the broadest of criteria: the complete contents of a document. We've managed to confer a lot of intelligence on search engines, even letting them identify languages and handle word forms, but we're still a very long way from teaching them to read, categorize, and organize documents without us having to specify which part is what.

This combination of volume and increasing complexity of formatting has led developers to wonder if there might be a better way. HTML has come a long way, quickly, but the limitations of a markup language designed for formatting are beginning to chafe. As the browser wars continue, designers are beginning to demand an alternative to letting the browser determine the presentation of individual tags. The limitations of search engines become more apparent every time the Web doubles in size. Finally, as the Web grows more omnipresent, the limitations of HTML for presenting information that doesn't easily fit the standard text and graphics model are becoming more pressing. Developers need to be able to create their own tags, and they need to be able to do so in a way that works with other people's browsers.

Back to the Origins: Structure and SGML

When Tim Berners-Lee created HTML in 1991, he based it on a more powerful but vastly more complex markup language called SGML, the Standard Generalized Markup Language. SGML had been around in various forms for 20 years, but its complexity had hobbled its adoption by organizations outside of publishing, government, and large-scale information processing. SGML markup, management, and processing was a specialized skill, mastered by a small group of government, corporate, and academic users.

Developers who complain that the HTML standards are developing too slowly should look back at the tortured pace of SGML's development. First conceived in the late 1960s, the Generalized Markup Language (GML) was created at IBM in 1969 by researchers coincidentally named Goldfarb, Mosher, and Lorris.

Charles Goldfarb went on to chair the American National Standards Institute (ANSI) committee on Computer Languages for the Processing of Text in 1978, after GML had become an important standard in publishing. In 1980, the committee released its first working draft, and by 1983 the sixth working draft was adopted by users including the Internal Revenue Service and Department of Defense, which mandated that its largest contractors use SGML as well. In 1984, the committee expanded into a group of collaborating committees developing standards for the International Organization for Standardization (ISO) as well as ANSI. In 1986, eight years into the standards process, SGML became ISO 8879:1986. Work on SGML continues, of course. A group of committees evaluates changes regularly, including projects on scripted style sheets, multimedia, link extensions, and a variety of document management issues.

Unlike HTML, SGML doesn't specify how text should be presented. SGML is not a formatting language, nor even a particular markup language. SGML is a specification that allows people to create their own markup languages. It specifies content identifiers that make it easy to format text consistently and which allow document management systems to locate information quickly. SGML is well-suited for projects that involve large quantities of similarly structured data, such as catalogs, manuals, listings, transcripts, and statistical abstracts. SGML is a favorite of the federal government, as well as IBM and other large companies. It makes it easy for a centralized team to develop specifications for data structures, to create a Document Type Definition (DTD) that can then be applied to documents throughout the organization.

More importantly in many cases, documents created with SGML are easy to port to different formats. Because SGML uses content-based markup rather than format-based markup, it's easy to change the formatting rules depending on whether a document is being output to a dot-matrix line printer, a laser printer, a four-color press, a CD-ROM, a Web site, or even audio speakers. Design teams determine formatting that can work with or follow up the work of the original DTD designers to present information in different styles that are appropriate to particular output media. Computerized storage systems can also treat the documents as small databases, querying them with searches based on content tags and index information. Companies that use the same information repeatedly —for proposals, for instance—can benefit greatly from having prefabricated text ready to be dropped into new documents. It doesn't make the writing any better, but it does make it easier to find.

HTML: Decaf SGML?

Most of what SGML contributed to HTML was syntax: a markup language that used the now familiar <TAG ATTRIBUTE=VALUE> Content here </TAG> style. Some of SGML's intent to separate content from formatting survived as well, as evidenced by the wildly divergent interpretations of common tags by different browsers. By describing elements with terms like <EM> for emphasis and <ADDRESS> for address information, Berners-Lee created a simple formatting language that was flexible enough to handle many different kinds of information. The <H1> through <H6> tags spoke of levels of headings, providing a somewhat natural structure to documents. The <HEAD> and <BODY> tags separated meta-information (the <TITLE>, at first) from the visible text of a document. Most important, the <A HREF="destination.html"> anchor tags provided a simple yet powerful structure for hypertext links.

HTML did a wonderful job of simplifying SGML and putting markup into the hands of amateurs, a necessary move for broadening markup's appeal. Ironically, Tim Berners-Lee never really intended for users to have to enter codes by hand. The initial experiments at CERN used a simple markup processor that managed the codes invisibly. While HTML remained a small collection of tags with only a few attributes, this friendly model made it easy for authors to get started using the Web to exchange papers and share information.

As we've seen, however, HTML was ill-suited to a world that had been spoiled by the control WYSIWYG tools had already given designers. Although it was clear that hyperlinks and the Web's incredible ease of use were good things, there were rumblings from the start about what these academics had done to create a useless formatting language. At the beginning of the browser wars, it was clear that HTML's extremely simple formatting tools were not going to be accepted in the long run by designers and developers who wanted to create documents on the Web that were as detailed (allowing for screen resolution) as documents on paper. The inherent flexibility of simple standards lacked appeal. Tags whose sole duty was formatting sprawled across the HTML landscape, with <B> and <I> and eventually <FONT> receiving much more use than <EM> or <ADDRESS>. Designers hand-crafted HTML, mixing and matching tags to achieve the precise appearance they wanted without regard to document structure. Because the HTML tags were used only to specify formatting, with no alternative formatting structures, HTML was doomed to life as a formatting language instead of a structured framework for documents. All the problems categorized earlier began to grow, springing from fundamental flaws in the originally brilliant nature of HTML.

Using SGML to Leapfrog HTML

The creators of the original standards and their successor organization, the W3C, scrambled to catch up for a while. "Netscape extensions" provided designers with controls that the early versions of HTML had lacked and fueled the phenomenal growth of Netscape. Only recently has the W3C caught up to the browser developers and cut them off at the pass, with the next set of powerful standards. Cascading Style Sheets was the first blow. CSS made it possible for designers to declare their formatting intentions for a document without having to cook up a tortured mix of tags and graphics. CSS frees tags from the burden of carrying formatting information and permits them to carry content information once again.

XML emphasizes the importance of that content information by making it possible for designers to create and manage their own sets of tags. Designers can apply this in concert with CSS to create tags that produce formatting if they like, but the main emphasis is on managing content, including hypertext links, which received enhanced specifications. XML arose from the concerns of the SGML working group at the W3C, which felt that HTML was heading in the wrong direction. Rather than propose a replacement, they proposed ways to allow developers to extend HTML, maintaining backward compatibility while moving forward with more manageable techniques. XML provides a subset of SGML functionality rather than just a set of tags that use SGML syntax. It remains a simplification (and there is some grumbling from SGML users about how gross a simplification it may be), but it promises to restore the initial promise of HTML, adding a little more complexity in an attempt to simplify the complicated mess that determined the current state of Web page creation.

In this book, we'll take a close look at the tools XML provides and how developers can apply them to common tasks. HTML developers should find much of the information familiar, although much of the content (creating DTDs, for instance) will be fairly alien. This book isn't targeted at SGML developers, but readers familiar with SGML should find many familiar concepts integrated with the wilder world of the Web. Although the book focuses on creating documents with XML, we'll also cover techniques for managing XML and integrating it with other Web technologies. XML may seem abstract at first, but its practical implications should become more evident as you proceed through the book and try the examples. We'll see how XML documents can be used as databases even though they are very unlike the previous generations of strictly hierarchical or tabular structures, and we'll explore the new architectures XML makes possible.

CHAPTER 2

HTML and CSS: WYSIWYG Pages

Before we move on to XML, let's examine HTML. Although I pointed out HTML's inadequacies in the previous chapter, HTML has popularized markup languages, and its existing structures deserve a full examination. By looking at HTML from the perspective of XML, you should understand what's to come without being too put off by the brave new world of XML. Cascading Style Sheets are also important to both projects. Delivering much of the holy grail of HTML WYSIWYG development, CSS frees markup from the formatting structures that have complicated it for so long.

HTML is an application of SGML. An SGML Document Type Definition (DTD) provides a formal definition of rules for markup. A DTD is available for each of the versions of HTML that have appeared, although some HTML elements (the BR element that indicates line breaks in particular) are hard to express in the more tightly structured world of SGML. HTML's syntax has always been looser and more forgiving; for example, closing tags have traditionally been optional. Only recently, with the development of HTML creation tools, has closing every tag become common. Browsers could usually tell where one element ended and another began, even though they often would display them differently based on the particular syntax used. Other tags could also be used flexibly, but with more varied results—some browsers collapsed when fed open tags, while others displayed documents in ways that looked completely different from what the document looked like on other browsers. Combined with the loose definitions for how browsers should format particular tags, this flexibility kept many designers up nights as they struggled to recreate formatting in multiple browsers, never finding the half-broken tag that was causing them grief.

HTML Roots: Old, Original Specifications

Before there were tables, frames, font tags, client-side image maps, and all the other magical tools of HTML as we now have it, there was a small set of tags that provided formatting based on the needs of the average academic paper. (The Web, after all, was created by CERN as a place for physicists to exchange their findings.) HTML, unlike SGML, had definite formatting intentions for its tags, but they weren't as specific as those available in the typical WYSIWYG word processor or desktop publishing package.

Nested under the opening HTML tag are the two major pieces of an HTML document: the HEAD element and the BODY element, each of which carries a different kind of information. The HEAD element contains data about the document—things like the TITLE, the BASE element that can set the base URL for all hyperlinks in the document, and the META elements. The META elements can contain information, also called metadata because it's data about data, about the author of the document, the organization that created it, keywords for search engines to find, and information that page creation and document management software can use to keep track of a page's place in the broader organization of a site. Later, we'll explore another tag used in the HEAD, the LINK tag.

The BODY element is where nearly all the action takes place. Information in the HEAD, apart from the title at the top of the browser window, will normally remain invisible to the user. Information in the BODY section produces the actual look of the Web page and gets most of the attention. Most users of Microsoft

Word leave the file properties box (which acts like the HEAD element) turned off; it's not worth the bother of entering search keywords for every single file. What matters to the average user is the text in the document, with all its formatting. The BODY element in HTML is similar to the main body of a word processing document. Within the BODY element, all text and tags are sequential, following the usual left-to-right down-the-page (or possibly another pattern if you use non-European character encodings). Most of the elements within the body define formatting or create things like images, Java applets, form fields, buttons, and checkboxes. HTML elements provide markup for the appearance and placement of text and other objects on a page—nothing in the body of the document specifies meta-information.

The original HTML tags defined document formatting structures in a general way. The structures were logical rather than appearance-based. H1 indicated a top-level header, not 24-point Helvetica bold underlined. EM meant emphasis, not bold, italic, or underlined. Because the Web was originally designed to run on a wide variety of equipment, from NeXT cubes to VT-100 terminals to PCs and Macs, its originators stayed away from such format-specific tags, leaving it to browser implementers to decide how to format each tag. Some early browsers even allowed users to specify styles for tags as part of their browser preferences.

A simple document created with an early version of HTML might look like this:

```
<HTML>
<HEAD><TITLE>Simple Document, early
HTML</TITLE></HEAD>
<BODY>
<H1>Introduction to HTML</H1>
<P>This page has been created purely with logical
tags. No additional formatting has been specified
by the designers.</P>
```

```
<P>While it might be nice to specify text like we
could in Quark XPress, we'll settle for applying
<EM>emphasis</EM> where appropriate,
<CITE>citations</CITE> when necessary, and maybe
highlight a <VAR>variable</VAR> along the way. We
can also indicate code listings:</P>
<CODE>
10 PRINT "HELLO WORLD"<BR>
20 END<BR>
</CODE>
<P>Bulleted lists are easy too:</P>
<UL>
<LI>HTML Structures</LI>
<LI>CSS Structures</LI>
<LI>XML Structures</LI>
</UL>
<P>Numbered and lettered lists are also fun:</P>
<OL>
<LI>Item #1</LI>
<LI>Item #2</LI>
</OL>
</BODY></HTML>
```

Even in the latest browsers, this simple example produces varied results. In Figures 2.1 and 2.2, you can see that Netscape Navigator 3.0 rendered EM, CITE, and VAR in italics, while Internet Explorer 3.0 rendered VAR in a monospace typeface and used a different background color as well.

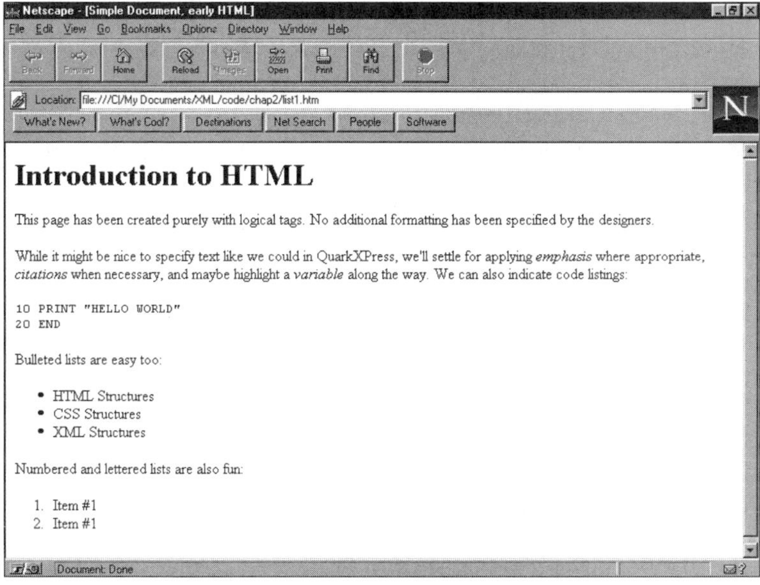

Figure 2.1 Logical tags in Netscape Navigator 3.0.

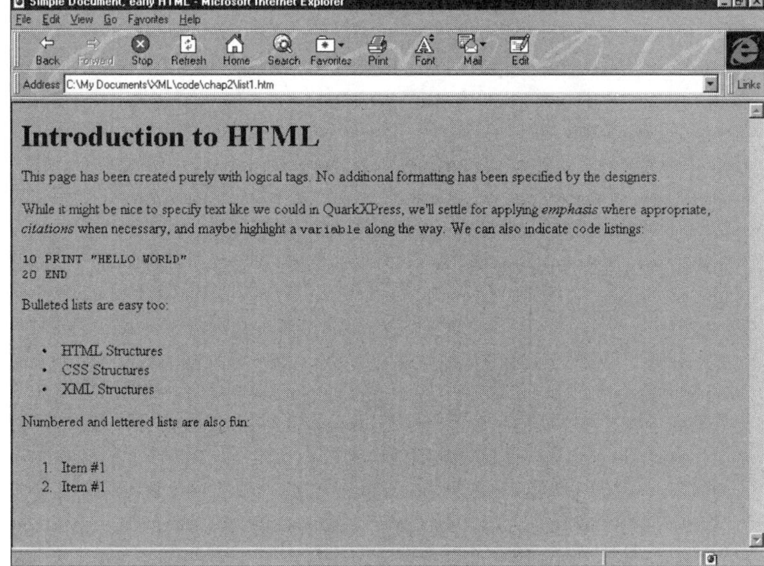

Figure 2.2 Logical tags in Microsoft Internet Explorer 3.0.

These kinds of changes made designers extremely unhappy. Used to WYSIWYG tools, they quickly demanded stronger, more consistent formatting controls. The FONT element gave them many of the tools they wanted, whereas tables, frames, and new attributes for wrapping text around graphics made it easy to place that formatted text more precisely where they wanted it to go. Best of all (apart from some cross-platform font issues), the browsers would render the pages nearly identically. The following code uses formatting codes rather than logical codes to produce text somewhat similar to that of the previous example.

```
<HTML>
<HEAD><TITLE>Formatted Document, later
HTML</TITLE></HEAD>
<BODY BGCOLOR="#FFFFFF">
<FONT FACE="Arial, Helvetica"
SIZE=7><B>Introduction to HTML</B></FONT>
<FONT FACE="Arial, Helvetica" SIZE=3>
<P>This page has been created with specific
formatting tags instead of logical tags.</P>
<P>Since we'd like to specify text like we could
in QuarkXPress, we'll use bold for <B>emphasis</B>
where appropriate, italic for <I>citations</I>
when necessary, and maybe highlight a <FONT
FACE="Courier"><B>variable</B></FONT> with bold
Courier. We can also indicate code listings with
Courier:</P>
</FONT><FONT FACE="Courier" SIZE=2>
10 PRINT "HELLO WORLD"<BR>
20 END<BR>
</FONT>
</BODY></HTML>
```

This time, the document looks nearly identical in Netscape (see Figure 2.3) and Internet Explorer (Figure 2.4). All the fonts are the same size, all the formatting is identical, and we don't need to worry about as much variation across browsers.

As convenient as this may be, it has some unfortunate side effects and doesn't completely address all aspects of page design. Our simple example didn't really abuse HTML, but pages that use tables and documents exported from traditional WYSIWYG document creators (Microsoft Word, for instance) can end up with a profusion of FONT elements that sometimes take up more space than the actual content. They don't address all aspects of page layout, which is another giant problem they pose for designers. Netscape and Microsoft still address many layout issues, especially whitespace, in different and uncontrollable ways. Tag-based formatting isn't enough.

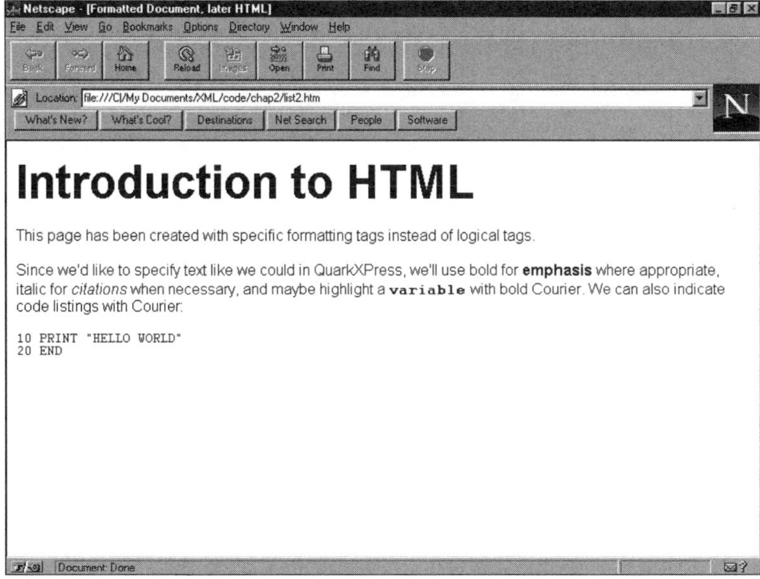

Figure 2.3 Explicit formatting with Netscape Navigator 3.0.

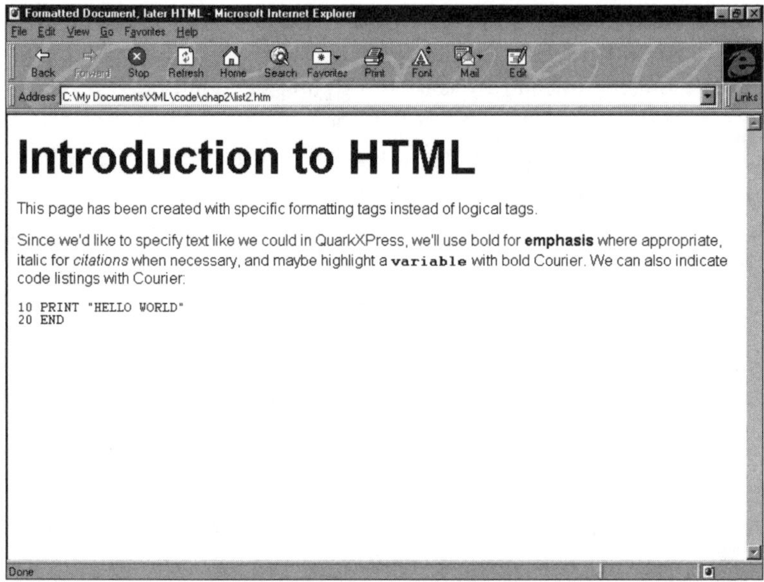

Figure 2.4 Explicit formatting with Internet Explorer 3.0.

Structured Formatting: Cascading Style Sheets

As part of a general effort by the W3C to return HTML to its more structured past and to address the needs of Web designers for whom control of overall appearance is the largest roadblock to effective Web use, the W3C released the Cascading Style Sheets Level 1 specification in late 1996. Microsoft jumped on the bandwagon immediately, implementing some CSS features in Internet Explorer 3.0 and adding considerably more robust functionality in 4.0. Netscape, which has proposed its own competing JavaScript Style Sheets standard, has also lined up behind CSS, implementing much of it in Netscape Communicator 4.0.

None of the browsers currently available from Microsoft or Netscape allow developers to assign styles to XML elements. This book will explore how to use XML and styles together, but keep in mind that you cannot just run these examples through a browser...yet. Because the XML specifications and other W3C standards refer frequently to Cascading Style Sheets, I will use *style sheets* to refer to CSS, rather than *JavaScript Style Sheets,* in this book. As we'll see later in this chapter, CSS may not be around forever either. Competing proposals for formatting control are also on the agenda at the W3C, and many of them are based on existing SGML standards.

For our first style sheets demonstration, we'll spruce up our earlier logical tag demonstration, providing specific formatting definitions for all the tags involved. It's the same HTML we used before, with the addition of a simple STYLE element:

```
<HTML>
<HEAD><TITLE>Formatting with CSS, modifying
standard HTML</TITLE>
<STYLE TYPE="text/css"><!—
H1 {font-family: Arial, Helvetica; font-weight:
bold; font-size: 24pt}
EM {font-weight: bold; font-style: normal}
CITE {font-style: italic}
VAR {font-family: Courier; font-weight: bold}
CODE {font-family: Courier}
LI {font-family: Arial, Helvetica}
—></STYLE>
</HEAD>
<BODY>
<H1>Introduction to HTML</H1>
<P>This page has been created purely with logical
tags. No additional formatting has been specified
by the designers.</P>
```

```
<P>While it might be nice to specify text like we
could in QuarkXPress, we'll settle for applying
<EM>emphasis</EM> where appropriate,
<CITE>citations</CITE> when necessary, and maybe
highlight a <VAR>variable</VAR> along the way. We
can also indicate code listings:</P>
<CODE>
10 PRINT "HELLO WORLD"<BR>
20 END<BR>
</CODE>
<P>Bulleted lists are easy too:</P>
<UL>
<LI>HTML Structures</LI>
<LI>CSS Structures</LI>
<LI>XML Structures</LI>
</UL>
<P>Numbered and lettered lists are also fun:</P>
<OL>
<LI>Item #1</LI>
<LI>Item #2</LI>
</OL>
</BODY></HTML>
```

As you can see in Figures 2.5 and 2.6, we have considerably more control over the appearance of this document in both Netscape Communicator 4.0 and Internet Explorer 4.0. (Earlier browsers, except Internet Explorer 3.0, will ignore the STYLE element because we placed comments around its content. Internet Explorer 3.0 will interpret the tags but won't let them override what it plans to do with the tags, resulting in bold italic for the EM tag, for instance.)

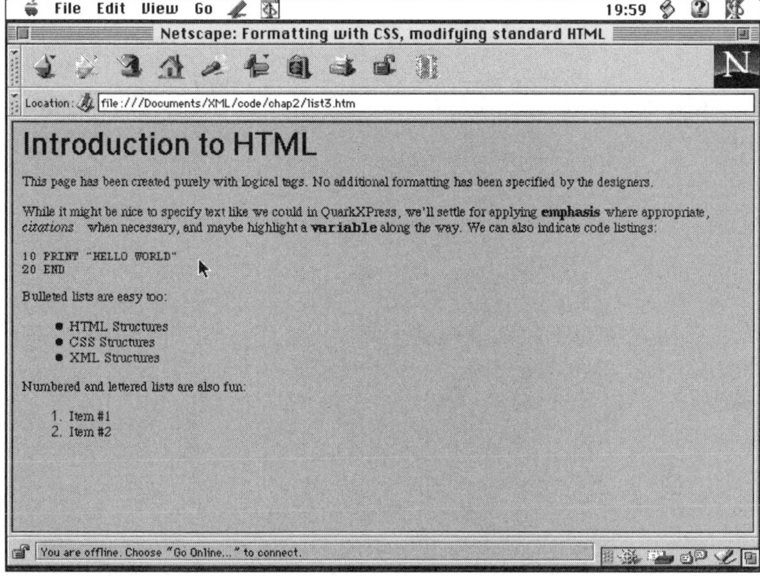

Figure 2.5 Simple style sheet in Netscape Communicator 4.0.

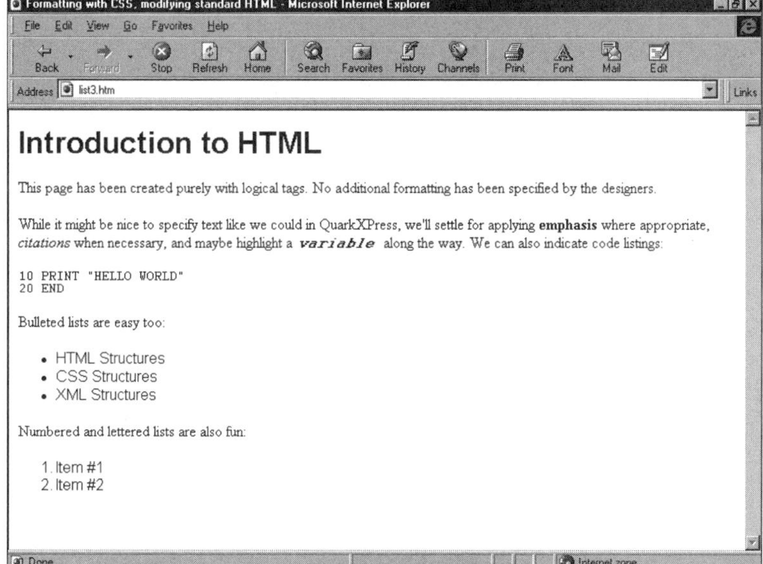

Figure 2.6 Simple style sheet in Internet Explorer 4.0.

Style sheets allow developers to specify formatting precisely, giving them exact control over fonts, colors, positioning, and whitespace issues. Table 2.1 lists a small selection of CSS properties that will be especially helpful with XML, when the vendors get around to implementing CSS for XML.

Table 2.1 A Few Useful CSS Properties

Property	Values
color	Accepts a color value (in *#rrggbb* or an alternate W3C format) or a named color.
display	**Inline** is for elements that don't have line breaks before and after, like <EM>. **Block** is for elements that have line breaks, like <P>. **List-item** declares that the element is an item in a list, much like <LI>. The **none** option is useful for hiding elements that need to be included for program reasons but should be invisible to users. (None is the only value available for Microsoft Internet Explorer 4.0.)
font-family	Specifies a font family. May be specific (Helvetica, Arial) or generic (**serif**, **sans-serif**, **monospace**). Note that font family names may be case-sensitive.
font-size	An absolute (12pt, 2in, small) or relative (larger, smaller) font size.
font-style	**Normal**, **italic**, or **oblique**.
font-variant	**Normal** or **small-caps**.
font-weight	**Normal**, **bold**, **lighter**, or multiples of 100, where normal is 400 and bold is 700.
white-space	**normal**, **pre**, or **nowrap. Pre** tells the browser to use all whitespace in the document, including line breaks, without requiring tags. **Nowrap** tells the browser not to break lines unless explicitly told to with a , <P>, or other line-break-forcing element.

This table is not complete by any measure. For a complete list, visit the CSS Level 1 specification at http://www.w3.org/TR/REC-CSS1. These styles provide a basic set of tools for making XML pages attractive. CSS doesn't provide all the tools developers need (like the ability to create tables, for instance), but it does provide a flexible set of properties that can be applied to virtually any HTML or XML element.

The rules for applying style sheets offer developers considerable flexibility, and, to a limited degree, the ability to create their own formatting tag vocabularies. Style sheets are called cascading because you can apply multiple style sheets to the same document. The style sheets are applied in a sort of reverse precedence, where the most recent definition is applied instead of the first. Styles (and style sheets) can be applied in several ways. We have already seen a STYLE element included in the HEAD element. This way is very useful if you're creating styles that should affect an entire document—but only one document. If you want to make styles apply to multiple documents, you should create a sheet, a separate file containing style information that gets connected to the HTML pages with a LINK element. Going the other direction, you can apply styles to individual elements, allowing you to use styles to format documents much the way the old FONT tag allowed.

First, we'll apply styles to individual elements, using a few different techniques. The easiest way to format text is to create a surrounding SPAN or DIV element that includes all the style information. DIVs create paragraph-like structures with space afterward, whereas SPANs let you format text without creating line breaks. Neither solution applies much formatting by itself, making it easier for you to produce predictable results.

Netscape 4.01 doesn't always support SPANs in a predictable way. Simple formatting usually works, but complex formatting doesn't always happen. I'm sure they'll fix that soon; just test your pages before releasing them. Netscape also supports DIVs differently: they appear without the line break that should follow them.

```
<HTML>
<HEAD><TITLE>Formatting with CSS, atomized DIVs
and SPANs</TITLE></HEAD>
<BODY BGCOLOR=#FFFFFF>
```

```
<DIV STYLE="font-size:24pt; font-weight:bold">This
is a big DIV.</DIV>
<P>This is a normal paragraph with an odd <SPAN
STYLE="font-size:14; font-weight: bold; font-
style: oblique; color: red">SPAN</SPAN> stuck in
the middle of it.</P>
</BODY></HTML>
```

This should produce the results shown in Figure 2.7.

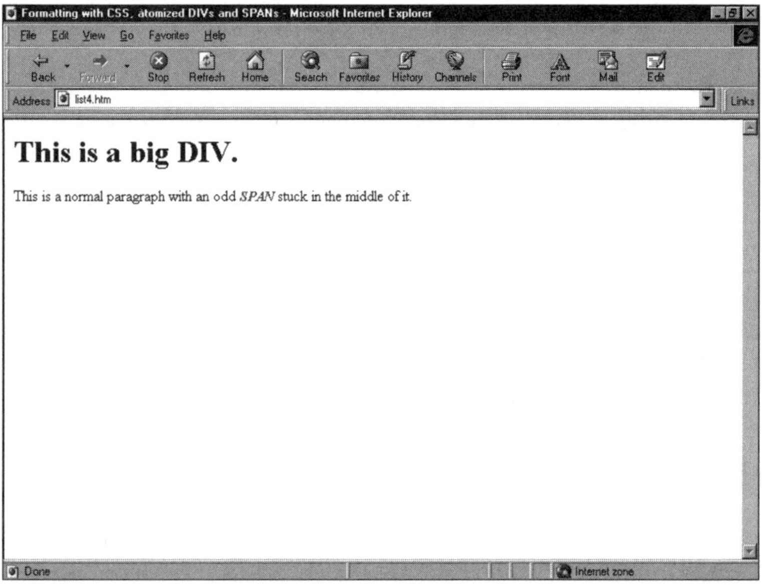

Figure 2.7 Style attributes in Internet Explorer 4.0.

Even though you can use styles in this way to achieve formatting nirvana, you'll quickly find yourself frustrated if you need to apply the same formatting repeatedly. Using a single style to produce the same result multiple times is quick and easy—and you don't need to corrupt existing tags. The SPAN and DIV tags have two additional attributes—ID and CLASS—which let you create styles for multiple instances of the same format. The ID attribute is used to identify individual elements, so all ID values should be unique. (As we'll see later, there are ways in XML to enforce that.) The CLASS attribute is used to identify groups of multiple elements. Five different DIVs could all share the same CLASS attribute value, and therefore be formatted the same way. A tag can have both a CLASS value and an ID value; any formatting specific to the ID will have precedence over the formatting for the CLASS.

All tags are supposed to have ID and CLASS attributes available, and you can usually count on it with both Internet Explorer 4.0 and Netscape Communicator 4.0. For our demonstrations, we'll stick to SPANs and DIVs.

Our next example creates a document with a STYLE element that controls several SPAN and DIV elements in the BODY of the document. Note the way that CSS uses CLASSes and IDs differently. Although CSS will let you get away with it, you still should probably avoid using the same name for a CLASS and an ID in a document.

```
<HTML>
<HEAD><TITLE>Formatting with CSS, using CLASS and
ID</TITLE>
<STYLE>
DIV.bold {font-size:24pt; font-weight:bold }
DIV.italic {font-size:24pt; font-style:italic }
SPAN.test {font-weight:bold}
SPAN#freaky {color: green; font-size:90pt; font-
style:italic}
</STYLE>
</HEAD>
<BODY BGCOLOR=#FFFFFF>
<DIV CLASS="bold">This is a big bold DIV.</DIV>
```

```
<DIV CLASS="italic">This is a big italic
DIV.</DIV>
<P>This is a normal paragraph with an odd <SPAN
ID="freaky">SPAN</SPAN> stuck in the middle of it,
as well as a <SPAN CLASS="test">bold</SPAN> bump
and another <SPAN CLASS="test">bold</SPAN> bump in
the middle of it.</P>
<DIV CLASS="style1">This is another big bold
DIV.</DIV>
</BODY></HTML>
```

This example is a little easier to do and produces the results shown in Figure 2.8.

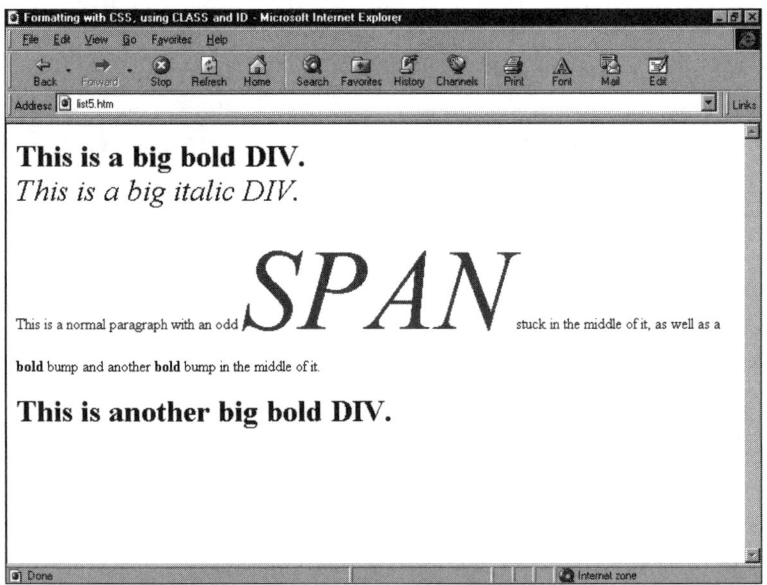

Figure 2.8 Class and ID styles in Internet Explorer 4.0.

Even though STYLE elements can help you with repeated formatting in the same document, managing the formatting of a large number of documents this way is extremely difficult. A Web site that's built to very specific rules will need incredible amounts of fine-tuning every time a designer wants to change a typeface or a color. Style sheets are the answer to this site-level problem, allowing you to manage your styles on the grand scale.

Building style sheets is very much like building STYLE elements, except that all the style information goes into a separate file that you link to all the documents that need it. CSS files look a lot like what we've done before:

```
DIV.style1 {font-size:24pt; font-weight:bold }
DIV.style2 {font-size:24pt; font-style:italic }
SPAN.test {font-weight:bold}
SPAN#freaky {color: green; font-size:90pt; font-
style:italic}
```

After you've saved this style sheet (as demo.css, for example), you can apply it to your pages. Instead of using the STYLE element, you'll need to use the LINK element. LINK has been around since HTML 2.0, but until recently, it was used only rarely. We'll use it to connect our style sheet to our previous bit of HTML:

```
<HTML>
<HEAD><TITLE>Formatting with CSS, using DIVs,
SPANs, and LINKs</TITLE>
<LINK REL=stylesheet HREF="demo.css"
TYPE="text/css">
</HEAD>
<BODY BGCOLOR=#FFFFFF>
<DIV CLASS="style1">This is a big bold DIV.</DIV>
<DIV CLASS="style2">This is a big italic
DIV.</DIV>
<P>This is a normal paragraph with an odd <SPAN
ID="freaky">SPAN</SPAN> stuck in the middle of it,
```

```
as well as a <SPAN CLASS="test">bold</SPAN> bump
and another <SPAN CLASS="test">bold</SPAN> bump in
the middle of it.</P>
<DIV CLASS="style1">This is another big bold
DIV.</DIV>
</BODY></HTML>
```

You need to use the REL attribute of the LINK element to specify that this is a style sheet. The HREF attribute just provides the URL at which the browser can find the style sheet file. TYPE specifies the MIME type of the document. Style sheets that use CSS are of type "text/css." As shown in Figure 2.9, the results for this style sheet look the same as they did when we included the style information in the HEAD element.

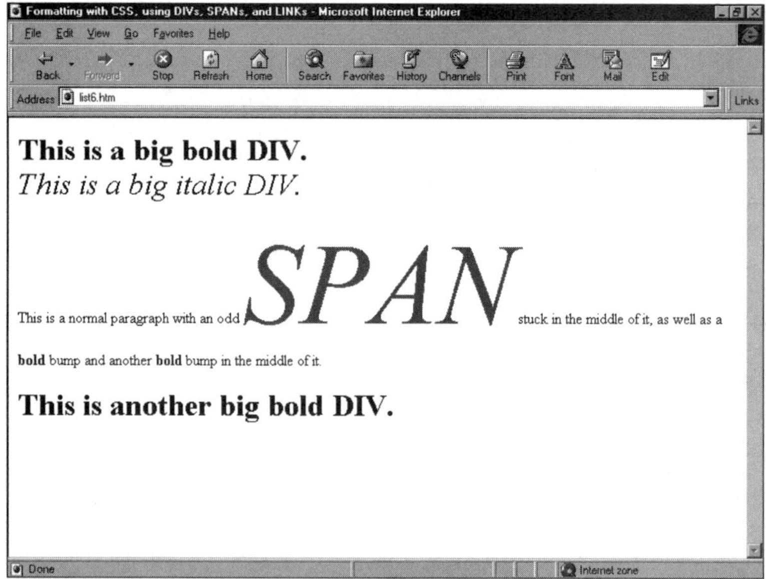

Figure 2.9 CSS with separate sheets.

You can also provide two additional attributes. MEDIA helps the browser decide what style sheet to use for which output application. Generally, you'll provide this information when you're applying multiple style sheets to the document. Accepted values are screen, print, projection, Braille, aural, and all. MEDIA is useful, among other things, for creating styles that include or remove illustrations and other nontextual material from your documents. The TITLE attribute lets you give your style sheets user-friendly names, which make it easy for users to choose among multiple style sheets. For example, you might have style sheets titled "large-print", "normal", and "microtype."

The other important thing to remember about style sheets is that they cascade. Although this may conjure up images of waterfalls and rapids, it really just means that an HTML element will accept formatting from the style that is closest to it. The most immediate style is embedded directly in the element, as a STYLE attribute. That overrides all other styles. The next style in order of precedence is a STYLE element in the HEAD element of the document. Receiving less precedence yet are any styles loaded through the LINK element, even though browsers may allow users to choose among multiple styles connected to a document. In that way, users can choose large print if they need it, or a style that hides all the graphics in a document for an unvarnished look at the text.

You can also link style sheets from within a <STYLE> tag, using the @IMPORT URL(*stylesheetURL*) syntax. LINK is preferred, however, because of its greater flexibility.

In practice, organizations can create style sheets for use by their entire group, but individual pages can override the look of the site. For example, a large company could create a standard style sheet for all its documents but allow departments to create their own style sheets that override the corporate standard. Individual page designers (at the risk of getting fired, of course) could then apply the corporate and the department style sheets to their documents, while making changes through STYLE elements and attributes.

XSL: A Different Approach to Styles

Inso, Microsoft, and ArborText have submitted another style sheet proposal, eXstensible Style Language (XSL), to the W3C. XSL offers developers considerably more control over the appearance of their documents than CSS does, at the price of a somewhat more complex and rather verbose syntax, complete with links to JavaScript. At this writing, the proposal has no official status beyond a submission; the W3C has not established a working group around the proposal nor has it announced plans to do so. The full submission is available at http://www.w3.org/TR/NOTE-XSL.html. XSL is derived in large part from the Document Style Semantics and Specification Language (DSSSL), which is commonly used to provide formatting information for SGML documents.

XSL goes beyond CSS by creating formatting structures for documents as well as elements. XSL allows developers to create styles that take into account (or even modify) an element's position in a document, its ancestry (by which other elements it is contained), and its uniqueness. Most XSL development will need only the declarative XSL markup, which is demonstrated later, but developers who find this too constricting can supplement their styles with JavaScript code, and XSL style sheets can be extended into formatting macros.

XSL extends much of the markup syntax of XML to styles. XSL treats the marked-up document as a flow object tree, a set of elements with definite relationships to each other. The document as a whole is the root, with subelements rising from that root as layers of elements. The document is the parent element for the elements that appear in it; these child elements may themselves be parents to child elements, which may contain their own children, and so forth. (A bush is probably a more accurate description.) This allows XSL to consider the positions of elements within the entire document to produce extremely flexible rules for applying formatting.

Rather than applying style properties based on a separate style attribute, XSL uses the markup itself to create construction rules, style rules, and modes. The position of an element inside of another element, its position within the document as whole, or even whether it is the first element of its type can affect the style it receives. XSL rules are actually elements that contain information about how to format other elements. The markup for XSL identifies patterns and then uses them to create flow objects with construction rules and to apply formatting with style rules.

Flow objects are a concept taken from DSSSL, providing a formatting model that allows display in multiple media and also supports text flow in multiple directions (an important issue we'll revisit in Chapter 5). Flow objects represent formatting types—characters, scrolls (which create line breaks), line fields (for lists), and a variety of other formatting and table-building information. Fortunately for developers with HTML experience, XSL allows the use of a core set of HTML elements as flow objects. Elements supported include:

- SCRIPT
- PRE
- HTML
- TITLE
- META
- BASE
- BODY
- DIV
- BR
- SPAN
- A
- HR
- FORM
- INPUT
- SELECT
- TEXTAREA
- TABLE
- CAPTION
- COL
- COLGROUP
- THEAD
- TBODY
- TFOOT
- TR
- TD
- IMG
- MAP
- AREA
- OBJECT
- PARAM
- FRAMESET

Effectively, this model allows developers to create XML tags and then order a browser (or other formatting device) to treat the XML tag as a specified HTML tag. In this way, XML tags can inhabit tables and even pass parameters to OBJECT elements. Developers more familiar with DSSSL will likely spurn the HTML flow objects for the more precise objects of DSSSL, but both sides should be happy about the situation. Style rules can also use the full set of CSS style properties, building another bridge between XSL and the old HTML/CSS order.

Patterns are fairly simple and allow developers to apply rules to elements based on their location, the other elements contained within them, their attributes, or even their uniqueness within a document. Because of the significant instability of the XSL standard, only a few brief examples will be presented and explained (there is no XSL browser yet to demonstrate). Our first example applies a construction rule to all the <HEADLINE> elements in a document:

```
<xsl>
     <rule>
          <!—Pattern follows —>
          <target-element type="headline"/>
          <!—Action follows —>
                  <DIV font-size="24pt" font-
family="sans-serif">
          <children/>
          </DIV>
     </rule>
</xsl>
```

This rule will tell the formatting program to treat all HEADLINE elements as DIV elements with the specified CSS formatting. (<children/> is a kind of placeholder representing the elements contained by the HEADLINE element.) This has the added advantage of making it easy to create block elements using XML, avoiding the whitespace problems that currently plague browsers attempting to display XML.

Similar, though lighter-weight tasks can be carried out with style rules. Styles don't affect the position of an element in the flow object tree; all they do is apply formatting. The preceding construction rule turned the HEADLINE elements into a DIV and applied formatting; the style rule will only apply formatting. For example,

```
<xsl>
<style-rule>
<target-element type="price"/>
<attribute-name="sale" value="true"/>
<apply font-weight="bold" font-color="red"/>
</style-rule>
</xsl>
```

This code will seek out any elements resembling <PRICE SALE="true"> and format them with bold red type to make certain that customers can't miss them. A similar rule could mark up the name of a product on sale:

```
<xsl>
<style-rule>
<element type="product"/>
<target-element type="productname"/>
<element type="price"/>
<attribute-name="sale" value="true"/>
<apply font-weight="bold" font-color="red" font-
size="24pt"/>
</style-rule>
</xsl>
```

If that isn't enough control over what elements get formatted, position and only qualifiers are available to let you format elements based on their position in a group or their uniqueness in a document. Developers who want even more control can add actions written in JavaScript (using the ECMA-262 standard for that language). XSL is only getting started, but it promises developers control far beyond that offered by CSS.

CHAPTER 3

XML: Building Structures

Knowing that there's a complete set of formatting tools available we can use to make documents appear as they were intended, we can forget about what the documents look like for a little while. Using XML requires a different focus, demanding that designers examine the way that their documents are built rather than the way they are formatted. If you remember diagramming sentences in English classes (it's okay if you hated it), you've been through the drill before, although on a different level than we'll be using here. Instead of looking at structures on the sentence level, we'll be examining structures at the document level, identifying titles, sections, subsections, paragraphs, lists, figures, item numbers, and item descriptions rather than nouns, verbs, and prepositions. XML offers developers the opportunity to create documents with built-in frameworks that make it much easier to create consistent results time after time.

Browsers and Parsers

The explosive growth of the Web was made possible by several different factors: the simplicity of HTML, the relative ease of setting up an HTTP (Web) server, and the rapid proliferation of browsers, of which Netscape and Microsoft Internet Explorer are just the most prominent. Even the earliest browsers, created at CERN in 1991, were meant to give users quick access to documents, letting them move from document to document without any complex transactions getting in the way. This was one of HTML's largest breaks with SGML; it was just as significant as using markup tags for formatting as well as structure. HTML browsers didn't worry about checking document syntax; instead, they parsed the document (the computer equivalent of reading the document) and presented their results. The results weren't, and aren't, always pretty. Finding a missing end tag in a large, heavily formatted document is a difficult task at best, requiring designers to compare their codes with the results generated by a particular browser. HTML browsers have always been very forgiving, but the results they present are not.

Outside the main stream of browser development were a few browsers that did validate HTML to some extent. For instance, Arena, a W3C testbed browser, had an option to indicate broken tags. The direction taken by the market, however, was clearly in favor of putting something on the screen, however odd, rather than pestering readers with error messages.

SGML was always more focused on parsing documents than presenting them. A parsing program takes a large file, usually text, and breaks it down into its component parts. In SGML, this meant that a program would examine a file, compare it to a DTD, break the document into its component parts, and validate the document against the definition. "Broken" SGML is easy to find, although the reasons for its being broken are frequently more difficult to determine. Because SGML parsers usually validate files, and because SGML is not directly concerned with formatting, programs for managing SGML paid a lot more attention to making sure that an SGML document was properly coded than to presenting it attractively. Bad markup could prevent a document management system's sophisticated tools for storing, indexing, and reusing information from accepting the document at all.

Browsers combine a parsing engine with a presentation engine. HTML browsers don't validate HTML even against their internal definitions. Instead, they parse the file and do what they can with the tags they can understand. If they can't understand a tag, they ignore it. If they're missing a closing tag, they take their best guess at where it would most likely have been. Attributes may have an effect or may be ignored, depending on whether the browser understands them. This uncontrolled model has made it much easier for amateurs to publish Web pages, increasing the number of authors dramatically. The downside is a lot of poorly written HTML. This same situation has allowed the browser developers to get away with private additions to the language, since one company's additions wouldn't "break" another company's browser. The page might not look as good, because the tags are ignored. Although pages might look best on a particular browser, the worst that could happen to a user opening them in the "wrong" browser was missing or oddly presented information. Designers who wanted to make everything look perfect in every browser were bound to be disappointed, but at least a lowest common denominator of development was available.

XML doesn't go nearly as far as SGML in requiring conformance to standards, but it may still come as a shock to HTML developers. XML standards refer to processors (parsers), not to browsers, because much XML development will be intended for machine-readable data applications rather than graphically exciting web pages. Netscape and Microsoft have both announced plans for integrating XML into their browsers, but browsers are only one part of the XML toolset. XML still allows for a good deal of HTML-style free-form development, but it enforces the rules much more strictly, as we'll see. Developers will be happiest in the long run if they use the strongest set of tools available for structure building available, but not all applications may need that level of effort. It's still possible to create documents easily in a format that both validating parsers and browsers can understand.

Browsers are only a tiny part of the XML vision. They remain extremely useful, presenting XML workers with a friendly and accessible tool for looking at their code, but the browser is only a window to a much larger project.

Building Blocks

XML uses structures that are very similar to HTML, which isn't surprising given their shared roots in SGML. Underneath those structures is a language for defining structures that gives XML the power HTML lacks. We'll start by examining the structures on the surface of HTML and then dig down until we've uncovered enough to begin building some simple XML documents.

Elements and Tags

Even though HTML designers have used **elements** and **tags** fairly interchangeably, the difference between them is significant. A tag is a piece of markup: <P>, <B>, or <LI> for example. An element is a fully formed application of those tags. A paragraph element might look like this:

```
<P>This is a <EM>sample</EM> paragraph element. It
includes several other elements, including an
emphasis (EM) element that includes the word
'sample' and a <B>bold</B> element that includes
the word bold.</P>
```

This text includes six tags (three opening, three closing) but only three elements. The paragraph element includes two other elements. The nesting rules which have frustrated designers since HTML first appeared, rely on this distinction between tags and elements. The following code is illegal HTML, even though some browsers will render it properly anyway:

```
<B>This is bold. <I>This is bold italic.</B> This
is italic.</I>
```

In my word processor, I get away with this every day. I don't need to convert text back to normal before I'm allowed to add additional formatting; formats are understood to be additive and can layer on top of each other. If the <B> and <I> tags were simply for formatting, this code would work the same way. It doesn't work that way in HTML (or XML or SGML), however. That kind of code attempts to create elements whose beginning and end tags overlap, as shown in Figure 3.1.

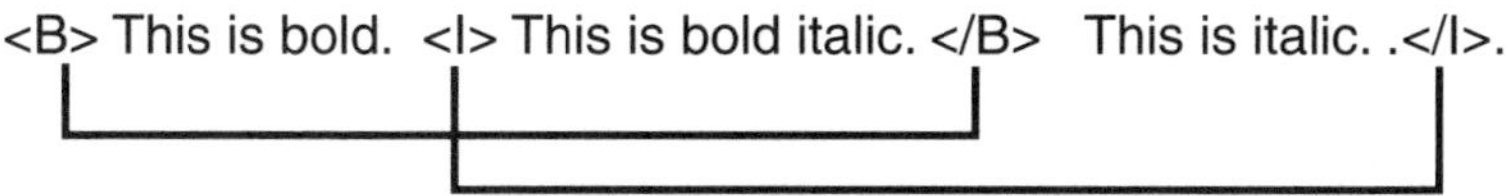

Figure 3.1 Overlapping elements are prohibited.

Overlapping elements produce all kinds of ambiguity, especially when content (and formatting) get more complicated. In HTML tthe proper way to produce the result shown in 3.2 is:

```
<B>This is bold.</B> <I><B>This is bold
italic.</B></I> <I>This is italic.</I>
```

or

```
<B>This is bold.</B> <I><B>This is bold
italic.</B> This is italic.</I>
```

or

```
<B>This is bold. <I>This is bold italic.</I></B>
<I>This is italic.</I>
```

This way takes more tags, but the beginning and end tags do not overlap. The first sample variation use the most markup but is probably the safest way to create this text, especially if you anticipate cutting and pasting or otherwise moving it around. The other two variations use fewer markup tags and take advantage of HTML's ability to nest tags and allow elements to absorb the formatting of the element surrounding them.The only change is whether the bold italic element is an italic element nested in the bold element preceding it or a bold element nested in the italic element that follows it. Figure 3.3 shows the three variations on nesting taking place here.

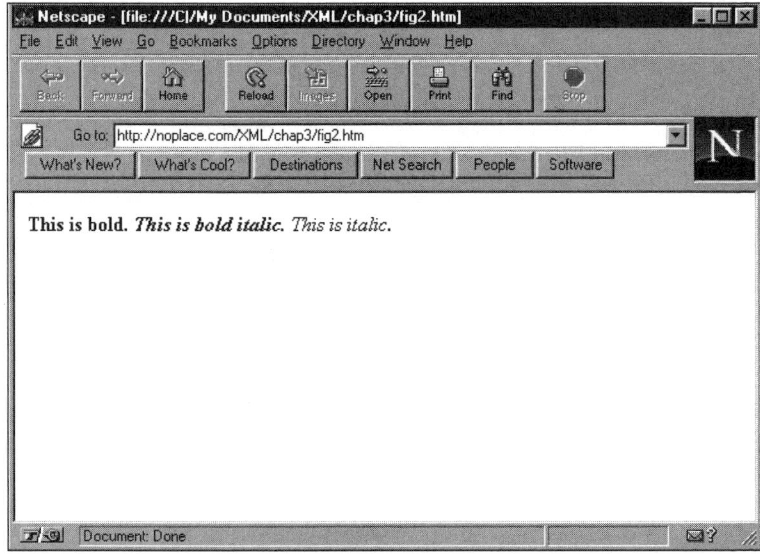

Figure 3.2 Bold, bold italic, and italic.

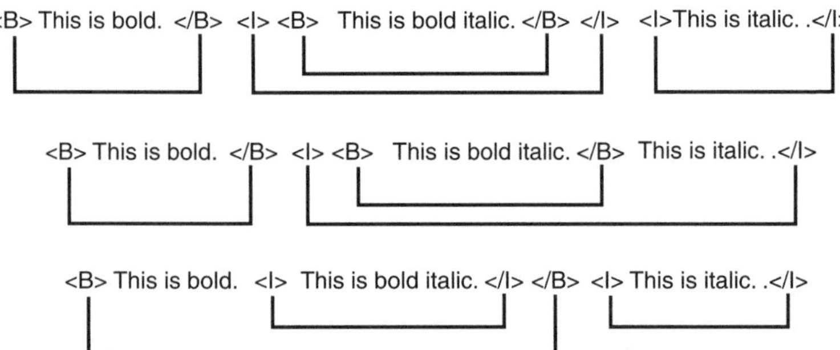

Figure 3.3 Acceptable element creations.

I always recommend creating the most containerized solution (like the first variation here), so that you can pick up elements and move them around without worrying about losing half your structures.

XML is more particular than HTML in a few other significant respects. HTML is very forgiving about leaving off closing tags and quotes around attributes and can even sometimes forgive stray <, >, and & symbols in the text. The browsers tend to parse HTML as well as they can but do not worry too much about where an element is supposed to end. Many HTML elements, including the commonly used IMG, HR, and BR elements, don't normally have closing tags. XML is not this forgiving. For starters, unlike HTML (and even SGML) it's case-sensitive. Tags must match in capitalization as well as meaning. To be well formed, the minimal acceptable level of XML compliance, a document must have closing tags of some kind, for all opening tags, as well as quotes around all attributes. Leaving these tags and quotes off should generate an error when the page is loaded. "Empty" elements, which don't bracket any text, must either be given closing tags (as in
</BR>) or have a slash at the end of their tag (<BR/>), which acts as an equivalent. Most HTML browsers are much happier about the useless end tag than the mysterious slash at the end of the normal tag, so that's probably a better way to handle this situation until XML browsers become the standard. Markup symbols in the text may not generate errors, but they will certainly cause problems and keep the document from being technically well-formed. The entities for encoding <, >, and & are the same in XML as they were in HTML (<, >, and &), easing that transition.

At this point, it is unclear how tightly browsers and even parsers will enforce these rules. Given their HTML heritage, browsers may remain more forgiving than the standard. Despite that likely forgiveness, I strongly recommend complying with this rule. You'll have better-structured documents that are easier to debug and manipulate as a result.

Elements and Attributes

Although some elements are extremely simple (for example <B> or <BR> in HTML), others need much more information. Writing <IMG> in an HTML document produces nothing, because an IMG tag needs an SRC attribute to figure out what image it's supposed to display. Most elements, even the simplest ones, now have attributes in the latest HTML standard, 4.0. Attributes give designers much more control over elements, allowing them to specify formatting, label elements for scripting, make elements respond to user actions, and define default behaviors.

XML is much pickier about the use of quotes in code than HTML is; get used to always surrounding attribute values with quotes to avoid annoying and mysterious errors. Single quotes and double quotes are both acceptable. Even though double quotes are more common, single quotes are handy if an attribute must include a double quote.

It's not always clear when information belongs in an attribute or when it deserves an element of its own, especially when it comes to formatting tags. Although the W3C tends to favor putting formatting information into elements rather than creating new elements, it hasn't always been that clear. Compare for example, the following two pieces of HTML code:

```
<P><FONT FACE="Arial">This paragraph is in Arial,
except for <B><FONT FACE="Times New Roman">this
piece,</FONT></B> which is in Times New Roman
bold.</FONT></P>
```

and

```
<P STYLE="font-face:Arial">This paragraph is in
Arial, except for <SPAN STYLE="font-face:Times New
Roman; font-weight: bold">this piece,</SPAN> which
is in Times New Roman.
```

The second style is the newer standard, applying style information rather than font tags. It requires the creation of many fewer elements, which (as we'll see later) is a tremendous aid when you begin to apply style sheets and manipulate elements dynamically through scripting. The FONT element has been officially "deprecated" in HTML 4.0: it is no longer recommended. Although it's still a part of the standard and will probably be available for many browser versions to come, the next version of the HTML standard will probably not mention it.

The element/attribute distinction will be very important when you begin working with the upcoming Document Object Model, which promises to bring more dynamic HTML to the browser. The elements you create in your documents can be scripted as objects. The properties of those objects are simply the attributes of the elements, making it easy to change appearance, position, and even content interactively even after the page has loaded.

The logic behind what defines an attribute and what defines an element isn't always clear. Lists could have been defined in such a way that the list items were attributes of the main list element, but this would have created gigantic opening tags with multiple repetitive parts sprawling across pages. Because it doesn't make much sense to build pages that way, the creators of HTML opted to define certain types of elements, lists, that contains other elements, the list items. On the other hand, the INPUT element creates several different kinds of interface pieces (fields, checkboxes, radio buttons, etc.), using the same element name and a different set of attributes for each item. Defining the INPUT element is complex and messy, requiring several pages to explain the possible combinations of relevant attributes needed to create inputs. The INPUT element is an example of overextending one element with attributes to accomplish a task that would probably be easier to manage with separate elements.

It's hard to overdose a document with attributes in well-formed XML, because the lack of standards makes it difficult to develop them and make them meaningful. The STYLE attribute will probably be the most popular attribute in the beginning, helping XML developers to format their documents for browsers. However, as browsers and other parsers develop better hooks for XML, attributes will become more important. Attributes will allow XML tags to pass more information to dedicated programs about the way their information should be presented, and even whether it should be presented.

Finding the right balance of attributes and elements is difficult for beginning element designers. HTML doesn't always provide the best examples, and there are few other widely used formatting languages. Consenquently, developers should: create some sample documents and then try to mark them up. When you think you've reached a decent balance, show someone else your document and see if they can understand the markup and describe how the document is composed. If they can describe it back to you in familiar terms, you've probably done well. To really refine your strategy, ask the other person to mark up a new document using the rules you've provided. Although you may feel that you need this flexibility, in the long run it will keep you from using many of XML's more advanced potential. Work this way with well-formed XML for a while, then transform your impromptu standard into a written DTD. It will make your documents much easier to manage.

Professional designers team with others on a regular basis for this type of consulatation, but individual designers who need to build their own document structures often don't have those resources available. Designers working with HTML are concerned about whether the document looks right when it appears on a reader's screen; designers working with XML are concerned about whether the document is easy to create on the author's screen. Using elements and attributes inappropriately is the fastest way to snarl what might seem like a reasonable representation of document structure.

XML and HTML

The W3C refers to XML as a part of its Architecture domain, but describes HTML, Style Sheets, and Document Object Models as part of its User Interface domain. The reality is more complicated than that: XML promises to have a significant impact on the user interface as well as on HTML itself. XML is not an official replacement for HTML, but it definitely includes and extends HTML in a way that probably will stop HTML development in the fairly near future. The architecture designation is appropriate to a certain extent, though, because XML is more a tool for creating structures than for applying those structures to a particular interface. As we'll see throughout the book, these roles can blur, making it difficult to tell which parts of XML are architecture and which are more directly interface-related.

XML is larger than HTML. HTML is an application of SGML, a particular set of tags defined by a DTD written for SGML parsers. XML is a subset (technically, "an application profile or restricted form") of SGML, containing a subset of SGML's tools for defining instances. Most of HTML can be defined in XML. Consequently, it's reasonably easy to integrate XML and existing HTML sites. XML allows you to extend HTML, maintaining compatibility for the most part (remember the note above about closing tags), and allowing you to move well beyond the limited set of tags available in the older markup language.

Most HTML documents can be moved into XML very easily. We will do just that to our first XML document—an HTML document preceded with a processing instruction that declares this document to be XML as well as HTML:

```
<?xml version="1.0"?>
<HTML><HEAD><TITLE>Our first XML
Document</TITLE></HEAD>
<BODY BGCOLOR="#FFFFFF">
<H1>Welcome to XML</H1>
```

```
<P>Welcome to your first well-formed XML document.
There isn't too much exciting going on here, but
there will be soon.</P>
</BODY></HTML>
```

The first line is a processing instruction, a creature from SGML not normally seen in HTML. In this case, the instruction merely declares that this is an XML document. Although well-formed documents should have an XML declaration to announce that they are in fact XML, this statement may not always be required. The version identifies this as a document that uses version 1.0 of XML, making it easy for later versions to identify themselves to browsers and parsers. If you don't specify the version number, 1.0 is the default. Specifying version may not seem important, but it will keep your documents functioning when the rules change, which is likely to happen at some point. The XML declaration will get additional coverage in Chapter 5. The only other modification we made to the HTML was guaranteeing that all the tags are evenly matched (all start tags have end tags). For new documents, this is generally easy to enforce, but legacy HTML will present many problems, especially hand-coded HTML. (Most of the WYSIWYG HTML tools available will apply closing tags by default.) The old HTML will still work in a browser; however, it just won't get read as XML. If you have questionable HTML, either fix it or don't mark it as XML.

Creating your own Markup: A Well-Formed Document

You can use the XML declaration we just declared to build your own XML documents. It's working without a safety net, because there are no structures to protect you from your own mistakes, but it does give you a reasonable place to start designing your elements. Some designs are best constructed by looking at the top levels of the problem and carefully analyzing them, whereas others are best created by working from the bottom up. Choosing sample documents and marking them up in an experimental process may help you choose your elements and attributes more carefully.

The documents in this section are well formed—they use syntactically correct markup to produce XML that a computer can interpret, but they don't include a DTD that specifies requirements for all of these tags and makes a document valid. Well-formed documents are more of a convenience and an agreeable means for maintaining backward compatibility with most HTML documents than a recommended way of working. Even though creating your own tags can be downright liberating, it's only part of what XML intends to accomplish. The discipline that a DTD imposes can be irritating, but it makes interpreting and reusing document content much easier. Well-formed XML documents are more organized than HTML; however, you'll only realize the full potential of XML when you take advantage of its more powerful tools for creating structures that apply to a set of documents rather than just a single document.

For the examples in this section, we'll use two simple documents: a recipe and a catalog page. The recipe is fairly simple: title, ingredients, and instructions. Still, there are a few layers of structure here that must be organized if this document is to work. The ingredients and the instructions are both lists, although the instructions could be presented as a paragraph if that is more convenient. Ingredients often have alternates. Even the instructions can vary: most instructions are about preparation, but some are serving suggestions. Marking up this recipe is a little more complicated than formatting it for a browser:

```
<?xml version="1.0"?>
<RECIPE AUTHOR="Simon St.Laurent">
<RECIPENAME>Super-Duper Grilled
Cheese</RECIPENAME>
<DESCRIPTION>Succulent grilled cheese sandwiches
that go beautifully with soup but are still
delightful on their own.</DESCRIPTION>
```

```
<INGREDIENTLIST>
<TITLE>Ingredients: </TITLE>
<INGREDIENT>2 Tablespoons butter (or
<ALTERNATEINGREDIENT>non-stick
spray</ALTERNATEINGREDIENT> if preferred)
</INGREDIENT>
<INGREDIENT>8 slices wheat bread (or
<ALTERNATEINGREDIENT>other bread
</ALTERNATEINGREDIENT>)</INGREDIENT>
<INGREDIENT>1/4 pound jalapeño Monterey Jack (or
<ALTERNATEINGREDIENT>other
cheese</ALTERNATEINGREDIENT>)</INGREDIENT>
<INGREDIENT REQUIRED="no">2 bottles
beer</INGREDIENT>
</INGREDIENTLIST>
<INSTRUCTIONS>
<STEP>Melt butter in frying pan over low to medium
heat. </STEP>
<STEP>Slice cheese into thin slices. </STEP>
<STEP>Place cheese slices evenly on 4 slices
bread; cover with other slices. </STEP>
<STEP>Fry sandwich carefully in butter, flipping
repeatedly to avoid burning. </STEP>
<STEPCLASS="Serving">Cut sandwiches into quarters
diagonally. </STEP>
<STEPCLASS="Serving">Serve hot with beer. </STEP>
</INSTRUCTIONS></RECIPE>
```

The markup doesn't need to be done this way precisely; you may have tag names that you prefer or an industry standard for cookbooks may appear, in which case you should probably follow the standard. The key things to notice about this markup are that all elements have opening and closing tags and that a few of the elements have attributes that mark them as optional steps or serving suggestions. A real cookbook could be considerably more detailed and would probably have more sophisticated recipes. This document doesn't have any formatting, which will be a problem in most Web browsers. You must create style sheets or add line breaks (using <P> or <BR> tags) to make this display properly in a browser. XML tends to treat whitespace within elements as important, but implementations at present may vary.

In XML, parsers are supposed to respect line breaks (even without <BR> tags), spaces, and other whitespaces. At this point, no web browser behaves this way. For the short term at least, you must use HTML formatting elements or the CSS white-space and display styles to produce any documents that you want humans to read. XML also has its own mechanisms for declaring whether or not to pay attention to whitespace, which we'll cover in Chapter 5.

Our next example is a simple catalog entry. Catalogs are generally more than a simple price list, even though price and part lists are an important part of the document. It isn't unusual for one entry in a catalog to sell multiple items—a product and accessories for example. This catalog example can be applied to a catalog with a standard format for the sales pitch and a standard set of information for pricing and shipping information. Again, you could do the markup differently, and if an industry standard exists, you're probably better off using or even extending that standard rather than creating your own.

```
<?xml version="1.0"?>
<CATITEM CATEGORY="Clock">
<ITEMNAME>Jimbo's Super Clock</ITEMNAME>
<DESCRIPTION><STORY>Ever wake up in the morning to
discover that your alarm clock didn't go off
because the power failed? Or that your roof
leaked, it rained, and the stupid thing just plain
```

```
shorted out when it got wet? Now you don't have to
worry about waking up two hours after you were
supposed to be at work.</STORY>
<FEATURES>Our latest, greatest Super Clock is a
dream come true. It plugs into the wall but has
its own set of batteries and protection from short
circuits. The batteries even warn you when they're
starting to fade - and they come with a twenty-
five year guarantee! This clock is completely
watertight, a sealed sphere of time in a stainless
steel case. The clock face is large enough to read
from a distance, and lights up with a touch for
those nights when you're stumbling in the dark.
The alarm starts off quiet, but gets louder and
louder when you don't turn it off - guaranteed to
wake even the soundest sleepers. Snooze features
let you sleep just a little bit more, but it won't
let you sleep in for more than an hour past the
alarm. This clock is ready to adorn your bedroom,
and even includes connections for lamp controls to
brighten your morning, and electroshock clips for
those who can't wake up any other
way.</FEATURES></DESCRIPTION>
<PICTURE SRC="supclock.gif"/>
<ITEM><PRODNAME>Jimbo's Super Clock</PRODNAME>:
<PART>SC45-A</PART> <PRICE>$199.95</PRICE>
(<AIRF>$19.95</AIRF> freight/air,
<GROUNDF>$7.95</GROUNDF> ground) <WARRANTY>Twenty-
five year</WARRANTY> Warranty. Made in
<ORIGIN>Canada</ORIGIN></ITEM>
<ITEM><PRODNAME>Lamp Controller</PRODNAME>:
<PART>LC45-X</PART> <PRICE>$25.95</PRICE>
(<AIRF>$9.95</AIRF> freight/air,
<GROUNDF>$4.95</GROUNDF> ground) <WARRANTY>Ten
```

```
year</WARRANTY> Warranty. Made in
<ORIGIN>Canada</ORIGIN></ITEM>
<ITEM><PRODNAME>Electroshock Clips</PRODNAME>:
<PART>ES45-L</PART> <PRICE>$59.95</PRICE>
(<AIRF>$9.95</AIRF> freight/air,
<GROUNDF>$4.95</GROUNDF> ground) <WARRANTY>One-
year</WARRANTY> warranty. Made in
<ORIGIN>USA</ORIGIN></ITEM>
</CATITEM>
```

As you can see, this starts to get very complicated. For simplicity's sake, I've left out all formatting information, but you can add it with HTML tags if you want to see this in a browser. This catalog information could also be intended for print, a CD-ROM, or even an infomercial. With appropriate style sheets or other formatting tools, you could turn this into an attractive layout on a printed page, a Web page, a screen on a CD-ROM, or a script for an informercial complete with the price and a picture of the item for the order information section of the screen. Although XML may seem picky, requiring you to close all your tags and pay close attention to your syntax, you'll quickly find that the document management flexibility you gain by adhering to this discipline is considerably more useful than the document creation flexibility you lost.

A Nonvalidating Parser—Lark

Although it's a lot of fun to hand-code documents when you're developing the tags yourself, most XML probably will be coded using programs similar to the ones developers currently use for HTML. (Much XML will be generated directly out of databases, cutting individual coders even further out of the process.) XML has much stricter standards to meet and is considerably less forgiving of missing tags than HTML. Figuring out where you forgot a tag can be frustrating under the best of circumstances, and the tools at present are fairly primitive.

One of the best of the early tools for checking your work is Lark, a nonvalidating parser for XML documents. (Validating parsers check the XML markup against a DTD, whereas non-validating parsers only check to make sure that the document is well-formed. Lark isn't exactly beautiful, but it does a very good job of presenting the structure of documents and exposing the parts in the way that a parser or browser will interpret them. (If you want to frighten yourself, apply it to some HTML documents and see how many errors it finds. Lark ignores the HTML empty elements, so using <BR> without closing tags will not register as an error.) Lark is a Java application developed by Tim Bray, one of the editors of the XML specification, and is available with much (though not all) of its source code at http://www.textuality.com/Lark/.

Lark is a command line utility at this point (Version 0.9D), with no graphical user interface. To run it, you'll need a Java virtual machine that can run outside of a browser. For this example, I'll use the jview utility that comes with Microsoft Visual J++ for Windows 95, but similar tools are available in the Sun Java Development Kit (JDK), the Macintosh Runtime for Java SDK, and OS/2 Warp version 4, among others. Most people have only seen Java through an applet window in a browser, but Java is quite capable of working in text-only command line environments as well. The jview application takes as parameters the name of the Java application (which is the same as the name of its class file, without the .class extension) and any parameters the application may need. Running a Java application without any parameters usually produces a message outlining what parameters are available. The Java application of the Sun JDK works similarly, producing identical results in my testing. I'll use both at various times in the book.

If you don't own Visual J++, don't want to download the 8.75 MB of the Sun JDK, and don't need to develop Java applications, Sun offers a slimmer Java Runtime Environment (JRE) at http://java.sun.com/. It's still 2.2 MB, but that might be enough of a trim to make it manageable.

Lark is useful for reading document structures only. Even though it does a wonderful job of matching up tags and building document trees, Lark doesn't compare the structures in your document to the structures in a DTD. We'll examine tools that handle that in the next chapter. Lark is definitely a tool worth keeping around, however, especially if you plan to be creating your own document structures or must convert legacy HTML to XML.

Lark does have problems with certain parameters and XML entities. Check the Lark documentation for the full details.

Our Lark example begins with a simple XML document. This document is a weather report, with only basic information encoded.

```
<?xml version="1.0"?>
<WEATHERREPORT>
<DATE>7/14/97</DATE>
<CITY>NORTH PLACE</CITY>, <STATE>NX</STATE>
<COUNTRY>USA</COUNTRY>
High Temp:<HIGH SCALE="F">103</HIGH>
Low Temp:<LOW SCALE="F">70</LOW>
Morning:<MORNING>Partly Cloudy, Hazy</MORNING>
Afternoon:<AFTERNOON>Sunny and Hot</AFTERNOON>
Evening:<EVENING>Clear and Cooler</EVENING>
</WEATHERREPORT>
```

To have Lark parse this, we need to tell the Driver class to analyze our XML file. In Windows 95 (if you have Visual J++ installed, and the Lark files are in C:\lark), the command and its results look like the following output. Users of the Sun JDK will use the command 'java' instead of 'jview'.

If you don't own Visual J++, don't want to download the 8.75 MB of the Sun JDK, and don't need to develop Java applications, Sun offers a slimmer Java Runtime Environment (JRE) at http://java.sun.com/. It's still 2.2 MB, but that might be enough of a trim to make it manageable.

Lark is useful for reading document structures only. Even though it does a wonderful job of matching up tags and building document trees, Lark doesn't compare the structures in your document to the structures in a DTD. We'll examine tools that handle that in the next chapter. Lark is definitely a tool worth keeping around, however, especially if you plan to be creating your own document structures or must convert legacy HTML to XML.

Lark does have problems with certain parameters and XML entities. Check the Lark documentation for the full details.

Our Lark example begins with a simple XML document. This document is a weather report, with only basic information encoded.

```
<?xml version="1.0"?>
<WEATHERREPORT>
<DATE>7/14/97</DATE>
<CITY>NORTH PLACE</CITY>, <STATE>NX</STATE>
<COUNTRY>USA</COUNTRY>
High Temp:<HIGH SCALE="F">103</HIGH>
Low Temp:<LOW SCALE="F">70</LOW>
Morning:<MORNING>Partly Cloudy, Hazy</MORNING>
Afternoon:<AFTERNOON>Sunny and Hot</AFTERNOON>
Evening:<EVENING>Clear and Cooler</EVENING>
</WEATHERREPORT>
```

To have Lark parse this, we need to tell the Driver class to analyze our XML file. In Windows 95 (if you have Visual J++ installed, and

```
.T: [ 259+12 ]
Afternoon:
.<AFTERNOON> [ 271, 307 ]
..T: [ 282+13 ] Sunny and Hot
.T: [ 307+10 ]
Evening:
.<EVENING> [ 317, 352 ]
..T: [ 326+16 ] Clear and Cooler
```

The output is a textual tree diagram, if all goes well and Lark doesn't announce errors. (Fortunately, it provides comprehensible error messages that can help you find any errors that creep into your code.) Lark has chopped the document into tags and other text and indicated with periods and a T the layer to which each piece belongs. Lark also provides character counts that a developer could use to convert this parsing information into data fit for a browser or for some other kind of computerized interpreter. This basic tree structure is the fundamental model for all SGML-based markup, including HTML and XML, and can extend through many more layers in more complex documents.

CHAPTER 4

Plan in the Present, Save in the Future

Now that you've seen what XML looks like and the enormous power it gives the designer, it's time to look at the implications of what's been covered so far. XML allows designers to create their own tags. Cascading Style Sheets can combine very nicely with XML to let you define your own formatting language. You can do almost anything you want without having to pay attention to what someone you've never met said on a committee years ago in a distant land. XML is an extremely powerful tool, capable of amazing things. Unfortunately, XML is something like a chainsaw—incredibly powerful, capable of getting the job done without too much effort, and amazingly dangerous. Chainsaws demand regular maintenance and skilled users or they inflict tremendous damage. XML (probably) won't cause you bodily harm, but it can inflict tremendous damage on poorly thought-out projects.Users who thought they could just start it up and go to work without learning about the tool and how best to apply it are in for some dark days.

XML has the potential to become the worst disaster yet to hit the Web. Sites composed of poorly written XML may look okay on the surface, but they will rapidly deteriorate into maintenance nightmares that require small armies of developers who must sort out the incompatibilities between pages on the same site. Millions of people may choose to spend their time reinventing the wheel, wasting time that could have been spent coding productively.

Companies may continue to waste thousands of dollars converting information from one poorly thought-out system to another. HTML isn't always beautiful, but badly written XML can be much uglier.

XML is about much more than creating documents that look good on someone's screen. Unfortunately, that means that many more people must be involved in the process. When the Web first began creeping into businesses, it usually started in whatever group or person handled computers and networking and migrated slowly toward marketing and design. Even though different divisions of a company might all contribute to a Web site, their areas didn't all have to look identical, and data could arrive in different formats. Web applications so far have been mostly driven by relational databases, both of which have their own format and structures. XML promises to unify all these different pieces, making the transfer of information between divisions and departments much smoother and the transfer out to the Web much easier.

If you just want to use XML to extend your existing Web development toolset and have no interest in document management, you can, and the rest of this book will show you how. Keep in mind, however, that you'll be losing many of XML's advantages and still be spending your time building converters and hand-coding pages, much as you were with HTML. The ability to create your own tags is exciting, but it's only the beginning of what's possible. Additionally, you're exposing yourself to larger problems in the long run if you've written and used your own DTD for documents and your company develops a new, incompatible one that you are required to use.

Making this process work requires cooperation from many parts of an organization or even an industry. SGML has been mired down in committees from its very beginning, and XML will probably inspire many committee meetings of its own. This organizational quagmire doesn't have to mean endless meetings and continual reorganization or perpetually slipping release dates for the new company Web site. XML can greatly enhance collaboration, but it takes a certain amount of collaboration to get things moving at the beginning.

Developing an XML DTD doesn't have to be a companywide initiative, bringing together hundreds of people from across a firm, but involving more people than the Web development staff is an important first step.

Who's Involved in XML?

Because XML has the potential to become a standard format for virtually all documents in an organization, many people who never thought about data formats before (and probably don't want to think about them now) are likely to be affected by XML development. Companies that have standardized on commercial document management (mostly word processing) tools have the opportunity to switch to a far more flexible and indeed customizable solution. Planning for a change of this magnitude will probably take years of consideration and slow conversion from the old ways to the new.

The good old days where the Web development team was a strange group of techies and designers isolated in a former storage room are coming to an end. When the Web moves inside the company, rather than just projecting data outward, the development team can no longer live at the borders of the organization. Intranets have already begun this process. Employees who might not even have computer backgrounds have become grassroots Webmasters, using personal Web servers and other small-scale tools to distribute data. Some corporations have established central Web servers for departments or divisions, giving the smaller organizations responsibility for their own content.

XML has the potential to penetrate enterprises far more deeply than even the latest wave of Intranet applications, becoming a standard format on nearly every desktop. XML is more than just a format for Web and printed documents. XML can provide a database format, a container for control instructions, a generic interchange format, and a variety of other applications that will undoubtedly come along. XML's extreme flexibility gives it incredible power to reach into nearly every data processing application, not just word processing and Web development.

This reach means that XML developers must talk to many more people inside an organization than Web developers have had to in order to develop standards that meet the organization's needs. Organizing Web development has been mostly a matter of interface design and content automation—taking content from various sources, converting them to HTML, and presenting them attractively. Organizing XML development requires close examination of content design and workflow automation. Presentation may still be important, but XML allows developers to ask that documents use XML and a standard DTD as their native format, avoiding the costs of conversion and opening up powerful new possibilities for document management. This obviously won't happen immediately; the process may take years, but it probably won't happen at all if developers lurch forward with poorly designed document structures that cause more mayhem than they fix.

Avoiding that mayhem requires considerable consultation with users. Even if your Web development efforts have been moved from the computing department to marketing, it's time to go back to computing and talk about what can be done to ensure compatibility in the long run. Designers who have spent the past few years forcing HTML to present pages precisely the way they want them must talk with database managers whose data are organized in enormous tables and agree on some common solutions. Companies that may have standardized on a particular desktop applications suite to avoid the headaches of constant file conflicts may find that their large investment was merely an interim solution and that the real tools for document interchange are only starting to appear. Convincing users of the need to change will be a difficult process, even if software vendors extend support (as several have promised) for the new tools XML makes available.

Haven't I Heard This Before? XML and SGML's Promises

The promise of a universal file format is hardly new. SGML has been promising similar breakthroughs for the last 15 years, and has very little to show for it except for significant use in mammoth organizations like the IRS, Department of Defense, and IBM. SGML is capable of everything that XML can do and considerably more. Despite its power, though, the only variety of SGML that has caught the public's interest is HTML, which has very little of SGML's power. Why should XML be any different?

XML has several advantages over SGML. It's largest advantage is that HTML has paved the way for it. The syntax of nested elements and attributes is now familiar to a very large number of people who had not seen it 5 years ago. HTML developers are also frequently frustrated by the limitations of the blunt tools they have had to use and are looking for significant improvements in their toolsets. XML and CSS seem to offer that, allowing Web developers to create pages to their own specifications rather than those of browser developers. Although XML is much more than a tool for Web development, the Web is probably the doorway by which it will enter the most organizations.

XML's second advantage is that it is considerably simpler than SGML. Even though it will probably sprout extensions and eventually come to resemble its overgrown parent, XML provides developers with much less to learn initially and fewer odd subtleties to master over the long run. Although XML has been developed by a W3C working group that grew out of an SGML group, the XML developers seem determined not to replay SGML's reputation for mind-boggling complexity. XML promises to remain a markup language standard that ordinary users can comprehend, requiring XML gurus only occasionally.

The last significant advantage that XML has is the SGML community, which seems interested in promoting this new descendant. The SGML community is in the process of adjusting a few of the SGML standards to ease XML's way to full compliance. Although many SGML books remain high-level textbooks, costing $50 and up, SGML knowledge has filtered down to a broader base, including several trade computer books. SGML consultants who know the document management side of the product can offer their services to companies in need of a makeover. It remains to be seen whether the significantly different SGML and HTML communities can work together at this intersection, but the expertise is available.

Focus on Structure

The most difficult demand that XML makes of developers is that it standardizes their document structures. This doesn't mean that every single document must look the same; it means that developers must examine the components that go into their pages and create standards. HTML provided some tools for creating structures, like paragraphs, lists, and headings, but never demanded that developers apply structures rather than formatting. HTML tags had to work in concert at times, but a headline tag never required that a paragraph follow it, for example. XML can make such demands and (with a validating parser) enforce them. Taking full advantage of XML requires developers to examine their document and data structures closely and to restate them more explicitly.

Document Structure

This chapter is somewhat structured. It opened with a title, followed by some paragraphs. A heading followed, with some more paragraphs, and another heading appeared, followed by an introductory paragraph and a subhead. The text you are reading now is the paragraph below that subhead, so we are several layers down in the document hierarchy, as shown in Figure 4.1.

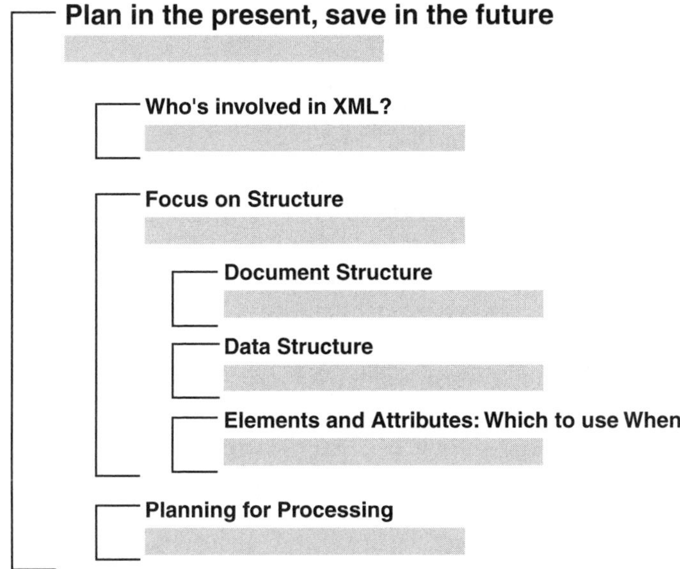

Figure 4.1 A map of this chapter.

Not every document has a structure as complex as this chapter, but most documents have some kind of structure. Memos, for example, begin with the names of the recipient(s) and the sender(s), as well as the date and other company information. The text that follows is less structured. Letters frequently provide more information, at least in a business environment, frequently including the sender and recipient's addresses as well as a statement addressing the letter (Dear John), a closing (Sincerely), a signature, and a clear copy of the name of the sender. Attachments may be noted, as may typists and others involved in the preparation of the document. Documents may be more complex than these basic examples, but they are very rarely any simpler.

Don't take this discussion to mean that your Web development team should be enforcing standards for company memos and other documents, even though that might eventually be a reasonable goal. Many companies' attempts to standardize formats of commonly used documents have been met with resistance. For a wide variety of reasons, people do not like to format their memos the same way as everyone else. When developing standards for company documents, try to allow for some flexibility— at least on stylistic matters like font and size, if not on header information. Pushing standardization too hard is likely to keep the standard from ever being applied, especially in these early stages when friendly tools for applying them have yet to appear.

HTML took a relatively simple approach to documents, identifying distinct components and creating tools for reproducing them. However, it did not link the parts in any particular way (with the significant exceptions of lists, forms, and tables). Most elements in the BODY section of an HTML document can appear anywhere, in any order. There are no rules declaring that H2 elements must appear only after H1 elements; H2 elements can appear anywhere in the document, with or without other headlines. The only limitations in HTML are those that create block elements. For example, H2 elements don't work well inside H1 elements. <H1>This is the top<H2>This is the middle</H2>This is the end</H1> doesn't produce a single line with two sizes of header. Figure 4.2 shows the results.

Apart from this kind of misbehavior, HTML puts very few constraints on the way its document parts are used. List elements were expected to appear in a list, but the browser would cope if they weren't; the same was true of form elements. Table elements (rows and columns) don't make sense outside the context of a table and would be ignored. HTML's lack of structural constraints makes it much easier for beginners to create pages that resemble their creators' expectations. Even if HTML had such structures, they wouldn't have been enforced because HTML has no requirement for document validation.

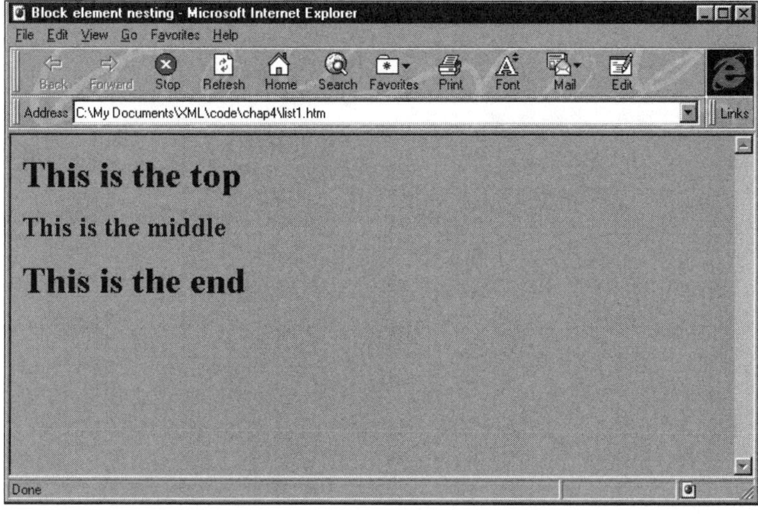

Figure 4.2 Block element nesting misbehavior.

XML allows developers to create document structures many times more complex than those available in HTML. Document structures are useful because they guarantee that documents have all their required elements, and that document authors haven't run completely amok, creating their own wild formats and putting information into the "wrong" places. These structures allow document management systems to check on completeness and to assist formatting engines in producing visually appealing representaions of XML documents. Combined with style sheets, document structure elements make it possible to use XML to create readable, highly formatted Web pages, complete with headlines, subheads, paragraphs, citations, indented blocks, and all the structures previously available in HTML.

Document structures are easy to identify by looking at a document. Their primary mission is to provide a roadmap to the information, allowing readers to find the information they need at a glance. Not suprisingly, most SGML implementations have been targeted at documentation projects, which tend to produce enormous amounts of information that need structure to help readers find their way through. Documentation usually follows strict conventions, often resorting to paragraph numbering for easy references (i.e., see paragraph 1.3.2 for detailed information about widgets). Projects that already have strong structures are easy targets for markup languages; the real challenges are less structured documents that contain multiple types of information.

When developing DTDs based on document structures, developers should check to see what has already been done. Large companies and other organizations may already have their own SGML standards. Organizations of every size may need to adhere to standards to allow them to circulate information easily. Document structures are much less likely than data structures to demand their own unique DTDs (a memo is pretty much a memo, whatever organization or individual produced it).

Developers in need of some inspiration may want to examine the work of the Text Encoding Initiative (TEI) (http://www.uic.edu/orgs/tei). This academic organization has produced an enormous set of standards for scholarly document encoding. Written to provide standards for the conversion from printed books to electronic formats that scholars could use more readily, the TEI DTDs provide extensive frameworks for all kinds of materials from prose to poetry to plays to commentaries. TEI standards regularly cross the boundaries between document structure encoding and data encoding. In fact, they demonstrate how blurred the distinctions can be. Nevertheless, their adaptations of markup structures to a variety of document types are generally well thought-out and informed by implementation as well as planning.

In general, good document structure systems are usually more obvious than good data structure systems. Most organizations have already given some thought to these issues, and many have even considered their impact on document presentation, storage, and management. Desktop publishers have had to develop a sense of the structures of their materials, Web developers have had to build homes for a variety of different types of information, and technical writers and other documentation writers have generally had to work with preset document structure expectations. XML offers developers the chance to codify these structures and possibly make them more interoperable. XML's freedom from formatting information gives it the flexibility to deal with all these situations, making it possible for newsletter information to reappear on a CD-ROM, the Web, or even in a printed company history without too much mangling and rebuilding along the way. Building abstract document structures makes producing and managing documents much easier in the long term.

Data Structure

If the document structures provide a table of contents for documents, the data structures provide the index. Document structures organize your document to help readers understand the structure of an argument or follow an extended discussion without getting lost. Data structures reflect the content directly, with little concern for where they appear in an overall document structure. A DTD may require that they appear in a particular document structure, but they often have more freedom to "float" within a document.

The ability to create structures based on data content gives XML most of its practical advantage over HTML. Even though document structures are useful, they have little direct effect on the ways that the information in documents can be reused by computers. They may allow management systems to identify the locations of information more precisely, but they do very little to help them actually retrieve the information. Document structures help humans read documents, but they do very little to help computers find the critical pieces of data they need without human assistance. A table in the middle of a document may be easily identified as a table, but without additional information, a computer cannot extract data from that table for reuse in analysis. Table headers may be useful to a certain extent, but as soon as multiple tables with similar headers appear in a document,which is a common situation, the computer is stuck once again when it tries to determine what information is relevant.

XML promises to help both computers and humans asses the data in a document and extract it for reuse or modification. Best of all, XML allows users to collect data that are scattered throughout a document as well as that which is carefully collected in a table or other formatting structure. When working on a suitably marked-up document, parsers can return information in a variety of formats, transforming textual data into more structured database and spreadsheet formats. Even though XML lacks tools for manipulating data within a document (calculated fields, for example), it provides the raw materials necessary for building applications around an independent data format.

Elements based on content provide document-structuring abilities as well. Apart from the fact that they can (in concert with style sheets) provide formatting based on content, these elements can be linked together with DTDs to provide datasets, not just individual atoms of data. In the catalog example from Chapter 3, for example, the last few lines were the actual ordering and shipping information:

```
<ITEM><PRODNAME>Jimbo's Super Clock</PRODNAME>:
<PART>SC45-A</PART>  <PRICE>$199.95</PRICE>
(<AIRF>$19.95</AIRF> freight/air,
<GROUNDF>$7.95</GROUNDF> ground) <WARRANTY>Twenty-
five year</WARRANTY> Warranty. Made in
<ORIGIN>Canada</ORIGIN></ITEM>
<ITEM><PRODNAME>Lamp Controller</PRODNAME>:
<PART>LC45-X</PART> <PRICE>$25.95</PRICE>
(<AIRF>$9.95</AIRF> freight/air,
<GROUNDF>$4.95</GROUNDF> ground) <WARRANTY>Ten-
year</WARRANTY> Warranty. Made in
<ORIGIN>Canada</ORIGIN></ITEM>
```

```
<ITEM><PRODNAME>Electroshock Clips</PRODNAME>:
<PART>ES45-L</PART> <PRICE>$59.95</PRICE>
(<AIRF>$9.95</AIRF> freight/air,
<GROUNDF>$4.95</GROUNDF> ground) <WARRANTY>One-
year</WARRANTY> Warranty. Made in
<ORIGIN>USA</ORIGIN></ITEM>
```

Each ITEM element includes a set of other elements, all of which can be made required with a DTD. These sets of elements could be treated as rows in a database, as follows:

PRODNAME	PART	PRICE	AIRF	GROUNDF	WARRANTY	ORIGIN
Jimbo's Super Clock	SC45-A	$199.95	$19.95	$7.95	25 years	Canada
Lamp Controller	LC45-X	$25.95	$9.95	$4.95	10 years	Canada
Electroshock Clips	ES45-L	$59.95	$9.95	$4.95	1 year	USA

These datasets can be stored in any order within the database. The sequence in which information is presented in XML is not bound by the sequence within the database, nor is the database bound by the sequence in the XML. Use whatever sequence seems most appropriate for each media. Making datasets like these work effectively requires more coding than the well-formed piece we originally used, but this certainly provides a much stronger starting point than was possible with HTML. The relational model of tables of data will not always be appropriate to XML, which offers considerably more flexibility, but the groundwork for easy transfers between the two information models is easy to build.

Previously, tools for for data interchange using basic text (usually ASCII) formats relied on one of two scenarios—fixed-length fields or delimiters. Fixed-length fields are designed for older technologies, like mainframes that stored all their information in tightly coded tables. For situations where information fits a tightly marked container and can be counted on never to exceed a preset maximum length, fixed fields can be handy. The receiving machine needs to know the boundary positions between the fields; then, it can chop the long string of characters it receives into usable fields. If one character slips, however, the data become useless. Delimiters use a different technique for indicating boundaries, inserting a previously agreed on character (like a comma) between each field and a different character (often a carriage return) between each record. The first line of the file containing the data is usually a list of field names, themselves delimited. Delimiters remain very popular; even one of the latest tools available for data presentation, Internet Explorer 4.0's Tabular Data Control (TDC), relies on delimited text data.

Neither of these solutions is very useful for data that need to be mixed with less structured information or data that aren't strictly text and numbers. (Given a large enough binary file, the code for the delimiter is likely to creep in at some point, disrupting the program trying to read the delimited file. This could happen with XML as well, even though XML provides an entity mechanism that should prevent it from happening with either valid or well-formed XML.) Both solutions have served well as interim techniques for managing information transfers, but XML promises a much more flexible and indeed much more reliable mechanism for information transfers.

Consider the following data table:

FirstName	LastName	ClassName
John	Nickelson	Introductory French
John	Nickelson	Introductory Geometry
Sarah	Angleton	Advanced Calculus
Carrie	Milton	Introductory French
Carrie	Milton	Advanced Calculus
Timothy	Shore	Introductory Geometry

If exported to a text file, delimited by commas, the information would look like:

```
FirstName,LastName,ClassName
John,Nickelson,Introductory French
John, Nickelson,Introductory Geometry
Sarah,Angleton,Advanced Calculus
Carrie,Milton,Introductory French
```

```
Carrie,Milton,Advanced Calculus
Timothy,Shore,Introductory Geometry
```

In an XML file, this information could appear mixed with other information that carries additional meaning to both humans and computers:

```
<?XML VERSION="1.0" RMD="NONE"?>
<HEADER><HEADLINE>Alert!</HEADLINE>
To:<TO>All teachers</TO>
From: <FROM>Registrar's Office</FROM>
Re: <SUBJECT>Students left off rosters</SUBJECT>
Date: <DATE>9/13/1997</DATE></HEADER>
<MESSAGE>The following students were inadvertently
left off the course lists previously distributed.
Please add them to your lists. If you have any
questions, please contact the Registrar's
Office.</MESSAGE>
<COURSELIST>
<COURSEITEM>
<STUDENT IDNUM
="A0653B"><FIRSTNAME>John</FIRSTNAME>
<LASTNAME>Nickelson</LASTNAME></STUDENT>
<CLASSNAME>Introductory French</CLASSNAME>
</COURSEITEM>
<COURSEITEM>
<STUDENT IDNUM
="A0653B"><FIRSTNAME>John</FIRSTNAME>
<LASTNAME>Nickelson</LASTNAME></STUDENT>
<CLASSNAME>Introductory Geometry</CLASSNAME>
</COURSEITEM>
```

```
<COURSEITEM>
<STUDENT IDNUM
="A0653C"><FIRSTNAME>Sarah</FIRSTNAME>
<LASTNAME>Angleton</LASTNAME></STUDENT>
<CLASSNAME>Advanced Calculus</CLASSNAME>
</COURSEITEM>
<COURSEITEM>
<STUDENT IDNUM
="A0653D"><FIRSTNAME>Carrie</FIRSTNAME>
<LASTNAME>Milton</LASTNAME></STUDENT>
<CLASSNAME>Introductory French</CLASSNAME>
</COURSEITEM>
<COURSEITEM>
<STUDENT IDNUM
="A0653D"><FIRSTNAME>Carrie</FIRSTNAME>
<LASTNAME>Milton</LASTNAME></STUDENT>
<CLASSNAME>Advanced Calculus</CLASSNAME>
</COURSEITEM>
<COURSEITEM>
<STUDENT IDNUM
="A0653E"><FIRSTNAME>Timothy</FIRSTNAME>
<LASTNAME>Shore</LASTNAME></STUDENT>
<CLASSNAME>Introductory Geometry</CLASSNAME>
</COURSEITEM>
</COURSELIST>
```

The XML version, even the section that carries the same information as the delimited text version, is considerably more verbose; however, it is capable of serving multiple purposes. With the help of a style sheet, this document can be posted to a Web site, printed, or sent as e-mail to MIME-enabled mailreaders. Even though transmissions directly to humans are important, the automation potential of this document is even greater. First of all, it provides both document and data structures, which overlap and reinforce one another. The traditional style of the memo is preserved, and the HEADER element contains information that is normally carried at the top of a memo. However, the information is marked up to indicate smaller chunks of data, allowing a document management system to store this memo and provide access to it in a number of ways. Readers can find it in lists sorted by recipient, sender, date, subject, or even headline. Searches can find information here on students whose first name is "Carrie" or by students taking "Introductory Geometry." An enterprising teacher maintaining a database of students can connect the XML information provided in the COURSELIST elements and import the list directly, without retyping student names. A good parser could even grab the student's ID number from the IDNUM attribute of the STUDENT element and store it along with the name and class information, allowing the teacher to link to other information in a central database regarding that student. Perhaps most exciting of all, the school's central database can generate these files automatically, creating an easy way for administrators to "push" information out to teacher's own databases without maintaining constant connections or linking everyone to a gigantic central system. If you can imagine a cut-and-paste mechanism that reliably transferred information between dramatically different systems and applications, you can see a small bit of the promise of XML.

These systems don't exist yet; even the few places that use SGML extensively probably haven't connected their data from the central documents to distributed databases via memos. Office automation on this level promises to build many new data-driven workflow applications, as well as finally reduce the amount of repetitive data entry that remains a constant task even in today's ubiquitous computing environments. According to the September 1997 *Byte*, 90% of business data currently lives outside of databases, as memos, spreadsheets, letters, proposals, documentation, and assorted other forms of information. Connecting those documents with a document management system (as opposed to a database) is the real promise of XML. Making the document management system meaningful will require considerable effort building infrastructure, a significant part of which is creating DTDs that provide information about the information in the document.

Developing DTDs that reflect data structures is frequently more difficult than developing document structures. Like relational databases, data structures are very clear in highly structured environments, but they can be extremely murky in ordinary documents. Deciding what counts as data and finding ways to mark it meaningfully are both difficult. Different sectors of an organization may apply data very differently. For example, the individual parts listed on an order are critical information to a shipping department. Nevertheless, they are only of marginal interest to accounts receivable and are interesting only in the aggregate to corporate management. Different priorities can lead to different proposals for data structures and data management, much as they have in other applications of information technology.

Despite the potential for chaos, some basic rules for data design remain useful in deciding which pieces of data rate their own elements and how they should be broken down. Data should always be broken down to the smallest parts that will ever be needed, much as is done in creating a normalized relational database. The preceeding example could have provided the first name and last name as one element, NAME, instead of two elements, FIRSTNAME and LASTNAME. This would certainly be easier for the document creators, who must mark up each element separately, but would cause problems for anyone else who needed to sort the class lists by last name. More complex structures can be built by nesting these smaller pieces in container elements (the STUDENT element, in this case). If the information was actually coming from a database, this structure would be easy to automate, both for exporting the data to XML and for importing it from XML. Hand-coders and document authors forced to deal with the complexity of nested tags may disagree, requiring compromise in many cases. To accomodate the varied uses of different users, compromise on the nesting of subelements within larger container elements may also be necessary.

Making these data structures work requires more than just creating a DTD; it requires continuous negotiation between developers and their user communities. Developers who are lucky enough to build standards only for themselves will be a distinct minority in the XML community. Making XML's promise of content-based documents come to pass will require considerable political as well as technical skill and will often require a team that can handle both sides of the equation.

Elements and Attributes: Which to Use When

A constant problem in developing DTDs concerns elements and attributes. HTML required many attributes to make its formatting precise, and HTML developers are comfortable manipulating attributes. Despite that comfort level, it is probably better to refrain from using attributes in XML except where they contribute to a specific goal. As we discussed in Chapter 3, this decision is often unclear. Developers creating well-formed XML aren't likely to use many attributes except perhaps the STYLE attribute from HTML, but developers creating DTDs will need to address the issue constantly.

Attributes are an excellent tool for passing along extra information about your element to an automated processor— a parser, a browser, or a conversion tool. They are not a good place to actually store data. Nesting elements when you need to store data (for example, `<STUDENT FIRSTNAME="John" LASTNAME="Nickelson"> </STUDENT>`) could work only in a situation where XML was transferring data between two computers; it would produce only blank space on the screen if a user were to open it in a browser. In addition, you would lose the opportunity to nest additional information inside the attributes. Elements can contain other elements, but attributes can contain only one value. On the other hand, the IDNUM attribute used previously is an appropriate use of an attribute. IDNUM is a hexadecimal identifier for the student that has relevance only to a central database someplace. It shouldn't be part of the memo's visible content, but it may prove to be useful to a database, allowing it to connect to the original data source and collect more information. Generally, you should use attributes to store information that may not be useful to humans directly but may help computers process the element properly. If you don't, you'll be walking into a maintenance nightmare.

Remember that you don't need to use attributes to hide information from the user. The CSS display property can be set to "NONE" to keep elements from appearing in a browser window. XSL has similar mechanisms.

Planning for Processing

HTML required developers to understand not only the basics of how a browser read the code and processed it but also the opinions on how to entice people to read the results. XML requires a bit more: developers must understand a larger variety of tools. XML is useful for the same kinds of browsers and search engines that have processed HTML for the past few years, but it is also useful for document management systems, workflow systems, a variety of databases, and even script processing within a browser. XML creation is still a pioneering effort; developers have little to work with because programs that support XML have only now started appearing. Still, XML developers have a rich heritage of examples to draw on from the SGML world and the promise of ever-increasing XML support from major vendors.

CHAPTER 5

Mortar and Bricks: Document Type Definitions

Now that we've explored some of the theoretical aspects of XML document creation, it's time to open the toolbox. Although the tools for creating validated XML may look a little strange, the logic behind them is not that much more complicated than the logic of markup languages like HTML. Creating a Document Type Definition is not an easy process, but a well-written DTD is worth the effort in later savings. Even if you don't plan to write your own DTDs, knowing how to read them may prove to be useful during a late night of work on documents created with a poorly documented DTD.

Many of the features described here work in several different places. A few work only in external DTDs, some work only in DTDs (internal or external), and some work in documents only. SGML developers need to be careful because many tools that worked in a variety of places have been restricted to provide only a subset of their previous functionality.

Parsing: An Introduction

Basically, parsing is just the interpretation of text. Computers can't really read, but they can interpret text files. Markup languages simply aid this interpretation, specifying explicitly to computers (or occasionally to humans) the nature of chunks of text. In HTML this is fairly straightforward: putting text between a start tag and an end tag means that the text is to be formatted in a particular way. `<I>This is italic.</I>` should produce: *This is italic.* HTML browsers understand that all characters placed between the sequence `<I>` and the sequence `</I>` should be displayed in italic.

SGML and XML take a more sophisticated approach to interpreting text. HTML browsers interpret the text according to a hard-wired set of rules, created by the browser developer based on their interpretation of HTML and the various standards surrounding it. HTML browsers do the best job they can of parsing text, in the sense already described. XML and SGML parsers, on the other hand, check the document's markup to make sure it fits a set of rules. XML parsers check at least for well-formedness, the minimal set of rules described in Chapter 3. Both SGML and XML require documents to conform to a complex set of specifications outlined in document type declarations. Documents that conform to a DTD are said to be valid; parsers that can interpret DTDs and check documents against their strictures are called validating parsers.

The XML specification refers to two components of a larger system for reading and interpreting XML. The first is the XML processor, which is the parser described previously. The job of the XML processor is to load the XML and any related files, check to make sure that it follows all the necessary rules, and build a document tree structure that can be passed on to the application. The application is the part of the system that acts upon that tree structure, processing the data it contains. The application could be a browser that displays the information in the tree structure on the screen or a printing application that formats the information to a printer. It also could be a reader application that turns the computerized text into audio for blind users. The application doesn't need to produce output that humans can use. Instead, it could treat the XML as control information for machine tools or a set of orders that need immediate shipping. The XML application can implement just about any data-dependent process.

This separation of markup from formatting makes interpreting XML more complex than interpreting HTML. The <I> tag means the same thing on any HTML browser—start italics here—but it's not that simple with XML. <I> could mean start italics, or it could indicate an ice cream flavor, or it could signal comments about IBM. In fact, it could signal just about anything. In HTML, the browser combines the parser and the application and follows a somewhat strict set of rules for how it interprets particular tags. XML is quite flexible about the final interpretation of the marked-up data, although it is far more strict about the markup itself.

Creating DTDs is a necessary step for building robust applications. DTDs provide critical information that allows XML processors to parse the code and make certain that it contains all the information the application needs, in a form the application is prepared to accept. The DTD provides a critical link between the data files given to the XML processor and the data that are transmitted from the XML processor to the application. DTDs help computers understand structures that may seem obvious to humans.

In this chapter and throughout the book, the focus is on creating DTDs and valid documents. Because XML is so new, there aren't very many applications for it. Developing real applications that apply XML is beyond the scope of this primer, although several road maps will be presented. The XML examples will demonstrate how to use various parsers—XML processors that can interpret the structure of a document. In Chapter 3, we already saw the Lark parser, a nonvalidating parser that can check a document for well-formedness but doesn't interpret DTDs. In this chapter, a validating Java parser from Microsoft, MSXML, will be the primary parser used to demonstrate XML code. Other parsers are available, including SP, an SGML parser that can parse XML documents as well.

A brief explanation of the MSXML program is in order before we leap into DTD development. The MSXML program is a free software demonstration available from Microsoft at http://www.microsoft.com/standards/xml/. It can be used as part of a more complete Java parsing program or run from the command line using

Microsoft's jview or a similar program. The MSXML program takes several arguments. The -i argument forces the program to validate the XML code against the DTD. If they don't match up, the parser returns some reasonably cryptic error messages indicating where the error happened and giving some basic explanations of what went wrong. The -d argument tells the parser to return its interpretation of the document to standard output, displaying it on the screen. The -t argument tells the parser to return its interpretation of the text, minus the markup tags, which it displays at the end, after the output from the -d argument. (An additional argument, -n *num*, allows developers to tell the parser to run a specified number of times to make it easier to time performance.)

MSXML can be connected to another application, which may then act on the object model MSXML creates from its parsing. Java applications should be able to use MSXML quite easily this way. We'll discuss this potential further in Chapter 11.

MSXML was built on the August 1997 working draft and may not yet reflect the latest updates to the standard. In Chapter 12, we'll see a whole new interface for it.

Starting Simple

The details involved in building DTDs can be daunting, even to experienced HTML coders, SQL developers, and C++ and Java programmers. XML has toned down SGML's dire reputation for complexity, but XML still has many strange detours and odd passageways. The various parts of the XML standard refer to each other constantly, requiring page flipping on an enormous scale. To avoid marching forward into quicksand, we'll start simple, with lightweight documents that demonstrate some of XML's power. This first section will use many parts of XML without explaining them in depth; the detailed explanations are in the following sections. Unfortunately, the explanations aren't likely to make much sense until you've seen some of this in action. This brief section is here to present a general idea of the appearance of an XML document, not to explain the details. All the details will appear in later sections of this chapter.

Initially, our examples use an internal DTD. Like style sheets, DTDs can appear in the document they describe or in separate files. Most large-scale projects will use external DTDs stored in central file structures, but this simple document probably won't be managed. The document begins with the XML declaration, followed by a document type declaration that includes a few elements, attributes, and entities.

```
<?xml version="1.0" encoding="UTF-8"?>
<!DOCTYPE simple [
<!ELEMENT DOCUMENT (#PCDATA)>
<!ENTITY Description "This is a very simple sample
document.">
]>
<DOCUMENT>This is an entity inside an
element:&Description; </DOCUMENT>
```

Running this through the MSXML parser yields the following:

```
C:\msxml>jview msxml -t -i -d
http://127.0.0.1/simp1.xml
<?XML VERSION="1.0" RMD="INTERNAL" ENCODING="UTF-8"?>
<!DOCTYPE SIMPLE [
    <!ENTITY Description 'This is a very simple sample
document.'>
    <!ELEMENT DOCUMENT PCDATA>
]>
<DOCUMENT>
    This is an entity inside an element:This is a very
simple sample document.
</DOCUMENT>
This is an entity inside an element:This is a very
simple sample document.
```

MSXML interpreted the declarations, allowing the creation of the DOCUMENT elements and expanding the &Description; entity. This code doesn't do much yet, but it provides a basic framework upon which a structure can grow. The XML declaration on the first line of the document tells the parser the version number of the XML used, that the only markup declarations to be used are inside the document, and that the document is encoded in a manner compatible with the UTF-8 standard, which includes the standard Latin-1 set of characters for most European languages. The document type declaration on the next line (<!DOCTYPE *name* [...]>) creates a "simple" definition, which includes two key pieces—an element and an entity. The element declaration on the third line (<!ELEMENT *name data*) announces a DOCUMENT element that can contain parsed character data (#PCDATA), and the entity declaration on the fourth line (<!ENTITY *name EntityDefinition*>) provides a particular value to go with the name "Description". The actual markup includes only a single DOCUMENT element. This element contains some text and an entity reference, which is the entity name (from the declaration) preceded by an ampersand and followed by a semicolon. From these humble beginnings, we can create more complex types that begin to define a sample document.

Our next example will add several attributes to the DOCUMENT element, providing some information for a document management system to use for tracking. The <!ATTLIST *name data...*> declaration will allow the DOCUMENT element to carry a tracking number and a security level.

```
<?xml version="1.0" encoding="UTF-8"?>
<!DOCTYPE simple [
<!ELEMENT DOCUMENT (#PCDATA)>
<!ATTLIST DOCUMENT
     trackNum CDATA #REQUIRED
     secLevel (unclassified|classified)
"unclassified">
```

```
<!ENTITY Description "This is a very simple sample
document.">
]>
<DOCUMENT trackNum="1234">This is an entity inside
an element:&Description; </DOCUMENT>
```

The attribute list declaration (<!ATTLIST *name values*>) should go under the element to which it refers, although it technically doesn't have to because it names the element. The two attributes are of different types. The trackNum attribute can have any value of type CDATA. CDATA (as we'll see in much more detail later) is character data that isn't parsed at all. Most attributes will be of type CDATA. The attribute declaration also announces that it is required (#REQUIRED). Attributes may also be optional (indicated by #IMPLIED, or a default value) or have fixed values assigned to them by default (#FIXED followed by the default value). The second attribute, secLevel, can accept only one of two values—unclassified or classified. (The | symbol always indicates an OR statement in XML markup.) The default, which is specified after the listing, is unclassified. The actual document element contains the required trackNum but not the secLevel attribute, so the default value of unclassified will apply.

```
C:\msxml>jview msxml -i -d http://127.0.0.1/simp2.xml
<?XML VERSION="1.0" ENCODING="UTF-8"?>
<!DOCTYPE SIMPLE [
    <!ENTITY Description 'This is a very simple sample
document.'>
    <!ELEMENT DOCUMENT PCDATA>
    <!ATTLIST DOCUMENT
        TRACKNUM #REQUIRED
        SECLEVEL ( )>
]>
<DOCUMENT TRACKNUM="1234">
    This is an entity inside an element:This is a very
simple sample document.
</DOCUMENT>
```

The MSXML program has displayed the attributes differently, dropping out the value sets and the default value. Otherwise, most of this parsed well. If you add a secLevel attribute with a value of "NONE" to the DOCUMENT element, MSXML will return the following output, among a series of errors as the problem rebounds through the hierarchy of classes processing the code:

```
Error: null(9,42)
Context:  - <null> - <DOCUMENT>
com.ms.xml.ParseException: Attribute value mismatch
NONE
```

Now that the example element has attributes, let's give it some additional elements to oversee. XML allows developers to specify other elements as data types and to govern how many times they appear. Our example will acquire a title, an author, and a description of the document. The title must appear one time only, the author field must appear at least once, summary elements are optional, and a special note element may appear only once or not at all. All these elements must appear in the order listed.

```
<?xml version="1.0" encoding="UTF-8"?>
<!DOCTYPE simple [
<!ELEMENT DOCUMENT (TITLE,AUTHOR+,SUMMARY*,NOTE?)>
<!ATTLIST DOCUMENT
     trackNum CDATA #REQUIRED
     secLevel (unclassified|classified)
"unclassified">
<!ELEMENT TITLE (#PCDATA)>
<!ELEMENT AUTHOR (#PCDATA)>
<!ELEMENT SUMMARY (#PCDATA)>
<!ENTITY Description "This is a very simple sample
document.">
]>
<DOCUMENT trackNum="1234">
```

```
<TITLE>Sample Document</TITLE>
<AUTHOR>Simon St.Laurent</AUTHOR>
<SUMMARY>This is an entity inside an
element:&Description;
</SUMMARY></DOCUMENT>
```

This produces a fairly rigid document structure, built by the (TITLE,AUTHOR+,SUMMARY*,NOTE?) part of the DOCUMENT element declaration. Because all the entries are separated by commas, they must appear in the order listed. (Separating them with ampersands requires them to appear, but in any order.) TITLE, because it has no suffix, must appear once and only once. The plus following AUTHOR requires it to appear at least one time, and possibly many more. The asterisk following SUMMARY allows any number (including zero) of SUMMARY elements to appear at this point. The question mark after NOTE makes it an optional element, but it can only appear once. MSXML returns the following document structure:

```
C:\msxml>jview msxml -d -i http://127.0.0.1/simp3.xml
<?XML VERSION="1.0" ENCODING="UTF-8"?>
<!DOCTYPE SIMPLE [
    <!ENTITY Description 'This is a very simple sample
document.'>
    <!ELEMENT TITLE PCDATA>
    <!ELEMENT AUTHOR PCDATA>
    <!ELEMENT SUMMARY PCDATA>
                        <!ELEMENT        DOCUMENT
(((TITLE,(AUTHOR,AUTHOR*)),SUMMARY*), NOTE?)>
    <!ATTLIST DOCUMENT
        TRACKNUM #REQUIRED
        SECLEVEL ( )>
]>
<DOCUMENT TRACKNUM="1234">
    <TITLE>
        Sample Document
    </TITLE>
    <AUTHOR>
```

```
            Simon St.Laurent
        </AUTHOR>
        <SUMMARY>
            This is an entity inside an element:This is a
    very simple sample document.
        </SUMMARY>
    </DOCUMENT>
```

As you can see, MSXML has rearranged portions of the DTD. Although it typically makes more sense to humans to start with a top-level element and work down, outline style, the computer often prefers to list all the parts before combining them into a whole. XML is flexible enough to accommodate many ways of processing. (MSXML's logic for rearranging is not always so clear, but at least it seems to work.) MSXML has also changed the notation describing the contents of the DOCUMENT element, adding parentheses and breaking AUTHOR+ into the equivalent (AUTHOR, AUTHOR*) for its own convenience. Developers can also use parentheses to group element choices. Changing the sequence of the elements in this document will make the parser fail. For example, moving the SUMMARY element above the TITLE element produces:

```
C:\msxml>jview msxml -d -i http://127.0.0.1/simp3.xml
Error: null(13,9)
Context:  - <null> - <DOCUMENT>
com.ms.xml.ParseException: Pattern mismatch: SUMMARY
at state 0
        at com/ms/xml/Parser.error
```

Our next example will expand the DTD one level deeper, providing more information under the AUTHOR element. In this case, the author can identify both an organization (company or university) and a name.

```
<?xml Version="1.0" Encoding="UTF-8"?>
<!DOCTYPE simple [
<!ELEMENT DOCUMENT (TITLE,AUTHOR+,SUMMARY*,NOTE?)>
<!ATTLIST DOCUMENT
```

```
     trackNum CDATA #REQUIRED
     secLevel (unclassified|classified)
"unclassified">
<!ELEMENT TITLE (#PCDATA)>
<!ELEMENT AUTHOR (FIRSTNAME, LASTNAME, (UNIVERSITY
| COMPANY)?)>
<!ELEMENT FIRSTNAME (#PCDATA)>
<!ELEMENT LASTNAME (#PCDATA)>
<!ELEMENT UNIVERSITY (#PCDATA)>
<!ELEMENT COMPANY (#PCDATA)>
<!ELEMENT SUMMARY (#PCDATA)>
<!ENTITY Description "This is a very simple sample
document.">
]>
<DOCUMENT trackNum="1234">
<TITLE>Sample Document</TITLE>
<AUTHOR><FIRSTNAME>Simon</FIRSTNAME>
<LASTNAME>St.Laurent</LASTNAME>
<COMPANY>XML Mania</COMPANY></AUTHOR>
<SUMMARY>This is an entity inside an
element:&Description;
</SUMMARY></DOCUMENT>
```

The main change, apart from the addition of a few elements, is in the AUTHOR element declaration: <!ELEMENT AUTHOR (FIRSTNAME, LASTNAME, (UNIVERSITY | COMPANY)?)>. This declaration allows developers to create somewhat more flexible structures. In this case, the AUTHOR element must include (in this order) a FIRSTNAME element, a LASTNAME element, and either a UNIVERSITY element or a COMPANY element. (Using both elements will produce a parsing error.) MSXML seems happy enough about this arrangement:

```
C:\msxml>jview msxml -d -i http://127.0.0.1/simp4.xml
<?XML VERSION="1.0" ENCODING="UTF-8"?>
<!DOCTYPE SIMPLE [
    <!ENTITY Description 'This is a very simple sample
document.'>
    <!ELEMENT TITLE PCDATA>
    <!ELEMENT UNIVERSITY PCDATA>
                              <!ELEMENT       AUTHOR
(PCDATA|((FIRSTNAME,LASTNAME),(UNIVERSITY|COMPANY)?))>
    <!ELEMENT COMPANY PCDATA>
    <!ELEMENT FIRSTNAME PCDATA>
    <!ELEMENT SUMMARY PCDATA>
    <!ELEMENT LASTNAME PCDATA>
                              <!ELEMENT       DOCUMENT
(((TITLE,(AUTHOR,AUTHOR*)),SUMMARY*),NOTE?)>
    <!ATTLIST DOCUMENT
        TRACKNUM #REQUIRED
        SECLEVEL ( )>
]>
<DOCUMENT TRACKNUM="1234">
    <TITLE>
        Sample Document
    </TITLE>
    <AUTHOR>
        <FIRSTNAME>
            Simon
        </FIRSTNAME>
        <LASTNAME>
            St.Laurent
        </LASTNAME>
        <COMPANY>
            XML Mania
        </COMPANY>
    </AUTHOR>
    <SUMMARY>
        This is an entity inside an element:This is a
very simple sample document.
    </SUMMARY>
</DOCUMENT>
```

At this point, the document is getting very long, and most of it is just defining the document type. For our last example, we'll separate the

DTD file from the actual document. The document becomes considerably shorter:

```
<?xml version="1.0" standalone="no""UTF-8"?>
<!DOCTYPE SIMPLE SYSTEM
"http://127.0.0.1/simple.dtd">
<SIMPLE><DOCUMENT trackNum="1234">
<TITLE>Sample Document</TITLE>
<AUTHOR><FIRSTNAME>Simon</FIRSTNAME>
<LASTNAME>St.Laurent</LASTNAME>
<COMPANY>XML Mania</COMPANY></AUTHOR>
<SUMMARY>This is an entity inside an
element:&Description;
</SUMMARY></DOCUMENT></SIMPLE>
```

The <!DOCTYPE> declaration now points to a URL—http://127.0.0.1/simple.dtd.

The simple.dtd file contains all the declarations that used to be in the document itself:

```
<!ELEMENT DOCUMENT (TITLE,AUTHOR+,SUMMARY*,NOTE?)>
<!ATTLIST DOCUMENT
     trackNum CDATA #REQUIRED
     secLevel (unclassified|classified)
"unclassified">
<!ELEMENT TITLE (#PCDATA)>
<!ELEMENT AUTHOR (FIRSTNAME,LASTNAME, (UNIVERSITY
| COMPANY)?)>
<!ELEMENT FIRSTNAME (#PCDATA)>
<!ELEMENT LASTNAME (#PCDATA)>
<!ELEMENT UNIVERSITY (#PCDATA)>
<!ELEMENT COMPANY (#PCDATA)>
<!ELEMENT SUMMARY (#PCDATA)>
```

```
<!ENTITY Description "This is a very simple sample
document.">
```

To see the results, run MSXML as usual. It doesn't display all the declaration information, but as you can see by the expanded entity, it did find the DTD.

```
C:\msxml>jview msxml -d -i http://127.0.0.1/simp5.xml
<?XML VERSION="1.0" ENCODING="UTF-8"?>
<!DOCTYPE SIMPLE SYSTEM "simple.dtd">
<SIMPLE>
    <DOCUMENT TRACKNUM="1234">
        <TITLE>
            Sample Document
        </TITLE>
        <AUTHOR>
            <FIRSTNAME>
                Simon
            </FIRSTNAME>
            <LASTNAME>
                St.Laurent
            </LASTNAME>
            <COMPANY>
                XML Mania
            </COMPANY>
        </AUTHOR>
        <SUMMARY>
             This is an entity inside an element:This
is a very simple sample document.
        </SUMMARY>
    </DOCUMENT>
</SIMPLE>
```

Now that we've created a workable beginning DTD, let's examine the parts that go into defining an XML document. The following sections start with the techniques needed to connect an XML document to a DTD and then explore XML data and document structures in greater depth.

How Documents Find Their DTDs: The Prolog

Although not technically a part of a DTD, the opening prolog, which contains the <?XML?> processing instructions and the following document type declarations are the glue that bind DTDs to the code that applies them. These strange-looking new declarations perform some of the functions that the HTML and HEAD elements offer in HTML, but they answer somewhat different questions. They hold only a few pieces of information, all of which are key to telling the browser how to interpret the code that follows. Although the HEAD element could contain interesting information, that information affects only a few specific parts of the presentation, like the title and possibly some scripting information. Specifying what version of HTML was used in a document could be useful for designers or automated HTML editors, but the browser doesn't really care—it will interpret the code to its own specifications, not those of a committee far away. In XML, the opening tags tell the browser in fairly specific terms how to interpret the document.

<?xml?>: A Very Special Processing Instruction

Valid XML documents should always begin with the XML declaration. The XML declaration contains version information, encoding information, and information about which if any DTDs the document will use. Even though the contents of the XML declaration give only a very broad idea of the kind of XML document follows, they provide some critical basic information to the parsers that interpret the document.

The XML declaration uses SGML processing instruction syntax. Technically, processing instructions, which begin with <? and end with ?> tags, don't directly affect the SGML. (XML processing instructions must end with ?>, instead of the SGML standard of >.)

Instead, they provide instructions to outside programs, like formatters, that are less concerned with the syntactical structure of a document than they are with making it look as its designers intended. Most processing instructions intended for outside formatters have their own syntax; they needn't follow typical SGML syntax. Although it would be unusual,

```
<?Jimmy - use the burnt umber crayon for this. ?>
```

could be an acceptable processing instruction if the processing application was a child named Jimmy. A more typical processing instruction might be

```
<?FormatWhiz azure-embossed-type?>
```

FormatWhiz would probably (although not necessarily) be the name of the processing application, whereas the remainder of the instructions specify unusual formatting, possibly for a business card or wedding invitation.

Processing instructions have been condemned as a diabolical means of creating unnecessarily complicated SGML that doesn't transfer well between different parsers, but the XML working group appears to have settled on it as the most appropriate syntax for telling the parser how to handle the document that follows.

Even though using processing instructions in XML is permissible, always avoid processing instructions that begin with <?XML. They are expressly reserved for future use by the XML specifications.

The XML declaration includes several parts: the opening <?xml, version information, the standalone declaration, the encoding declaration, and the closing ?>. None of this information is technically required. XML declarations can have missing parts, and documents can still be well-formed without having an XML declaration. The version information and the declarations have default values that parsers can use. Unlike the HTML element, the XML declaration has no closing tag. </?xml> should never appear in a document. The XML declaration is an opening statement—an instruction—and nothing more.

The version information in this first version of XML is quite simple: version="1.0". Version 1.0 will be the default, providing a base for all future implementations of XML. Whatever happens to the standard, leaving out the version completely or specifying version 1.0 should mean that the documents and document type declarations written for version 1.0 will be interpreted as originally intended even when XML reaches version 7.3 or even 20.0. Unlike HTML, which arrived as version 0.9 when it became publicly available, XML has been at version 1.0 since the working drafts first appeared.

The standalone declaration announces whether a document contains references to external document type declarations. The value may be either "yes" or "no". If no standalone declaration appears, the default is "no." Valid documents are required to provide an honest answer for this declaration. Documents may make references to external entities, and still claim "yes", but may not refer to external DTDs. The Proposed Recommendation suggests that any XML document can be converted into a standalone document for processing if necessary, and some simple applications may well choose to reject all documents that are not standalone documents. In general, however, document developers who are building sets of valid documents will most likely anwswer "no" or leave out this declaration entirely.

The standalone declaration replaces the RMD declaration that appeared in earlier working drafts.

Encoding addresses complex issues related to internationalization. XML allows developers to specify which of several different character encoding schemes should be applied to a document. The default scheme is UTF-8, which includes direct representations of most of the characters used in English using values of 0–127 for the ASCII set of characters, and provides multibyte encodings for Unicode characters with higher values. UCS-2, which XML parsers are required to support, applies the Unicode/ISO/IEC 10646 standards, which extend the character space to 16 bits, allowing values from 0 to 65,535, a very significant expansion that allows the inclusion of most modern languages. (There are still significant problems with Chinese characters and a few other characters sets that remain under negotiation.) XML parsers can (although they aren't required to) support several other encodings, including ISO 8859-1 through ISO 8859-9, which represent most European languages, and EUC-JP, Shift_JIS, and ISO-2022-JP, which represent Japanese. The encoding scheme's name must always be enclosed in single or double quotes and described using the Latin character set.

Encoding has the same case-sensitivity problem that *version* has. Watch the standard and check your parser or browser documentation for the latest updates.

Unicode and Other Encodings

While most English-speaking developers have grown used to the standard character sets available for that language, developers elsewhere have strained to use their languages in computers that weren't really designed to accommodate them. After several years of development, the Unicode standard is finally gaining some use, chipping away at the 8-bit character sets that have dominated computing since the arrival of the (later extended) 7-bit ASCII character set. Unicode offers 16 bits, for 65,536 possible characters.

Although ASCII was adequate for most documents in English, the limitations of a 128-member character set rapidly became clear, even when expanded to 256 members, as computers began to spread to areas using other languages. Even Latin-based European alphabets have enough accented and other special characters to fill up the 256 spaces rapidly. Adding Cyrillic, Greek, Turkish, Hebrew, or Arabic characters to that moves well beyond the available space. Character sets for Asian languages have tens of thousands of ideographs. Creating standards that will work for all these languages is a complex task, often demanding political and technical compromise.

XML requires that parsers support UTF-8, UCS-2, and UTF-16. The encodings required or recommended for support in the standard are those in Table 5.1.

Table 5.1 Common XML encoding schemes

Encoding Scheme	# of Bits	Notes
UCS-2	16	Canonical Unicode character set
UCS-4	32	Canonical Unicode character set, using 32 bits
UTF-8	8	Unicode Transformation—8 bit
UTF-7	7	Unicode Transformation— 7 bit (for mail and news)
UTF-16	16, 32	Unicode format that 'escapes' 32-bit characters
ISO-8859-1	8	Latin alphabet No. 1 (Western Europe, Latin America)
ISO-8859-2	8	Latin alphabet No. 2 (Central/Eastern European)
ISO-8859-3	8	Latin alphabet No. 3 (SE Europe/miscellaneous)
ISO-8859-4	8	Latin alphabet No. 4 (Scandinavia/Baltic)
ISO-8859-5	8	Latin/Cyrillic
ISO-8859-6	8	Latin/Arabic

Encoding Scheme	# of Bits	Notes
ISO-8859-7	8	Latin/Greek
ISO-8859-8	8	Latin/Hebrew
ISO-8859-9	8	Latin/Turkish
ISO-8859-10	8	Latin/Lappish/Nordic/Eskimo
ISO 10646	32	32-bit extended set; includes Unicode as subset
EUC-JP	8	Japanese (uses multibyte encoding)
Shift_JIS	8	Japanese (uses multibyte encoding)
ISO-2022-JP	7	Japanese (uses multibyte encoding; for mail and news)

Developers used to working with the ASCII set of characters shouldn't have too much difficulty because most of these standards include that set. Because the default set is explicitly declared to be UTF-8, developers can expect most pages in English to display without additional difficulty. The Unicode UCS-2 standard begins with a code sequence that identifies it, and parsers should be able to auto-detect it. A well-written parser will be able to protect users to some extent from the seemingly random characters that currently fill screens when users visit pages written in different encodings than the default.

Unfortunately, displaying all these character sets still requires additional operating system support. Windows NT and Solaris 2.6 both offer native Unicode support, but developers on other platforms will need additional language kits that convert between formats. Collecting an adequate set of fonts to represent multiple languages remains a problem, but support is rapidly increasing. Programming languages have similar problems; most use an 8-bit space for character data. Java already uses Unicode as its default format for character information, giving developers a ready-made language for Unicode text processing. Unicode support is growing, and XML's use of it as a standard should widen its acceptance.

Document Type Declarations

After the opening prolog has announced that this is an XML document, the document type declarations announce what kind of XML document it is to be. Document type declarations glue the DTDs to the actual document or may even provide their own declarations about the structure of the document. Although internal DTDs (which are declared in the document they apply to) can be used and may be appropriate for certain situations, using an external DTD is usually preferable. Keeping DTDs separate makes them considerably more reusable and assures document managers that developers aren't taking liberties with the DTD to suit their own purposes, creating incompatible document types.

Whenever the acronym DTD appears in this book or in other XML document, always assume that it stands for document type definition, *not* document type declaration.

A document type declaration always begins with <!DOCTYPE, followed by the name of the DTD, followed by a declaration of the DTD or a link that points to where the DTD can be found, and finally a > to close the declaration. The name of the DTD doesn't need to correspond to the file name of the DTD file specified, but it should convey some sort of intelligible description of what the DTD is for and match the root tags of the document. After the name, the declaration can either provide a DTD within the declaration itself, enclosed in braces ([ ]), which we'll do in some of the following examples, or provide a link to a file containing the DTD. The reference to the DTD file is an external entity; external entities will receive additional coverage later in the entities section. For now, we'll just discuss how to apply them in this situation.

Some DTDs are public standards, available in standardized format to a large number of users. Others are locally developed, useful for a Web site, a business, or perhaps a small industry. For the first type, the PUBLIC keyword is more appropriate; for the second, the SYSTEM keyword should be used. The PUBLIC keyword first provides a public identifier (in quotes) that the parser can use to locate the standard if it is connected to a library of standards. Following that is a URL (also in quotes) that can lead the parser to a copy of the DTD. The SYSTEM keyword is followed only by the URL. Large document management systems may well have libraries of DTDs available to parsers, but developers of other types of projects may not have such resources. The following two document type declarations link the document to the same DTD, but the first also provides a public identifier for the DTD.

```
<!DOCTYPE manual PUBLIC "-//loopbackInc//DTD
manual//EN" "http://127.0.0.1/manual.dtd">
<!DOCTYPE manual SYSTEM
"http://127.0.0.1/manual.dtd">
```

DTDs may also be nested—one DTD file may call another. DTDs are cumulative, although an internal DTD will always have precedence over an external DTD.

The public identifier structure uses the same format as SGML public identifiers. If the entity or DTD described is an ISO standard, the identifier starts with "ISO." Otherwise, the first character is a plus (+) if the standard is officially approved by a standards body, or a minus (–) if it is not, followed by two forward slashes (//), after which an identifier of the owner of the DTD appears. After two more slashes the type of the document (DTD, for example, or TEXT) appears followed by whitespace and the name of the document. After yet another two slashes, the language identifier appears, using the codes specified in ISO 639 (EN, for example, is English).

Comments

Comments are another critical part of XML. They appear in both documents and DTDs. Comments in XML behave much like comments in HTML. Comments begin with <!-- and end with -->.

XML comments are not allowed to have two consecutive dashes (--) in their content because it may confuse parsers that interpret that as the end of an SGML comment. XML comments can appear in both documents and DTDs. XML comments are not allowed to appear inside of tags or in declarations and will not work in CDATA. (In CDATA sections, the comment symbols are treated as regular characters and will appear as part of the document.) The parser ignores the contents of comments. The following is a sample comment:

```
<!--This is a comment.  Please ignore me if you
are parsing.-->
```

Comments in XML are more likely to be used in DTDs than in documents, but they are critically important there. Comments are the signposts future editors will need to understand the structures you have created. Comments can explain otherwise mysterious entity references and are useful for labeling declarations, especially if element names are abbreviated. Comments may seem like wasted space to developers with perfect memories, but a DTD without comments is truly wasted space to the next developer who must work with it.

Data Structures

Before we can start building document structures, we must look at the data underneath. As HTML developers discovered when they tried to convert old files to HTML, the use of characters like <, >, and & for markup creates significant problems. A site I once converted from a Macintosh HyperCard stack, for example, worked very well except for the page on AT&T, which had missing characters throughout. XML applies a few SGML solutions to HTML's problems, adding some apparent complexity but solving the problems much more thoroughly.

Data Types

Although XML has simplified SGML's data types considerably, we need to consider a number of issues that never cropped up in HTML. XML allows for two types of data in documents: #PCDATA, or parsed character data, which is ordinary marked-up character data, and CDATA, which is character data without any markup. CDATA is useful for situations where a document contains no markup and many <, >, and & symbols. By default, XML assumes that all information is PCDATA, except for the contents of attributes, which are normally assumed to be CDATA. PCDATA and CDATA will receive considerably more use when we get to actually define some elements and attributes.

CDATA can also play a role directly in a document, marking a section as pure character data. To declare a section as CDATA, mark its beginning with `<![CDATA[` and its end with `]]>`. (This will fail if the data includes any `]]>` sequences, which should be a highly unusual occurrence.) For example, the CDATA section in

```
<?xml version="1.0" Encoding="UTF-8"?>
<DOCUMENT><![CDATA[@#X! <<<<  >>>> & <<<<<
>>>>>]]></DOCUMENT>
```

will be interpreted as the characters "@#X! <<<< >>>> & <<<<< >>>>>" and will not generate a parsing error. When queried for the text in this document, MSXML returns the CDATA information:

```
C:\msxml>jview msxml -t http://127.0.0.1/cdata.xml
@#X! <<<<  >>>> & <<<<< >>>>>
```

If this text wasn't "escaped" with the CDATA declaration, parsers would stop at the first < sign because it appears to open a tag with no proper closing. Even though using CDATA prohibits developers from using markup in a section of text, the tradeoff may be worth it if the section doesn't require markup anyway. If it needs markup, replace the offending characters with their entity equivalents, as discussed later in the chapter.

The use of CDATA to escape text is actually a specific example of a more general SGML technique—marked sections. Marked sections follow a <![*keyword*[*data...*]]> syntax. Even though developers may use this syntax for CDATA, the SGML RCDATA, TEMP, IGNORE, and INCLUDE keywords are not available in XML documents. IGNORE and INCLUDE marked sections, are, however, available within DTDs and will be covered later in the chapter.

One missing feature, which many developers have complained about, is that XML doesn't have any way to require that elements contain more specific types of data, like text or numbers or currency. Several proposals for this "stronger typing" are under development. One proposal would apply the standard types of SQL, the relational database standard, to XML elements. In the meantime, any such enforcement of data types will be the responsibility of the processing application, not the XML parser.

Entities

XML offers two kinds of entities—general entities and parameter entities. HTML developers will be familiar with using predefined general entities for encoding unusual characters and characters used for markup (the infamous <, >, and &). Although defined in DTDs, general entities are used to add information to documents, substituting their value for the entity reference, which takes the form &*name*;. Parameter entities are defined and used only in external DTDs. They can save developers typing, as do general entities, but they also can give developers tremendous power to include other DTDs and other information in their DTD. Parameter entities allow developers to reuse and subset older DTDs, avoiding the perpetual reinvention of the wheel and making the expansion of previously existing DTDs easier.

General entities are used through HTML to provide representations of characters that are either outside the basic ASCII character set or interfere with markup. XML has fewer problems with this for several reasons. The character encodings already described will allow developers to include characters from other languages and writing systems more directly, easing the need for those kinds of character-representation entities. The option to "escape" characters with CDATA sections also makes it easier to include the characters that interfere with markup, especially for large chunks. Still, CDATA is somewhat clunky for regular use. XML includes a few built-in entities, although not nearly as many as HTML. XML's five built-in entities are listed in Table 5.2.

Table 5.2 Entities built into the XML standard

Entity	Character Represented
&	ampersand (&)
<	less-than sign (<)
>	greater-than sign (>)
'	apostrophe (')
"e	quote (")

Even though these entities are certainly useful and help developers keep their content out of the way of markup, they offer only the tiniest taste of the powerful things XML can do with general entities. Developers can define entities just as they can define elements. General entities are simple and make many complex and annoying tasks very simple, especially when it comes to filling in boilerplate text. The syntax for defining a general entity is fairly simple:

```
<!ENTITY Name EntityDefinition>
```

The name of the entity must be composed of letters, digits, periods, dashes, underscores, or colon, and begin with a letter or an underscore. The entity definition may contain any valid markup and must be enclosed in quotes. The syntax for using an entity in the markup is also simple:

```
&Name;
```

The ampersand must appear at the start, and the semicolon must be at the end. No additional whitespace is permitted around or inside the entity.

Creating entities this way is useful for repetitive information that is prone to change during the lifetime of the document. For example, during the development of a manual for the first version of a product, the developers may not even know the name of the product. Rather than introducing possible errors by doing a search-and-replace when the product is finalized, the developers can use an entity reference to make sure that the product is referred to correctly. For example, the code name of a project might be "Crystal". In the prerelease version of the documentation, developers could create the following entity reference:

```
<!ENTITY ProdName "Crystal">
```

Whenever the product was referred to, they would then use an entity reference rather than the actual name of the product;

```
&ProdName; is a remarkable advance, guaranteeing
users happier days.
```

would be interpreted as

```
Crystal is a remarkable advance, guaranteeing users
happier days.
```

When the final product name was finalized, transforming Crystal into RF-2000-QJ-46, the developer could just change the entity reference:

```
<!ENTITY ProdName="RF-2000-QJ-46">
```

This text would then be interpreted as

```
RF-2000-QJ-46 is a remarkable advance, guaranteeing
users happier days.
```

It sounds a bit stilted, but determined developers could even create entities that address different grammatical positions (possessive, for example), if they needed to go that far. Entities are extremely useful for legal and other boilerplate documents. A simple contract where the only parts that change are the name of one of the parties and the amount of money involved could be written as

```
<CONTRACT>&boilerplate1; <PAYMENT>$100,000.00
(US)</PAYMENT>&boilerplate2;<RECIPIENT>Lucky
Author</RECIPIENT></CONTRACT>
```

Most contracts change more than this form would allow, but many contracts can be broken down into standard clauses, allowing the regular use of entities.

Nevertheless, the main use of general entities is still for presenting characters that aren't in the usual (normally ASCII) set. Character references allow developers to include characters that aren't easily inputted or that might not be understood consistently. For example,

```
<!ENTITY THORN   "&#222;" >
```

when used on systems using Latin-1 or Unicode encoding, will produce an Icelandic Thorn, a character not frequently seen on American keyboards. The built-in ampersand entity is declared as

```
<!ENTITY amp "&#38;">
```

Although developers could use these codes directly in XML without going to the trouble of creating an entity declaration, naming these characters tends to produce a much cleaner document. ISO 8879 (SGML) includes a full set of standard named entities used in SGML. The SGML markup uses codes, however, that most early XML parsers probably won't process. A full set of entity DTDs written for XML is available at http://www.jtauber.com/xml/entities.html and includes a wide variety of different characters and marks. You can either examine the code and add the parts you need to your own DTD or use parameter entities (described later) to include the entire entity DTD in your own DTD.

Entities have their own quirks. It is permissible to use markup inside of an entity, but using entities inside of entities takes some extra effort. The parser will examine the entity for markup when it is added to the document text, and errors in entity coding can produce mysterious parsing errors. Always test your entities before using them, and always make sure that the content of an entity is appropriate to its destination in the document.

One quirk in particular is worth additional mention. XML parsers interpret entities according to a strict set of rules, which tend to result in entities being parsed more than once. This can make it difficult to include entities within entities in certain situations. The situation comes about because some entities—all the parameter entities and character references—are parsed when the computer parses the DTD. When the entity is placed in the document, all entities are parsed. This situation is highly unusual (happening mostly when developers use the character reference equivalents for ampersands and less-than signs), but developers whose entities mysteriously wreak havoc on their documents should parse their entities separately and inspect their results.

The parameter entity, the other kind of entity, is for use only within DTDs. Parameter entities carry information for use in the markup declaration, often a set of common attributes shared by several elements or a link to an outside DTD. Parameter entities whose references are purely within the DTD are known as internal entities, whereas references that draw information from outside files are external entities. Even though parameter entities may considerably simplify the creation of a DTD, they should be used with caution. Entities by their nature require a lookup to determine their contents. This isn't too difficult for computers, but it can become extremely complex for unfortunate humans who have to sort out obfuscated XML.

Parameter entries use a percent sign (%) both in their references and in their declaration. The percent sign differentiates a general entity from a parameter entity. The syntax for a parameter entity declaration is

```
<!ENTITY % Name EntityDefinition>
```

(The space between the percent sign and the name of the entity is mandatory.) As was true for general entities, the name of the entity must be composed of letters, digits, periods, dashes, underscores, or colons and begin with a letter or an underscore. The entity definition may contain any valid markup and must be enclosed in quotes. The value of the entity definition must resolve to something that makes sense in the context in which the entity will be used; otherwise, the parser will fail to understand the DTD and will return errors.

Internal parameter entities are very similar to general entities. For example, a DTD for a document set that contained a variety of quoted materials might use a common set of attributes for all the different kinds of materials—letters, diaries, novels, poems, and quotations. To make the documents more readily searchable, all these elements need to have attributes that identify the language in which they are written and a copyright date to determine whether or not they remain in copyright. An entity declaration that provides these attributes might look like:

```
<!ENTITY % sourceinfo
"LANGUAGE CDATA #REQUIRED
COPYRIGHTDATE CDATA #REQUIRED">
```

Using that entity in a declaration only requires calling it with the *%name;* syntax:

```
<!ELEMENT LETTER (#PCDATA)>
<!ATTLIST LETTER %sourceinfo;>
<!ELEMENT QUOTATION (#PCDATA)>
<!ATTLIST QUOTATION %sourceinfo;>
```

(There is no space between the percent sign and the entity name when the entity is used; the space is used only when the entity name is declared.) The language and copyright date information will flow right into the QUOTATION and LETTER attribute declarations. When the parser encounters the %sourceinfo; notation, it will expand the entity to include the full value announced elsewhere in the DTD. QUOTATION and LETTER and any other elements that use the contents of the sourceinfo entity will require attributes indicating language and copyright date. This becomes more useful as the number of repetitive elements and the length of the attributes list grow.

External entities let developers link to materials entirely outside of their documents or their DTD and use the same syntax as the document type declaration described previously for linking to outside files. Entity values must use SYSTEM identifiers and may also use PUBLIC identifiers when appropriate. Most XML developers will probably find themselves linking to external documents using SYSTEM identifiers until document management systems become widely used enough for most document users to have access.

The contents of the files linked to by external entities are required only to make sense in the context in which they are used. Generally, they will consist of declarations or parts of declarations, although under certain circumstances they may also contain binary data, like GIF files. Parameter entities are frequently used to combine several DTD subsets or to include large lists of general entities. The files referred to by external entities may also include other external entities. Parsers will return an error if these references are circular—if document A refers to document B which refers to document C which refers to document A again, the parser will stop. External entities may resemble trees with many branches, but those branches are not allowed to grow back into the trunk. Too many branches, of course, will produce incredibly unwieldy DTDs, which are nearly impossible to understand.

Entities that refer to binary (nontextual) data are also required to use the NDATA keyword after the entity definition and to specify the type of data contained in the entity. An external binary entity referring to a GIF file, for example, should conclude with NDATA gif.

Our example for external entities will simply combine two lists of general entities for use in a single DTD. (Using parameter entities to nest more complex DTDs will be covered in later chapters.) It is always a good idea to include comments with external entity declarations—the URLs in SYSTEM identifiers and even the more complete information in PUBLIC identifiers are often cryptic. Our first entity file, companies.pen, includes the following:

```
<!ENTITY GLW "Corning Incorporated">
<!ENTITY IBM "International Business Machines">
<!ENTITY T "American Telephone and Telegraph">
```

Our second file, states.pen, includes the following:

```
<!ENTITY NC "North Carolina">
<!ENTITY ND "North Dakota">
<!ENTITY NJ "New Jersey">
<!ENTITY NM "New Mexico">
<!ENTITY NY "New York">
```

Our DTD, although simple, is also stored in an external file:

```
<!--The following entity connects to a list of
companies using stock ticker symbols as entity
references. -->
<!ENTITY % companies
"http://127.0.0.1/companies.pen">
<!--The following entity connects to a list of
states using postal abbreviations as entity
references. -->
```

```
<!ENTITY % states "http://127.0.0.1/states.pen">
<!ELEMENT DOCUMENT (#PCDATA)>
%companies;
%states;
```

The sample XML file that uses these references reads as:

```
<?xml version="1.0" Encoding="UTF-8"?>
<!DOCTYPE PARAMEXAMPLE SYSTEM
"http://127.0.0.1/penex.dtd">
<PARAMEXAMPLE>
<DOCUMENT>The company &GLW; is headquartered in
&NY;, as is &IBM;.  &T; is headquartered in
&NJ;.</DOCUMENT>
</PARAMEXAMPLE>
```

Parsing this should yield the following results:

```
<?xml version="1.0" Encoding="UTF-8"?>
<!DOCTYPE PARAMEXAMPLE SYSTEM "http://127.0.0.1/penex.dtd">
<PARAMEXAMPLE>
    <DOCUMENT>
            The company Corning Incorporated is
headquartered in New York, as is International
Business Machines. American Telephone and Telegraph is
headquartered in New Jersey.
    </DOCUMENT>
</PARAMEXAMPLE>
```

As we'll see in later chapters, parameter entities can be a very useful tool for simplifying complex markup and managing multiple DTDs.

Notation Declarations

Notation declarations are an announcement that data from an outside (non-XML) source is needed in the document and helps to pass processing to an application other than the parser. Notation declarations are sometimes used in combination with processing instructions to provide a means of handling nontextual information within a document. The notation declaration tells the processor what kind of information there is; the processing instruction announces what process should be used to handle it. Notation names can also be used as attribute values.

The syntax for notation declarations is similar to the document type declaration:

```
<!NOTATION Name ExternalID>
```

A notation declaration might read:

```
<!NOTATION eps SYSTEM "epsview.exe">
```

The parser does nothing to check the information at the location specified; it just passes the address on to the processing application. If the processing application can handle the information, that's wonderful. If it can't, it doesn't matter to the parser. The SYSTEM keyword is normally followed by a reference to an application that can present the data, but the processing application is definitely not required to use that application. (If a Macintosh or UNIX user was reading this file, a Windows executable wouldn't help them much anyway). Notations that the processing application cannot understand may be errors, but they aren't XML errors. The parser will continue its work without announcing an error. The application, of course, may announce its own errors.

Marked Sections in DTDs: IGNORE and INCLUDE

Developers who need to test different structures while keeping track of alternatives may want to use the IGNORE and INCLUDE marked sections in DTDs. (In SGML, these also work in documents, but XML has banished them to the DTD.) IGNORE and INCLUDE let developers turn portions of a DTD on and off. IGNORE and INCLUDE are particularly useful for developers who are combining several DTDs and need to limit the side effects of multiple files colliding, or for developers who need to create a single core DTD with optional subsets. IGNORE and INCLUDE sections may be nested inside other IGNORE and INCLUDE sections, but, like elements, their beginnings and ends may not overlap.

The syntax for IGNORE and INCLUDE resembles that of CDATA:

```
<![IGNORE[ declarations ]]>
<![INCLUDE[declarations ]]>
```

Neither IGNORE nor INCLUDE may appear in the middle of a declaration; both must address a single declaration or a set of declarations. For example,

```
<![IGNORE[<!ELEMENT YUCK (#PCDATA)>]]>
<![INCLUDE[<!ELEMENT HOORAY (#PCDATA)>]]>
```

would keep the YUCK element from being parsed and would allow the HOORAY element to be parsed normally. Applied in this way, IGNORE seems like a handy wait to edit out useless parts of a DTD, and INCLUDE seems to be just plain useless. Parameter entities give INCLUDE and IGNORE the power they need to be meaningful additions to the XML vocabulary. Instead of using INCLUDE and IGNORE directly to change code throughout a DTD, developers can use parameter entities to make all those changes in one place. This makes INCLUDE and IGNORE far more convenient and occasionally even necessary. The following example provides a simple demonstration:

```
<!ENTITY % invoice "IGNORE">
<!ENTITY % receipt "INCLUDE">
<![%invoice; [
```

```
<!ENTITY notice "Please remit the following
payment within thirty days.">]]>
<![%receipt; [
<!ENTITY notice "Thank you for your prompt
payment. The sums below have been collected and
recorded.">]]>
<!ENTITY address "555 Twelvetwelve Lane">
```

Depending on the values assigned to invoice and receipt, the general entity notice will provide either the voice of a bill collector or a grateful vendor. To change the output, just switch the values of the two entities. The value of the address entity, on the other hand, will be the same in either case. Similar markup could have continued throughout the DTD, with parts inappropriate for receipts being struck. Switching the DTD over to receipts would require editing only two lines of the file rather than demanding a search-and-replace of the entire document. In the next chapters, we'll explore more uses of this limited but powerful tool.

Logical Structures

After pages and pages of preliminaries, it's time to finally create some elements, attributes, and document structures. The tools covered previously are necessary to this work, but element and attribute declarations are the core of XML. Well-formed documents can be useful for certain situations, but the element structures they use exist only in the document and in the mind of the designer. DTDs are an opportunity for developers to make their vision concrete, creating specifications for documents and not just documents. A well-written set of elements and attributes will make it easy for programs to extract useful information as well as present it beautifully. Even though the other parts of the XML specification may assist in this task, the main work of XML is creating document structures using elements and attributes.

Elements

Before we discuss elements any further, we need to look at two related concepts—parent and child elements. HTML developers are accustomed to using elements without much concern for context, with the significant exceptions of list and table elements. Understanding context is a critical prerequisite to building a DTD that works efficiently. In XML, the context provider is the parent element, and the child element may provide context to elements nested inside of itself. For example, in the structure

```
<SECTION >
     <PARAGRAPH>
          <SENTENCE>
          </SENTENCE>
     </PARAGRAPH>
</SECTION >
```

the SECTION element is the parent element of the PARAGRAPH element, which in turn is the parent element of the SENTENCE element. Similarly, the SENTENCE element is the child element of the PARAGRAPH element, which itself is the child of the SECTION element. XML also includes a document entity, which provides a root from which the markup tree structures can grow. If SECTION was the first element in a document, it would be a child of the document entity. (There isn't any special way to define a document entity—it just provides parsers with a place to start.)

As we saw earlier in the chapter, creating elements is very simple. The element declaration syntax is

```
<!ELEMENT name content>
```

The name of an element must follow the same rules as the name of an entity: it must be composed only of letters, digits, periods, dashes, underscores, or colons. The name may be defined as a parameter entity, as may the content. The content of an element can be of four types: a mixed-content declaration, a list of elements, the keyword EMPTY, or the keyword ANY. ANY is the simplest declaration, announcing that this element can contain all kinds of data and markup:

```
<!ELEMENT BOXOSTUFF ANY>
```

Using this declaration, all BOXOSTUFF elements will allow any kind of element or data to be included in their content. A document created that used the BOXOSTUFF element declared previously could look like:

```
<BOXOSTUFF><DARKSPACE>emptiness</DARKSPACE>more
junk</BOXOSTUFF>
```

The DARKSPACE element would need to be declared elsewhere; otherwise, BOXOSTUFF would impose no rules on its contents.

Although using ANY is perfectly acceptable XML, I strongly recommend that developers try to be more specific about document structure. Because HTML and some other forms of markup were primarily used for formatting, tags that effectively used ANY were necessary. Forbidding the use of bold text in a paragraph would undoubtedly cause an uproar. XML changes all that. By providing developers an opportunity to create document structures, XML promises to help create more intelligent documents. A large part of that intelligence is the kind of error checking XML can provide when given a fully developed DTD, complete with rules defining which elements can go where. Try to restrict the use of ANY to early DTD development, replacing it with a more complete content specification as quickly as possible.

The EMPTY keyword is ANY's polar opposite. Instead of allowing any content, it allows no content. Elements defined with EMPTY content may have attributes but do not permit information to be stored between their beginning and end tags. The element declaration for an empty element is concise:

```
<!ELEMENT EMPTYSPACE EMPTY>
```

Using this empty tag in a document requires even less room:

```
<EMPTYSPACE/>
```

Most of the time EMPTY elements will be written as only an empty element tag ending with a /> (
, for example). Typical beginning and end tags are permitted, but no elements or data may come between the tags.

Most element declarations will contain lists of elements, setting rules for which elements are required, the sequence in which they appear, and how many times they may appear. (Remember that all elements in the list must always be defined separately in their own declarations.) Parameter entities may also appear in the list, making it easier for developers to create multiple similar structures. Table 5.3 lists a few symbols to provide rules for using elements (and attributes, as we'll see later).

Table 5.3 Symbols for specifying element structure

Symbol	Symbol Type	Description	Example	Example Notes
|	Vertical bar	Indicates or condition.	thisone | thatone	Either thisone or thatone must appear.
,	Comma	Requires appearance in specified sequence.	thisone, thatone	thisone must appear, followed by thatone.
?	Question mark	Makes optional, but only one may appear.	thisone?	thisone may appear.
	No symbol	One, and only one, must appear.	thisone	thisone must appear.
*	Asterisk	Allows any number to appear, even zero.	thisone*	thisone may be present; multiple appearances of thisone are acceptable.
+	Plus sign	Requires at least one to appear, but may appear multiple times.	thisone+	thisone must be present; multiple appearances of thisone are acceptable.

Symbol	Symbol Type	Description	Example	Example Notes
( )	Parentheses	Groups elements.	(thisone | thatone), whichone	Either thisone or thatone must appear, followed by whichone.

SGML developers may wonder what happened to the ampersand (&). XML, at least in version 1.0, does not support that content model group. Mixed declarations and use of or statements can provide similar capabilities in XML.

These options create a tremendous number of possibilities, as well as a dangerous temptation to create complex structures that attempt to cover every possible use of child elements that seems sensible. The following examples provide some simple examples and explanations of acceptable declarations.

The simplest element content is the rare circumstance where an element may contain only one other element. This might happen in cases where a frustrated developer needs to create a "wrapper" element for an element in an outside DTD that can't be modified. The declaration for WRAPPER would read:

```
<!ELEMENT WRAPPER (UNTOUCHABLE)>
```

In this case, the only acceptable use of the WRAPPER element would be as follows:

```
<WRAPPER><UNTOUCHABLE>untouchable
content</UNTOUCHABLE></WRAPPER>
```

A more likely declaration would include two elements in sequence. A briefing, for example, might include a title and some content. The declarations would be

```
<!ELEMENT TITLE (#PCDATA)>
<!ELEMENT CONTENT (#PCDATA)>
<!ELEMENT BRIEFING (TITLE, CONTENT)>
```

This allows for more sophisticated markup:

```
<BRIEFING>
<TITLE>Another dull briefing</TITLE>
<CONTENT>Today, too much happened for me to
adequately discuss it.</CONTENT>
</BRIEFING>
```

If the boss grew weary of such despondent headlines, the DTD could be modified to make the TITLE optional:

```
<!ELEMENT BRIEFING (TITLE?, CONTENT)>
```

In extreme cases, the CONTENT could also be made optional with the addition of a question mark. If briefings grew longer, the developer could allow writers to include multiple CONTENT elements under a single briefing element by adding a plus sign:

```
<!ELEMENT BRIEFING (TITLE?, CONTENT+)>
```

Substituting an asterisk for the plus sign would allow briefings to be shorter as well as longer, which would allow writers to create briefings with no CONTENT elements or thousands.

Although most simple documents, and some larger documents, contain single elements in reasonably obvious sequences, more complex documents need more combinations to allow for greater flexibility. Paragraphs and lists can often substitute for each other. A recipe, for instance, might include a list of ingredients or a story of a trip to the grocery store. The following declarations would make either approach valid:

```
<!ELEMENT STORY (#PCDATA)>
<!ELEMENT ITEM (#PCDATA)>
<!ELEMENT INGREDIENTLIST (ITEM+)>
<!ELEMENT INGREDIENTS (STORY | INGREDIENTLIST)>
```

The XML code for an ingredient section could then look like this for a more traditional recipe:

```
<INGREDIENTS><INGREDIENTLIST>
<ITEM>Butter,enough to coat frying pan</ITEM>
<ITEM>Hot dogs, as many as needed</ITEM>
</INGREDIENTS>
```

Authors who preferred to tell tales of their ingredients could use this format instead, and XML parsers would accept it:

```
<INGREDIENTS><STORY>
No one wants to talk about where hot dogs come
from, but I know their origins. They come from
trucks that unload them regularly into the backs
of grocery stores.  Clerks open the boxes and put
the hot dogs on the shelf.  It's really not that
complicated, and at least it's plastic wrapped.
Butter works the same way, but it comes in boxes
and wax paper.
</STORY>
```

The OR structure also makes it possible to create spaces where a limited number of elements may be used freely in combination. A discussion of poetry, for instance, might consists of quotes interspersed with commentary. The sequence wouldn't be especially predictable, but it would clearly fit within the structure of a chapter. The following declaration creates a CHAPTER element that comes complete with a title and allows multiple quotes and comments.

```
<!ELEMENT TITLE (#PCDATA)>
<!ELEMENT QUOTE (#PCDATA)>
<!ELEMENT COMMENT (#PCDATA)>
<!ELEMENT CHAPTER (TITLE, (QUOTE | COMMENT)*)>
```

The following XML document would parse properly, interpreting the (QUOTE | COMMENT)* as an invitation to use multiple QUOTE and COMMENT elements in any sequence.

```
<CHAPTER><TITLE>Bad Poetry Rocks</TITLE>
<QUOTE>I'm a poet and I didn't know it</QUOTE>
<COMMENT>This is the classic 'bad' poem.  Some
might claim that its natural rhythm makes it a
fine 'found' poem, but I must disagree.</COMMENT>
<QUOTE>Jack and Jill went up the hill</QUOTE>
<COMMENT>Who let the nursery rhymes in?</COMMENT>
</CHAPTER>
```

QUOTE elements and COMMENT elements could appear in any sequence. Two quotes followed by a comment would be legal, as would be ten comments with no quotes at all.

XML allows developers to create very elaborate sets of rules using the parentheses and the |, *, and + operators. It is possible to define entire documents so that all the child elements appear in the root parent element: it just takes an extremely twisted declaration, and results in markup that frequently isn't useful for very much. If a markup declaration becomes too complicated, it's usually a sign that it's time to break up the declaration and create some subelements. For example,

```
<!ELEMENT CRAZY((TITLE | ART)+, (HEADLINE |
PARAGRAPH | SUBHEAD | PICTURE | TABLE | POP-UP)*,
CONCLUSION)>
```

The CRAZY element is perfectly legal. It begins with at least one of a TITLE element or an ART element. The next section, which is probably the body of the article, can include HEADLINE, PARAGRAPH, SUBHEAD, PICTURE, TABLE, and POP-UP elements in any sequence and any order. After that mess is complete, a CONCLUSION element must appear to finish the article. This declaration might be better broken up into multiple elements with more structure:

```
<!ELEMENT CRAZY (HEADER, ARTICLE+,CONCLUSION)>
<!ELEMENT HEADER (TITLE?, ART?)>
<!ELEMENT ARTICLE (HEADLINE, CONTENT)>
<!ELEMENT CONTENT (PARAGRAPH | SUBHEAD | PICTURE |
TABLE | POP-UP)*>
<!ELEMENT CONCLUSION (#PCDATA)>
```

The CONTENT element can stay mixed up because every article is bound to vary, but the rest of the document receives considerably more structure.

Mixed-content declarations are the final option. Technically, the (#PCDATA) content used in most of the examples in this chapter is a mixed-content declaration all by itself. Mixed-content declarations can allow multiple elements to appear as child elements without requiring them to appear or making any specific demands on the sequence in which they appear. The simplest mixed-content declaration is one of the most frequent: declaring content to be PCDATA so that text and entities (but no other elements) may appear:

```
<!ELEMENT ORDINARY (#PCDATA)>
```

The ORDINARY element can now contain text or entity markup in any combination. XML offers only PCDATA for elements that need to contain text (and not just other elements). Consequently, this basic declaration will be used for nearly any leaf element. (Leaf elements have parent elements but no child elements; figuratively, they're the branches farthest out on the tree, where the action actually takes place.) In some situations, however, developers may want to allow other elements to appear in a leaf element. Not all leaf data are appropriate to every element. An ingredient, for instance, shouldn't contain a table of contents, but it might contain a note.

The declaration creating an element that could hold an ingredient description and/or a note would look like:

```
<!ELEMENT INGREDIENT (#PCDATA | NOTE)*>
```

This declaration would permit INGREDIENT elements to contain the textual information they need to present ingredients, as well as NOTE elements to explain ingredients that are strange or difficult to find.

DTDs that include a significant set of child elements that can be used in multiple parent elements can be simplified with parameter entities listing the elements. The parser should parse the parameter entity and add its markup to the element content declaration.

```
<!ENTITY % parts "prologue | detail | moral |
punchline | joke">
<!ELEMENT STORY (#PCDATA | %parts;)*>
<!ELEMENT TALE (#PCDATA | %parts;)*>
<!ELEMENT FABLE (#PCDATA | %parts;)*>
```

In this case, STORY, TALE, and FABLE elements can contain text and any of the PROLOGUE, DETAIL, MORAL, PUNCHLINE, or JOKE elements. These subelements may appear in any order and any number may appear. All other elements are prohibited from appearing in a STORY, TALE, or FABLE element.

The parameter entity could also include the parentheses and the #PCDATA declaration. Each approach has its advantages in a different situations.

Attributes

Attributes have provided much of HTML's power, but they will probably be used somewhat more sparingly in XML. Attributes are most useful for storing information holding more interest to computers than to humans. Even in HTML, attributes held critical formatting information for the browser, not information about the contents of the element. Attributes remain a key part of XML, however, offering flexibility beyond that of elements, and solidifying underlying structures. Attribute declarations use some syntax similar to element declarations but tend to offer more precise definitions of the content they allow.

Attributes are defined using the following syntax:

```
<!ATTLIST ElementName
     AttributeName Type Default
     (AttributeName Type Default...)>
```

The first value in an attribute declaration is the name of the element to which the attributes apply. Although it makes a DTD more readable to include the attribute declaration right after the element declaration, this is not required. In fact, there can be multiple attribute declarations for the same element; all declarations for that element will be combined into one large set. If the same attribute is declared multiple times in that set, only the first appearance will be used. This makes it easy to extend existing DTDs without having to change them drastically.

After the element is named, an attribute definition or a list of attribute definitions may follow. A definition consists of the name of an attribute, its type, and its default value (or a specification for that value). Names of attributes must obey the same rules as names for entities and elements: it must contain only letters, digits, periods, dashes, underscores, and colons. Attribute types are quite unlike the structures explored so far and define the kinds of data permitted in an attribute when used in an element instance. (An element instance is just a use of the element in the document.) Table 5.4 lists all the acceptable values for attribute types.

Table 5.4 Attribute Types

Type	Explanation
CDATA	The attribute may contain only character data. (Markup will never be interpreted in attribute values.)
ID	The value of the attribute must be unique, identifying the element. If two attributes within a document of type ID have the same value, the parser should return an error.
IDREF	The value of the attribute must refer to an ID value declared elsewhere in the document. If the value of the attribute doesn't match an ID value within the document, the parser should return an error.
ENTITY, ENTITIES	The value of an ENTITY attribute must correspond to the name of an external binary entity declared in a DTD. ENTITIES is similar but allows multiple entity names separated by whitespace.
NMTOKEN, NMTOKENS	The value of the attribute must be a name token much like CDATA, but the characters used in the value must be letters, digits, periods, dashes, underscores, or colons. NMTOKENS is similar but allows multiple values separated by whitespace.
NOTATION	The value of the attribute must refer to the name of a notation declared elsewhere in the DTD.
Enumerated, e.g. (thisone | thatone)	The value of the attribute must match one of the values listed. Values must appear in parentheses and separated by OR (|) symbols.
NOTATION (enumerated)	The value of the attribute must match the name of one of the NOTATION names listed. For example, an attribute with type NOTATION (picture | slide) would need to have a value of "picture" or "slide", and NOTATION declarations would need to exist for both picture and slide.

Most of the time, developers will need to use CDATA, ID, and enumerated types, although the other possibilities are available. The last necessary part of an attribute declaration is the default. The default may take one of four values:

Table 5.5 Attribute Defaults

Value	Explanation
#REQUIRED	Indicates to the parser that this attribute must have a value in all instances of the element. Failure to include the attribute will result in parsing errors.
#IMPLIED	Allows the parser to ignore this attribute if no value is specified. The XML working draft states: "The XML processor must inform the application that no value was specified; no constraint is placed on the behavior of the application."
#FIXED *value*	Announces that element instances that specify that a value for this attribute must specify *value*. If an element instance doesn't include this attribute, its value will be presumed to be the *value* specified.
defaultvalue	Provides a default value for the attribute. If the attribute is not declared explicitly in an element instance, the attribute will be assumed to have a value of *defaultvalue*.

Now that we have explanations of all these parts, it's time to show what they do. Attributes of type ID are becoming more and more common as scripting tools and other processors have scrambled to find a way to address elements individually in documents. Making these systems work effectively, however, usually requires that all elements (or at least the elements to be manipulated) have an ID value, usually listed in the id attribute. Declaring a required ID value for an element takes little effort:

```
<!ELEMENT DATABRICK (#PCDATA)>
```

```
<!ATTLIST DATABRICK
     id   ID   #REQUIRED>
```

All DATABRICK elements created in documents resulting from this DTD will be required to have unique values for their id attribute. Other attributes might allow a processing application to treat DATABRICK elements differently, based on their type. Defining a list of possible types will make it much easier for a processing application to run smoothly.

```
<!ELEMENT DATABRICK (#PCDATA)>
<!ATTLIST DATABRICK
     id   ID   #REQUIRED
     status    (proceeding | accepted | rejected
|deferred) "proceeding">
```

DATABRICK elements now have a status attribute that informs the processing application of their status. If an element is created that doesn't specify a value for this attribute, the DATABRICK is assumed to be "proceeding" along a path of eventual acceptance, rejection, or deferral to a later date. A document management system or a database could use this attribute to limit their activities to DATABRICK elements whose status is appropriate to their work.

In cases where an attribute's presence isn't critical to proper processing, implied default values are acceptable. An application that translates documents from one DTD to another might use a comments field of some kind to keep track of the activities it has performed on the document. Only documents that had been through this process would need such a comment; documents that had been created directly in the target DTD might have no such need. To create this comment attribute, you could use the following declaration:

```
<!ELEMENT MASTERPIECE (#PCDATA)>
<!ATTLIST MASTERPIECE
```

```
      TranslationNote      CDATA      #IMPLIED>
```

This might be adequate for many situations. It might be better, however, to supply a default value instead of leaving the parser to report no value.

```
<!ELEMENT MASTERPIECE (#PCDATA)>
<!ATTLIST MASTERPIECE
      TranslationNote      CDATA      "None">
```

"None" is a slightly stronger affirmation that no translation was done than is a notice that the attribute contained no value. It is easier to check for in a program and relieves the programmer of wondering whether the parser had a problem or there really was no value.

Fixed attribute types are somewhat unusual. They might be useful in situations where documents are fed into processors that use attributes for formatting to ensure that the results of processing all the documents created with this DTD will look similar. By specifying a fixed attribute value, a particular DTD can make certain to preserve its identity in collections of documents that use similar DTDs.

```
<!ELEMENT ARTICLE (#PCDATA)>
<!ATTLIST ARTICLE
      FormatModel      CDATA      #FIXED
"Contemporary">
```

Another DTD file uses a similar declaration, but with a different fixed value:

```
<!ELEMENT ARTICLE (#PCDATA)>
<!ATTLIST ARTICLE
      FormatModel      CDATA      #FIXED "Country">
```

A processing application could take note of the FormatModel attribute and choose a set of styles appropriate to that model. It could also use the information to sort the documents in a library, allowing browsers to choose only articles that fit their design mood of the moment.

Attribute values that refer to external data sources can also be useful for processing. Although the parser itself will do nothing with the information (except pass it along), a processing application can combine that information with the markup material to create, for example, a document with pictures:

```
<!NOTATION ourFormat1SYSTEM
"http://www.gronk.com/ourViewer.exe">
<!NOTATION ourFormat2 SYSTEM
"http://www.gronk.com/pictures/ourPlayer.exe">
<!ELEMENT DOCUMENT (#PCDATA)>
<!ELEMENT PICTURE empty>
<!ATTLIST PICTURE
     TYPE     NOTATION (ourFormat1 | ourFormat2)
"ourFormat1"
     IMAGE CDATA #IMPLIED>
```

In this case, the editor of a set of documents has decreed that all pictures must be in one of two formats. The XML document that used this DTD might look like:

```
<DOCUMENT>I hate my boss.  He makes me use this
picture all the time:
<PICTURE TYPE="ourFormat2" IMAGE="FROGS.fm2"/>
Sometimes he lets me use this image:
<PICTURE TYPE="ourFormat1" IMAGE="BIRDS.fm1"/>
But I hate it more, so I usually stick with the
frogs.
</DOCUMENT>
```

Now that we have the tools, it's time to start making them work. The next chapter will take all these strange parts and start applying them to real documents and practical situations.

CHAPTER 6

Re-creating Web and Paper Documents with XML

Now that we've covered all the parts involved, it's time to create some valid XML documents with reasonably complex DTDs. Despite the many parts involved, creating a DTD doesn't need to be painful. Developers converting documents from HTML or a word processor style sheet often find that their document structures are actually simplified. This chapter will examine the production and implementation of two example DTDs for document production, including DTD development, document coding, and style sheet creation for browser viewing of the documents.

None of the examples in this chapter include links to other documents. Links in XML are considerably more complex than those in HTML and will receive separate coverage in Chapter 10. For now, familiarize yourself with the syntax of XML DTDs and learn the structures that exist within a document rather than throughout a site.

To XML from HTML

Many businesses already store huge quantities of information in HTML. After spending hours to convert it to HTML from some other format, many of these information keepers probably aren't thrilled to be hearing about this great new development that promises to sweep away HTML. However, most of the HTML information already created will probably never be formally converted to XML, and if it is, that conversion is likely to be automated. Because HTML files have often been developed to look a certain way, the appearance of finished HTML on the screen has taken precedence over the structure underlying the code. Developers on a deadline must have something to show the client; if broken code doesn't bother the browsers in which it's viewed, it isn't likely to bother the client. Add to that the fact that much HTML is coded by hand (or by tools that litter the page with extra markup), and the odds of HTML pages being close to well-formed XML drop precipitously.

If all that is needed are technically valid XML documents, it might be appropriate to use one of the standard HTML DTDs as the document DTD. The DTDs are currently in SGML that isn't compatible with XML, but work is in progress on several projects to create XML versions of the HTML DTDs. Remember, though, that valid XML is not necessarily easily managed. Meaningful markup that reflects content rather than formatting is the main advantage of XML, and using the HTML DTDs will not provide that.

For many pages, the conversion process will probably take place by hand, as it would with paper documents. Tools may appear that can "learn" the format of a set of pages and extract the needed content, but sets of HTML pages that aren't generated by machines rarely follow a format consistently. The text on one page may include five paragraphs, whereas another page may have no text at all. For example,

```
<HTML>
<HEAD><TITLE>Joe's Catalog - Money
Counters</TITLE></HEAD>
<BODY BGCOLOR="#FFFFF">
<H1>Money Counting Equipment</H1>
```

```
<H2>Basic Money Counter</H2>
<H4>Count your cash without spending all of
it!</H4>
Joe's is pleased to announce this NEW addition to
our line.  People with piles of change can sort
their money easily, and wrap it for the bank.
Makes the change box a lot more useful!<BR>
Price:<B>$14.95</B>, <FONT SIZE=1>plus $4.95
shipping and handling. </FONT><P>
Also available: Paper Coin Wrappers, bag of 100:
<B>$2.95</B><P>
<H2>Standard Money Counter</H2>
<H3>Count and collect your cash
automatically!</H3>
This money counter wraps your change automatically
- just feed it the plastic change rolls.  You'll
feel just like the bank when you read its LED
display announcing how much change you've
gathered.<P>
Special guarantee: 100% accuracy on wrapping or
your money back!<BR>
Price:<B>$64.95</B>, <FONT SIZE=1>plus $7.95
shipping and handling. </FONT><P>
Also available: Plastic Coin Wrappers, box of 400:
<B>$10.95</B><P>
<H2>Super-Duper Money Counter</H2>
Tired of change?  This machine counts bills as
well.  Feed it the take from a cash register and
watch it count away.  Spits out old bills in a
separate tray for easy counting.  Saves hours of
effort spent counting pennines - and twenties!<BR>
Price:<B>$649.95</B>, <FONT SIZE=1>plus $29.95
shipping and handling.</FONT><P>
```

```
Uses plastic coin wrappers above, and Paper Bill
Wrappers, box of 1000: <B>$10.95</B><P>
</BODY></HTML>
```

Even though this document has some clear parts that could be converted easily to a DTD, the style of coding isn't exactly conducive to automatic conversion to XML. The text is littered with "extra guarantees" and "also availables" that neither appear consistently nor use the same format. This looks like an old hand-coded HTML document, which uses the <P> tag at the end of a paragraph rather than enclosing paragraphs in <P>...</P>. Although it might be possible to write a program that converts this, Joe will probably be better off either developing a DTD and having someone convert it by hand or settling for making it well formed by adding closing tags.

A DTD for Joe's catalog could read like the following:

```
<!ELEMENT CATALOGPAGE (HEADER,CATALOGITEM+)>
<!ELEMENT HEADER (#PCDATA)>
<!ELEMENT CATALOGITEM (ITEMNAME, ITEMSUBHEAD?,
ITEMDESCRIPTION*,ITEMPRICING,SUBITEM*)>
<!ELEMENT ITEMNAME (#PCDATA)>
<!ELEMENT ITEMSUBHEAD (#PCDATA)>
<!ELEMENT ITEMDESCRIPTION(#PCDATA)>
<!ELEMENT ITEMPRICING
(#PCDATA|ITEMNOTE|PRICE|SHIPPING)*>
<!ELEMENT PRICE (#PCDATA)>
<!ELEMENT SHIPPING (#PCDATA)>
<!ELEMENT ITEMNOTE (#PCDATA)>
<!ELEMENT SUBNAME (#PCDATA)>
<!ELEMENT SUBITEM
(#PCDATA|SUBNAME|PRICE|SHIPPING)*>
```

Joe's catalog page would need to undergo some extensive modification. For example, the DTD adds a SHIPPING element that wasn't formally represented before. Additional layers of elements must be added where there wasn't any markup before. For those reasons, Joe's catalog probably needs to be recreated by a human rather than a machine. The new page looks like:

```
<?xml version="1.0" standalone="no" encoding="UTF-
8"?>
<!DOCTYPE CATALOGPAGE SYSTEM
"http://127.0.0.1/joes.dtd">
<CATALOGPAGE>
<HEADER>Money Counting Equipment</HEADER>
<CATALOGITEM>
<ITEMNAME>Basic Money Counter</ITEMNAME>
<ITEMSUBHEAD>Count your cash without spending all
of it!</ITEMSUBHEAD>
<ITEMDESCRIPTION>Joe's is pleased to announce this
NEW addition to our line.  People with piles of
change can sort their money easily, and wrap it
for the bank.  Makes the change box a lot more
useful!</ITEMDESCRIPTION>
<ITEMPRICING>Price:<PRICE>$14.95</PRICE>, plus
<SHIPPING>$4.95</SHIPPING> shipping and
handling.</ITEMPRICING>
<SUBITEM>Also available: <SUBNAME>Paper Coin
Wrappers, bag of 100</SUBNAME>:
<PRICE>$2.95</PRICE></SUBITEM>
</CATALOGITEM>
<CATALOGITEM>
<ITEMNAME>Standard Money Counter</ITEMNAME>
<ITEMSUBHEAD>Count and collect your cash
automatically!</ITEMSUBHEAD>
```

```
<ITEMDESCRIPTION>This money counter wraps your
change automatically - just feed it the plastic
change rolls.  You'll feel just like the bank when
you read its LED display announcing how much
change you've gathered.</ITEMDESCRIPTION>
<ITEMPRICING><ITEMNOTE>Special guarantee: 100%
accuracy on wrapping or your money
back!</ITEMNOTE>
Price:<PRICE>$64.95</PRICE>, plus
<SHIPPING>$7.95</SHIPPING> shipping and
handling.</ITEMPRICING>
<SUBITEM>Also available: <SUBNAME>Plastic Coin
Wrappers, box of 400</SUBNAME>:
<PRICE>$10.95</PRICE></SUBITEM>
</CATALOGITEM>
<CATALOGITEM>
<ITEMNAME>Super-Duper Money Counter</ITEMNAME>
<ITEMDESCRIPTION>Tired of change?  This machine
counts bills as well.  Feed it the take from a
cash register and watch it count away.  Spits out
old bills in a separate tray for easy counting.
Saves hours of effort spent counting pennines -
and twenties!</ITEMDESCRIPTION>
<ITEMPRICING>Price:<PRICE>$649.95</PRICE>, plus
<SHIPPING>$29.95</SHIPPING> shipping and
handling.</ITEMPRICING>
<SUBITEM>Uses plastic coin wrappers above, and
<SUBNAME>Paper Bill Wrappers, box of
1000</SUBNAME>: <PRICE>$10.95</PRICE></SUBITEM>
</CATALOGITEM>
</CATALOGPAGE>
```

This code is clearly valid and makes Joe's catalog much more machine-readable.

```
<?xml version="1.0" encoding="UTF-8"?>
<!DOCTYPE CATALOGPAGE SYSTEM
"http://127.0.0.1/joes.dtd">
<CATALOGPAGE>
    <HEADER>
        Money Counting Equipment
    </HEADER>
    <CATALOGITEM>
        <ITEMNAME>
            Basic Money Counter
        </ITEMNAME>
        <ITEMSUBHEAD>
            Count your cash without spending all of it!
        </ITEMSUBHEAD>
        <ITEMDESCRIPTION>
            Joe's is pleased to announce this NEW
addition to our line. People with piles of change can
sort their money easily, and wrap it for the bank.
Makes the change box a lot more useful!
        </ITEMDESCRIPTION>
        <ITEMPRICING>
            Price:
            <PRICE>
                $14.95
            </PRICE>
            , plus
            <SHIPPING>
                $4.95
            </SHIPPING>
            shipping and handling.
        </ITEMPRICING>
        <SUBITEM>
            Also available:
            <SUBNAME>
                Paper Coin Wrappers, bag of 100
            </SUBNAME>
            :
            <PRICE>
                $2.95
            </PRICE>
        </SUBITEM>
    </CATALOGITEM>
```

```
    <CATALOGITEM>
        <ITEMNAME>
            Standard Money Counter
        </ITEMNAME>
        <ITEMSUBHEAD>
            Count and collect your cash automatically!
        </ITEMSUBHEAD>
        <ITEMDESCRIPTION>
            This money counter wraps your change
automatically - just feed it the plastic change rolls.
You'll feel just like the bank when you read its LED
display announcing how much change you've gathered.
        </ITEMDESCRIPTION>
        <ITEMPRICING>
            <ITEMNOTE>
                Special guarantee: 100% accuracy on
wrapping or your money back!
            </ITEMNOTE>
            Price:
            <PRICE>
                $64.95
            </PRICE>
            , plus
            <SHIPPING>
                $7.95
            </SHIPPING>
            shipping and handling.
        </ITEMPRICING>
        <SUBITEM>
            Also available:
            <SUBNAME>
                Plastic Coin Wrappers, box of 400
            </SUBNAME>
            :
            <PRICE>
                $10.95
            </PRICE>
        </SUBITEM>
    </CATALOGITEM>
    <CATALOGITEM>
        <ITEMNAME>
            Super-Duper Money Counter
```

```
        </ITEMNAME>
        <ITEMDESCRIPTION>
            Tired of change? This machine counts bills
as well. Feed it the take from a cash register and
watch it count away. Spits out old bills in a separate
tray for easy counting. Saves hours of effort spent
counting pennies - and twenties!
        </ITEMDESCRIPTION>
        <ITEMPRICING>
            Price:
            <PRICE>
                $649.95
            </PRICE>
            , plus
            <SHIPPING>
                $29.95
            </SHIPPING>
            shipping and handling.
        </ITEMPRICING>
        <SUBITEM>
            Uses plastic coin wrappers above, and
            <SUBNAME>
                Paper Bill Wrappers, box of 1000
            </SUBNAME>
            :
            <PRICE>
                $10.95
            </PRICE>
        </SUBITEM>
    </CATALOGITEM>
</CATALOGPAGE>
```

This is still not a complete solution, although it may be all the solution Joe's Catalogs wants. A more through DTD design might change the kinds of information presented and the order in which they appear, making the code look more like the Jimbo's Super Clock catalog example in Chapter 3 with its part numbers and freight information. The catalog as it stands now is reasonably useful for people to read, but it is still not very effective for use in an inventory system or catalog management tool.

Pages that are already generated by a computer will be fairly easy to convert. Search-and-replace mechanisms may be able to convert static machine-generated pages if all the material uses precisely the same markup. Better yet, if the data are still available in the original structure (database form, most likely) and are used to create pages on the fly, the scripts that create HTML can be easily modified to produce XML. Instead of placing certain formatting tags around a price, the script can place it within a <PRICE> element.

A few HTML documents are probably ready for XML now, and HTML developers can plan ahead by designing pages that will convert easily. In Chapter 2, we discussed how Cascading Style Sheets provided a CLASS model that HTML developers could use to create their own tags effectively. CSS has been available for over a year, and some sites have been created that take advantage of its capacities. Developers who used CSS classes to reflect categories of content and not just formatting will be in very good shape. The main difference between the structure created by CSS CLASS attributes and that of XML is in enforcement: CSS can't require classes to nest in a particular order. Still, because CSS provides formatting inheritance between elements (child elements will by default receive many of the style properties of their parents), many pages that were created with CSS reflect good XML structure and are in a good position to be converted. The following example uses a small segment of a catalog to show how CSS CLASS attributes could have worked for Joe:

```
<HTML>
<HEAD><TITLE>Joe's Catalog - Money
Counters</TITLE>
<STYLE TYPE="text/css">
DIV.HEADER {font-size:24pt;font-weight:bold}
DIV.ITEMNAME {font-size:18pt;font-weight:bold}
DIV.ITEMSUBHEAD {font-size:14pt;font-weight:bold}
DIV.ITEMDESCRIPTION {font-size:12pt}
```

```
DIV.ITEMPRICING {font-size:10pt}
SPAN.PRICE {font-weight:bold}
SPAN.SHIPPING {font-weight:normal}
DIV.SUBITEM {font-size:11pt}
SPAN.SUBNAME {font-weight:bold}
</STYLE></HEAD>
<BODY BGCOLOR="#FFFFF">
<DIV CLASS="HEADER">Money Counting Equipment</DIV>
<DIV CLASS="ITEMNAME">Basic Money Counter</DIV>
<DIV CLASS="SUBHEAD">Count your cash without
spending all of it!</DIV>
<DIV CLASS="ITEMDESCRIPTION">Joe's is pleased to
announce this NEW addition to our line.  People
with piles of change can sort their money easily,
and wrap it for the bank.  Makes the change box a
lot more useful!</DIV>
<DIV CLASS="ITEMPRICING">Price:<SPAN
CLASS="PRICE">$14.95</SPAN>, plus <SPAN
CLASS="SHIPPING">$4.95</SPAN> shipping and
handling.</DIV>
<DIV CLASS="SUBITEM">Also available: <SPAN
CLASS="SUBNAME">Paper Coin Wrappers, bag of
100</SPAN>: <SPAN CLASS="PRICE">$2.95</SPAN></DIV>
</BODY></HTML>
```

If the catalog was organized like this, converting over to XML might take the development of a bit of custom code that could take the DIV and SPAN elements, replace them with the appropriate elements (in this case, their CLASS attributes), and group them under appropriate parent elements. Most developers, however, won't be this lucky, unless they've just begun building their HTML documents.

A much more complete analysis of the needs of a catalog document will appear in the next chapter. Joe's Catalog has come over from HTML, but faces a much more dramatic restructuring.

Building a CSS for Joe's catalog isn't too difficult. The parts are easily identified, and the formatting already exists in the HTML version. Remember that linking a CSS to an XML document requires some extra markup. To keep your XML documents valid after the CSS has been linked, modify the CATALOGPAGE element and add the following lines to your DTD:

```
<!ELEMENT CATALOGPAGE (HEAD?,HEADER,CATALOGITEM+)>
<!ELEMENT HEAD (LINK)>
<!ELEMENT LINK (EMPTY)>
<!ATTLIST LINK
      REL CDATA #REQUIRED
      HREF CDATA #REQUIRED
      TYPE CDATA #REQUIRED>
```

The big question now is whether or not Joe wants to change the look of his catalog. If not, it's pretty easy to create an appropriate style.

```
HEADER {
      display:block;
      font-size:24;
      font-family:serif;
      font-weight:bold
}
CATALOGITEM {
      display:block;
      font-family:serif
}
```

```
ITEMNAME {
     display:block;
     font-size: 18;
     font-weight:bold
}
ITEMSUBHEAD {
     display:block;
     font-size:14
}
ITEMDESCRIPTION {
     display:block;
     font-size:12
}
ITEMPRICING {
     display:block
}
PRICE {
     display:inline;
     font-family:bold
}
SHIPPING {
     display:inline
}
SUBITEM {
     display:block
}
```

The main tool used here is the style display attribute, which allows us to declare whether elements should be their own paragraph (start a new line and have space above and below) or flow with the text. If the element rates its own paragraph or line, it's styled as block. If it doesn't, it is styled as inline. The list-item option provides yet another option: separate lines, with less spacing than a block.

Although CSS and XML seem like a natural fit, the browser developers haven't quite caught on to the possibilities yet, at least as of version 4.0 of either the Netscape or Microsoft browsers. Still, given the general expectations that CSS will be used with XML on a regular basis, it seems worthwhile to go ahead and create style sheets for the DTDs featured previously to demonstrate the kinds of tools you'll need to make XML as presentable as HTML. Also remember that neither browser fully implements CSS in version 4.0.

After you have built a style sheet, making changes is easy—just make the change at the style sheet, and all changes will flow through to the documents that call the style sheet. Extending the style sheet isn't as easy. Suppose that the PRICE element had to be displayed in red, but only for markdowns. Although it would be nice to have an attribute indicating the type of price listed, CSS will respond to the CLASS and ID attributes only. As a result, the category of the PRICE element must be kept in the CLASS element for the following style declaration to format all marked-down items in red:

```
PRICE.markdown {

     display: inline;
     font-weight:bold;
     color:red

}
```

With this style declared, the browser or other formattng application will turn the following price red, indicating a great bargain:

```
<PRICE CLASS="markdown">$1.25</PRICE>
```

This will work for a while—until someone decides that the price color should also change if it's eligible for a bulk discount. Prices need to be either "fixed" or "byquantity". Even though the following style might work for a little while, it can hardly be called elegant:

```
PRICE.set{
      display:inline;
      font-weight:bold;
      color:blue
}
PRICE.byquantity {
      display:inline;
      font-weight:bold;
      color:green
}
PRICE.markdownset {
      display:inline;
      font-weight:bold;
      color:red
}
PRICE.markdownbyquantity {
      display:inline;
      font-weight:bold;
      color:brown

}
```

What would be ideal is an extension to CSS that allows it to set formats based on the existence and values of attributes other than ID and CLASS, and that may happen. Otherwise, formatting this properly and elegantly will probably require XSL or some other heavy-duty style tool.

Building This Book

In writing this book, I used two kinds of style notation. Most of the styling is done using Microsoft Word's built-in style tools and a style sheet provided by MIS:Press. Some of the information, like Notes, Output, Warnings, and Sidebars, uses markup notation very similar to XML. Notes, for instance, started with <NOTE> and ended with </NOTE>. Although these solutions work reasonably well, there are many ways they could improve. XML addresses most of those needs, simplifying the style sheet structure and opening up new media to this document at the same time.

The styles defined in Word are a combination of structural information and formatting information, as shown in Table 6.1.

Table 6.1 A sample style sheet

Style	Usage
TOC0 CT	Chapter number and title. This text will be used in table of contents when generated.
TOC1 A	A head—the top level of headings in a chapter. This text will be used in table of contents when generated.
TOC2 B	B head—the level of headings under A heads. This text also appears in table of contents.
C	C head—level below B. Not in table of contents.
D	D head—level below C. Not in table of contents.
E	E head—level below D. Not in table of contents.
BT	Body text—first paragraph of text after a header, icon, list, figure caption, or other free-standing graphic. Not indented.
BT INDENT	Body text following a BT element. Indented.
BL/NL1 TOP	Bulleted or numbered list—top line. (Formatted with extra space above.)
BL/NL2 MID	Bulleted or numbered list—middle lines. (Formatted with no extra space above or below.)
BL/NL3 BOT	Bulleted or numbered list—bottom line. (Formatted with extra space below.)

Style	Usage
GL	Glossary text—word defined should be in bold, definition in normal text.
CC1 TOP	First line of multiline code listing. Formatted with extra space above.
CC2 MID	Middle lines of multiline code listing. No extra space above or below.
CC3 BOT	Last line of multiline code listing. Formatted with extra space below.
CC4 SINGLE	Single line of multiline code listing. Formatted with extra space above and below.
ICON	Icon text—used in combination with markup (<NOTE>, <WARNING>, etc.) to identify text that needs to be called out from body text.
FG	Figure caption—Figure *chapterNum.FigureNum* should be in bold, rest of text plain.
LC	Listing caption—goes above code listing.
TBC	Table caption—goes above table.
TBH	Table heads—use above each column.
TB	Table body.
UL	Unnumbered list.
SN	Source notes—footnotes or notes at bottom of table.

The structures defined with markup are mostly icons and bullets. Bullets are entered as <b> on PCs to avoid collisions between operating systems. Note icons are indicated as <NOTE>. A few structures are indicated with simple formatting. Keystrokes and menu items are supposed to be in **bold**, and titles are in *italic*.

Even though the current model has worked well for MIS:Press over the years, we may be able to indicate document structures more easily and more clearly in XML. Unless they begin to use XML-enabled publishing tools, this effort won't do much for them, but it may shed some light on how to restructure formatting styles into structural styles. Structural styles can escape from some of the redundancy that is required to make formatting styles work and make converting this document from format to format easier.

Pass 1: A DTD That Looks Like the Old Styles

We'll start by setting up a chapter structure. Chapters will eventually themselves become part of the larger book structure. The Chapter will include a title, a brief introduction, and a series of sections marked by A heads. In the interest of ensuring a smooth transition, the original style names are used where possible, although spaces must be stripped out:

```
<!ELEMENT CHAPTER (HEAD?,TOC0CT, INTRODUCTORY,
ALEAF*))>
```

The HEAD element uses the DTD described previously to allow style sheet linking. The TOC0CT element performs the same duty as the TOC0 CT style: it identifies the chapter title. It contains only text:

```
<!ELEMENT TOC0CT (#PCDATA)>
```

The INTRODUCTORY element is new, making explicit a chapter feature that wasn't included in the previous definition. All chapters start with text after the chapter headline to introduce the material to follow. The INTRODUCTORY element is required and must consist of at least one body text (BT) paragraph. (No code listings or other subelements should appear in the introduction for now.)

```
<!ELEMENT INTRODUCTORY(BT+)>
```

The BT element is a bit more complicated because the text in it can include italic items (like citations) and bold items (like keystrokes and menu clicks—user actions). To address these needs, we'll create a few elements and a parameter entity that includes them, making it easier for us to include them in other elements.

```
<!ELEMENT CITATION (#PCDATA)>
<!ELEMENT USERACTION (#PCDATA)>
<!ENTITY % textual-elements
"(#PCDATA|CITATION|USERACTION)*">
<!ELEMENT BT(%textual-elements;)>
```

The next target is the ALEAF element. To avoid confusion with the HTML tags A and B, I've added the word LEAF to the letters for all of these sections. Because the leaves may contain a variety of content types, it's time to plan ahead and create a parameter entity. The content-elements entity will contain a list of all types of content available to a LEAF element, which includes only the PARAGRAPH element at present.

```
<!ENTITY % content-elements "BT">
```

All the LEAF elements will contain a header and paragraphs or sublevels.

```
<!ELEMENT ALEAF (TOC1A,BT,(%content-
elements;|BLEAF)*)>
<!ELEMENT BLEAF (TOC2B,BT,(%content-
elements;|CLEAF)*)>
<!ELEMENT CLEAF (C,BT,(%content-
elements;|DLEAF)*)>
<!ELEMENT DLEAF (D,BT,(%content-
elements;|ELEAF)*)>
<!ELEMENT ELEAF (E,BT,(%content-elements;)*)>
<!ELEMENT TOC1A (#PCDATA)>
<!ELEMENT TOC2B (#PCDATA)>
<!ELEMENT C (#PCDATA)>
<!ELEMENT D (#PCDATA)>
<!ELEMENT E (#PCDATA)>
```

Note that we didn't include the LEAF elements as part of the content elements entity. This would have allowed authors to put ELEAF elements directly below ALEAF elements, violating the desired hierarchy. Instead, they remain separate, making it easier for the designer to see the structure. Using the (%content-elements | XLEAF)* structure allows zero or more layers of content: ALEAFs aren't required to have BLEAF elements, but you can't have a CLEAF element unless it's included in a BLEAF element. (Later in this chapter, we'll change this, simplifying the structure considerably.)

This provides the basic structure for a chapter, building a basic outline form that can go five levels deep. (If a chapter moves beyond five levels, it will be either time to reconsider the chapter's organization or add a level to the DTD.) It's time to go back and add content beyond basic text paragraphs. The easiest type of information to manage in this context is code. The current style sheet uses four different styles for code, depending on the position of the line of code. In XML, what matters most is not the position of the code, but that the information is code. Style sheets get to clean up the presentation and apply the extra space before and after the code element. Our code element, to match the style sheet, will be named CC. By default, our CC element's TYPE attribute will be "CODE" because very few books still have textual output. For those books that do, we provide an "OUTPUT" value option for the TYPE, allowing the designer to format these two similar types slightly differently. A CC element may contain a listing caption (LC) and must include at least one CLINE (code line) element, with multiple lines available to store code as necessary.

```
<!ELEMENT CC (LC?,CLINE+)>
<!ATTLIST CC TYPE (CODE|OUTPUT) "CODE">
<!ELEMENT LC (#PCDATA)>
<!ELEMENT CLINE (#PCDATA)>
```

The next set of styles that needs an interpretation is the list styles. Currently, this style sheet includes a combined set of entries for bulleted and numbered lists, along with a separate style for unnumbered lists. This presents several options. We could maintain the style sheet as it exists now, creating one element to handle numbered and bulleted lists and another for unnumbered lists. We could break up the numbered and bulleted lists, keeping all the list styles separate. Finally, we could combine all the elements under one large umbrella.

Even though the large umbrella idea produces cleaner code (and we'll use it in the next pass), for now compatibility is important. Given the latest developments in style sheets (especially XSL), however, it seems likely that we'll want to separate bulleted and numbered lists for separate style processing. That way the style mechanism can apply numbers and bullets as appropriate, making it easier for writers to move items around without renumbering. Unnumbered lists will remain their own category.

```
<!ELEMENT BL (BLINE+)>
<!ELEMENT NL (NLINE+)>
<!ELEMENT UL (ULINE+)>
<!ELEMENT BLINE (#PCDATA)>
<!ELEMENT NLINE (#PCDATA)>
<!ELEMENT ULINE (#PCDATA)>
```

The next style we'll implement is GL, which is for glossary text. GL by itself doesn't do very much and depends on the author to make the glossary entry bold. Because glossaries are one of the best types of documents for manipulation, it seems reasonable to improve on this. The new GL element will contain a GLITEM and a GLDEFINITION, which explains it.

```
<!ELEMENT GL (GLITEM,GLDEFINITION)>
<!ELEMENT GLITEM (#PCDATA)>
<!ELEMENT GLDEFINITION (%textual-elements;)>
```

ICON text—the ubiquitous note—is a somewhat difficult case. The ICON text by definition has a graphic floating to the left of it, but the graphic is not specified in the style sheet. Although it might be possible to create separate NOTE, SHORTCUT, WARNING, and TIP elements for each type of text instead of an ICON element, this doesn't correspond well to current practice. We could use an attribute to store this information, but it must be visible to authors and editors without much digging. For now, we'll create an ICON element that contains an empty element at its start to represent the graphic that will be added by the processing application, followed by BT information.

```
<!ELEMENT ICON ((NOTE|SHORTCUT|WARNING|TIP),BT+)>
<!ELEMENT NOTE EMPTY>
<!ELEMENT SHORTCUT EMPTY>
<!ELEMENT WARNING EMPTY>
<!ELEMENT TIP EMPTY>
```

Tables are the next challenge, and they are a challenge XML is not exactly prepared to face. Tables are all about content, but content that's been stretched across a few columns. The style sheet offers TBC for the table caption (which should go above the table), TH to hold the column headings, TBH for the column headings, TB for the table body text, and SN for source notes at the bottom. Ideally authors would be able to create their own mini-DTD for every table, identifying cell contents with their own element. Unfortunately, a publishing style sheet doesn't offer much room for that kind of extension. For now, we'll improvise, using the HTML-style TR and the style sheet's TB (treated much like TD in HTML). Unlike HTML, we'll require that TB elements always fit inside of TR elements.

```
<!ELEMENT TABLE (TBC*,TH?,TR+,SN*)>
<!ELEMENT TBC (#PCDATA)>
```

```
<!ELEMENT TH (TBH+)>
<!ELEMENT TBH (#PCDATA)>
<!ELEMENT TR (TB+)>
<!ELEMENT TB (%textual-elements;)>
<!ELEMENT SN (%textual-elements;)>
```

Creating table elements in XML is a tricky business. Declaring these elements is not nearly the end of the line for this process. Although XSL has a much more complete set of tools for formatting tables, this is an area in which CSS has a long way to go.

The last major element that needs to be dealt with is figures. Figure images are not embedded directly in the file. Only a limited number of formats are acceptable. Figures include three parts: the picture, the figure number, and the caption describing the figure. The picture will be an empty element with attributes that explain to the processing application where to find the figure and what kind of figure file it is. The kind of file is defined using an attribute that matches a previously defined NOTATION declaration. The figure number will be part of the caption.

```
<!NOTATION tiff SYSTEM "viewer.exe">
<!NOTATION bmp SYSTEM "viewer.exe">
<!NOTATION eps SYSTEM "viewer.exe">
<!ELEMENT FIGURE (FIGREF, FG)>
<!ELEMENT FIGREF EMPTY>
<!ATTLIST FIGREF
     SRC   CDATA      #REQUIRED
     TYPE  NOTATION (tiff | bmp | eps) "tiff">
<!ELEMENT FG (FIGNUM, %textual-elements;)>
<!ELEMENT FIGNUM (#PCDATA)>
```

Now that we've created all of these content elements, it's time to update the content-elements parameter entity to include them.

```
<!ENTITY % content-elements "(BT | CC | BL | NL |
UL | GL | ICON | TABLE | FIGURE)*">
```

Combining all this into one gigantic DTD file gives us something we can work with.

```
<!--Chapter DTD, version 1 -->
<!--Mandatory starting elements -->
<!ELEMENT CHAPTER (HEAD?,TOCOCT, INTRODUCTORY,
ALEAF*)>
<!-- Chapter Title -->
<!ELEMENT TOCOCT (#PCDATA)>
<!--Chapter Introduction -->
<!ELEMENT INTRODUCTORY(BT+)>
<!--Common text elements. -->
<!ELEMENT CITATION (#PCDATA)>
<!ELEMENT USERACTION (#PCDATA)>
<!--Textual elements allows mixing w/ regular data
-->
<!ENTITY % textual-elements
"(#PCDATA|CITATION|USERACTION)*">
<!--BT - Body text.  Used for each paragraph -->
<!ELEMENT BT(%textual-elements;)>
<!--Content elements allows multiple content types
in section contents-->
<!ENTITY % content-elements "(BT | CC | BL | NL |
UL | GL | ICON | TABLE | FIGURE)*">
<!--XLEAF elements behave like X-heads in
previous-->
```

```
<!--Note the structure for XLEAF elements - BLEAF
elements can only appear in ALEAF elements, CLEAF
elements can only appear in BLEAF elements, etc. -
->
<!ELEMENT ALEAF (TOC1A,BT,(%content-
elements;|BLEAF)*)>
<!ELEMENT BLEAF (TOC2B,BT,(%content-
elements;|CLEAF)*)>
<!ELEMENT CLEAF (C,BT,(%content-
elements;|DLEAF)*)>
<!ELEMENT DLEAF (D,BT,(%content-
elements;|ELEAF)*)>
<!ELEMENT ELEAF (E,BT,(%content-elements;)*)>
<!--Headers for leaf sections -->
<!--A Head - appears in Table of Contents -->
<!ELEMENT TOC1A (#PCDATA)>
<!--B Head - appears in Table of Contents -->
<!ELEMENT TOC2B (#PCDATA)>
<!--C, D, E heads do not appear in Table of
Contents-->
<!ELEMENT C (#PCDATA)>
<!ELEMENT D (#PCDATA)>
<!ELEMENT E (#PCDATA)>
<!--Declarations for marking code listings -->
<!ELEMENT CC (LC?,CLINE+)>
<!--TYPE attribute differentiates code listings
from text output-->
<!ATTLIST CC TYPE (CODE|OUTPUT) "CODE">
<!--LC is list caption -->
<!ELEMENT LC (#PCDATA)>
<!--CLINE represents a single line of code-->
<!ELEMENT CLINE (#PCDATA)>
```

```
<!--Declarations for lists (bulleted, numbered,
unordered lists) -->
<!ELEMENT BL (BLINE+)>
<!ELEMENT NL (NLINE+)>
<!ELEMENT UL (ULINE+)>
<!--List contents (bulleted, numbered, unordered
lists)-->
<!ELEMENT BLINE (%textual-elements;)>
<!ELEMENT NLINE (%textual-elements;)>
<!ELEMENT ULINE (%textual-elements;)>
<!--Glossary Declarations -->
<!ELEMENT GL (GLITEM,GLDEFINITION)>
<!--Word being defined-->
<!ELEMENT GLITEM (#PCDATA)>
<!--Definition-->
<!ELEMENT GLDEFINITION (%textual-elements;)>
<!--Icon/Note Declarations -->
<!ELEMENT ICON ((NOTE|SHORTCUT|WARNING|TIP),BT+)>
<!--ICON types-->
<!ELEMENT NOTE EMPTY>
<!ELEMENT SHORTCUT EMPTY>
<!ELEMENT WARNING EMPTY>
<!ELEMENT TIP EMPTY>
<!--Table Declarations -->
<!ELEMENT TABLE (TBC*,TH?,TR+,SN*)>
<!--Table Caption -->
<!ELEMENT TBC (#PCDATA)>
<!--Table Headers -->
<!ELEMENT TH (TBH+)>
<!ELEMENT TBH (#PCDATA)>
<!--Table Rows -->
```

```
<!ELEMENT TR (TB+)>
<!--Table Body (sim to HTML TD) -->
<!ELEMENT TB (%textual-elements;)>
<!--Table Source Note -->
<!ELEMENT SN (%textual-elements;)>
<!--Graphic Type Declarations -->
<!NOTATION tiff SYSTEM "viewer.exe">
<!NOTATION bmp SYSTEM "viewer.exe">
<!NOTATION eps SYSTEM "viewer.exe">
<!--Figure Declarations -->
<!ELEMENT FIGURE (FIGREF, FG)>
<!ELEMENT FIGREF EMPTY>
<!ATTLIST FIGREF
     SRC   CDATA     #REQUIRED
     TYPE  NOTATION (tiff | bmp | eps) "tiff">
<!--FG is figure description -->
<!ELEMENT FG (FIGNUM, %textual-elements;)>
<!ELEMENT FIGNUM (#PCDATA)>
<!--Style sheet linkage information -->
<!ELEMENT HEAD (LINK)>
<!ELEMENT LINK (EMPTY)>
<!ATTLIST LINK
     REL CDATA #REQUIRED
     HREF CDATA #REQUIRED
```

Unfortunately, a gargantuan DTD requires a gargantuan document to test it out. The following code is clearly only test code, not a real chapter (although I could increase the thickness of this book dramatically by including one). Nevertheless, this code should test out most of these elements in their natural habitats.

```
<?xml version="1.0" STANDALONE="no" encoding="UTF-
8"?>
<!DOCTYPE CHAPTER SYSTEM
"http://127.0.0.1/chapter.dtd">
<CHAPTER>
<TOCOCT>How to code XML</TOCOCT>
<INTRODUCTORY>
<BT>This is a chapter on how to code XML.</BT>
<BT>This is another bit of intro info.</BT>
</INTRODUCTORY>
<ALEAF>
<TOC1A>Subhead A1</TOC1A>
<BT>This is A1, from <CITATION>my
document</CITATION>.</BT>
<CC><LC>This is a listing</LC>
<CLINE>I don't know what to do in this
program!</CLINE>
<CLINE>I don't know what to do in this
program!</CLINE>
</CC>
<BT>You could have type
<USERACTION>exit</USERACTION> instead of running
the parser.</BT>
</ALEAF>
<ALEAF>
<TOC1A>Subhead A2</TOC1A>
<BT>This is A2. We'll start with a table, and move
on to a B leaf.</BT>
<TABLE><TBC>This is a sample table</TBC>
<TH><TBH>Column 1: Time</TBH><TBH>Column 2:
Money</TBH></TH>
```

```
<TR><TB>Never enough</TB><TB>Can always use
more</TB></TR>
<TR><TB>More than enough</TB><TB>Had enough to
begin with</TB></TR>
<SN>From <CITATION>The book of
nonsense</CITATION></SN>
</TABLE>
<BLEAF>
<TOC2B>Subhead B1</TOC2B>
<BT>A C leaf will follow, after the bulleted
list.</BT>
<BL>
<BLINE>This is the first item of a bulleted
list</BLINE>
<BLINE>This is the second item of a bulleted
list</BLINE>
</BL>
<CLEAF>
<C>Subhead C1</C>
<BT>This is a C leaf which contains a numbered
list and a figure.</BT>
<NL>
<NLINE>1. This is the first item.</NLINE>
<NLINE>2. This is the second item.</NLINE>
</NL>
<FIGURE><FIGREF SRC="image.tif" TYPE="tiff"/>
<FG><FIGNUM>101.12</FIGNUM> - The wild boar at
rest.</FG></FIGURE>
</CLEAF>
<CLEAF>
<C>Subhead C2</C>
```

```
<BT>This C leaf contains an unnumbered list and a
glossary item.</BT>
<UL>
<ULINE>This isn't in any order.</ULINE>
<ULINE>Who needs order?</ULINE>
<ULINE>Order just gets in the way.</ULINE>
</UL>
<GL><GLITEM>Order</GLITEM><GLDEFINITION> Something
that gets in the way
frequently.</GLDEFINITION></GL>
</CLEAF>
</BLEAF>
<ICON><NOTE/><BT>Hope you enjoyed the
chapter!</BT></ICON>
</ALEAF>
</CHAPTER>
```

The code rolls through the parser quite happily. The output is eight pages long and completely repeats the document except in formatting, so I will omit it here.

A Style Sheet for the Chapter DTD

A style sheet for the Chapter DTD won't be too hard to develop, even though the publishers may grumble about losing the fine control they had with previous desktop publishing tools, like QuarkXPress. Even though XML's supporting style technologies will allow some fairly intricate formatting, it's still a great distance from what designers are used to.

Remember that the browser developers haven't quite caught on to the possibilities of XML yet, at least as of version 4.0 of either the Netscape or Microsoft browsers. The browsers are also fairly far behind in implementing CSS. The following style sheets comply fully with the standards but will not work with most browsers at present.

Documents created with the Chapter DTD will probably be combined with other chapters as part of a larger structure, which may have its own formatting rules. For the purposes of this style sheet, we'll assume that chapters start and end on their own pages, and that the larger document's structure will not interfere with any of the styling that will be created later.

The format of this particular style sheet has very little to do with the way the document is presented in the final printing—it is just a generic representation that helps the author and the editors see the book. After the editing is over, the production staff could in theory just replace the style sheet with a style sheet customized for the look of a particular book and have the same elements fall into their proper place for printing.

The style for the CHAPTER element marks itself as a block element, making itself a separate unit of text from any surrounding material. It also sets the default font information for the entire document:

```
CHAPTER {
      display:block;
      font-family:serif;
      font-size:12pt;
      font-weight: normal;
      font-style:normal
}
```

I've avoided using actual font names throughout this style sheet, preferring to use the generic family names like serif and monotype. You can substitute real font names if you prefer, but keep in mind that not all computers will have your chosen set of fonts.

The TOC0CT opening headline is displayed in bold 24-point type. Note the padding-bottom attribute, which specifies the amount of space that should follow the headline.

```
TOC0CT {
      display:block;
      font-size:24pt;
      font-weight:bold;
      padding-bottom:9pt
}
```

The CITATION and USERACTION elements will italicize words within the text, but they don't create separate blocks. Setting the display to inline (which is the default) makes clear that these elements will not break up paragraphs.

```
CITATION {
      display:inline;
      font-style:italic
}
USERACTION {
      display:inline;
      font-weight:bold
}
```

BT is the primary element for displaying text. Each BT unit is the rough equivalent of a paragraph, so the BT element is clearly a block.

```
BT {
      display:block;
      line-height:24pt
}
```

The XLEAF elements all share similar formatting. They each begin a block element, separated from the previous element by a preset amount of space, set in the padding-top value.

```
ALEAF {
      display:block;
      padding-top:12pt
}
BLEAF {
      display:block;
      padding-top:9pt
}
CLEAF {
      display:block;
      padding-top:9pt
}
DLEAF {
      display:block;
      padding-top:9pt
}
ELEAF {
      display:block;
      padding-top:9pt
}
```

The headlines for the leaf elements are themselves block elements, each with their own set of formatting.

```
TOC1A {
      display:block;
      padding-bottom:6pt;
      font-size:18pt;
```

```
        font-weight:bold
}
TOC2B {
        display:block;
        padding-bottom:6pt;
        font-size:14pt;
        font-weight:bold
}
C {
        display:block;
        font-size:14pt;
        font-weight:bold;
        font-style:italic
}
D {
        display:block;
        font-size:12pt;
        font-weight:bold;
        font-style:italic
}
E {
        display:block;
        font-size:14pt;
        font-style:italic
}
```

The code elements, where we most dramatically simplified the original chapter style sheet, take most advantage of the power of CSS and XML. The extra spacing, which in Word required four different styles, is easily included in the definition of the CC element. Because the CC element encloses the caption and the code completely, it can supply the necessary padding at the top and bottom of the code listing without requiring that the author apply extra styling to the actual code.

```
CC {
      display:block;
      padding-top:9pt;
      padding-bottom:9pt;
      text-indent:.5in;
      font-family:monospace;
      line-height:18pt
}
LC {
      display:block;
      padding-bottom:6pt;
      font-weight:bold
}
CLINE {display:block}
```

The list elements can set the styles necessary for the list items they enclose, using Cascading Style Sheets' fairly comprehensive set of list styles.

```
BL {
      display:block;
      text-indent:1in;
      line-height:18pt;
      list-style-type:disc;
      list-style-position:outside
}
NL {
      display:block;
```

```
        text-indent:1in;
        line-height:18pt;
        list-style-type:decimal;
        list-style-position:outside
}
UL {
        display:block;
        line-height:18pt;
        list-style-type:square;
        list-style-position:outside
}
```

The content of those lists needs only to identify itself as a list item.

```
BLINE {display:list-item}
NLINE {display:list-item}
ULINE {display:list-item}
```

The GL element is a little more complex. Because glossary entries have a one-line item description followed by a multiline indented definition, the GL element sets its text indent to a *negative* 1 inch, which produces the required hanging indent.

```
GL {
        display:block;
        text-indent:-1in;
        padding-bottom:9pt;
        line-height:24pt
}
GLITEM {
        display:inline;
        font-weight:bold
```

```
}
GLDEFINITION {display:inline}
```

The ICON element simply indents its text 1 inch and applies appropriate padding and spacing. The NOTE, SHORTCUT, WARNING, and TIP elements don't need styles at this point because they have no content at all. In final production, they must be replaced with graphics.

```
ICON {
      display:block;
      text:indent:1in;
      padding-top:9pt;
      padding-bottom:9pt;
      line-height:18pt
}
```

The table items are a problem in CSS. CSS offers no row or column settings for its display element, and creating generic styles for building tables in CSS is nearly impossible. This task requires the flow objects of a more powerful style language, like XSL or DSSSL. The following is an approximation of a table, but CSS won't be able to make it look quite right.

```
TABLE {display:block;
      padding-top:9pt;
      padding-bottom:6pt
      }
TBC {
      display:block;
     font-weight:bold;
      font-style:italic;
      padding-bottom:9pt
```

```
}
TH{
      display:block;
      padding-bottom:9pt
}
TBH {
      display:inline;
      font-weight:bold
}
TR {
      display:block;
      line-height:18pt
}
TB {display:inline}
SN {display:block;
      font-size:10pt;
      padding-top:6pt;
      padding-bottom:6pt
}
```

FIGURE elements are always centered on the page. The FIGREF element that actually places the figure picture doesn't need a style, unless extra padding is necessary. The FIGREF will inherit the centering from the FIGURE element. The figure caption (the FG element) will also inherit the centering, and the FIGNUM will appear in bold.

```
FIGURE {
      display:block;
      text-align:center
}
FG  {
```

```
display:block;
font-style:italic
}
FIGNUM {
display:inline;
font-weight:bold
}
```

Eventually, we will be able to use styles like these to present complex XML documents in a browser with a minimum of difficulty. Changing styles with Cascading Style Sheets is extremely simple, making it easy to present documents in different formats aimed at different media. Although CSS doesn't provide all the answers (as we saw with the tables), it provides enough structure to build a reasonably well-formatted XML document.

Pass 2: Toward a Cleaner DTD

The real test of the previous DTD will come as authors and the production department put it to use, stretching it and finding its weaknesses. Several significant weaknesses arose during the previous discussion but were overlooked for the sake of compatibility with the previous version. A second round, unhindered by the political need of compatibility, may improve the DTD to make it more extensible. Three areas could definitely use some structural improvements—the leaf structure, lists, and icons—and many elements could use friendlier names.

These improvements are mostly technical improvements that demonstrate some of the more interesting features of XML. They are not guaranteed to improve user productivity, however. Some users may find the older structures easier to understand. DTD developers will frequently need to compromise between a more elegant technical solution and a solution that users find friendly. Automated tools for entering information will help bridge that gap, but their acceptance may take a while.

Even though the ALEAF/BLEAF/CLEAF structure makes sense to a reader who can scan through it, it requires a considerably larger number of elements than a more generic leaf version might. A more generic structure would use elements that behave similarly but that aren't labeled as A or B or C. Creating a generic leaf structure involves recursion—allowing an element to include another element of the same type within itself.

Recursion has several meanings in different contexts, many of which lead to endless loops. XML permits elements to include themselves in the list of accepted child elements, but it does not, for example, permit entities to refer to files that then refer to the original file. For most purposes, the following recursion is the practical limit of recursion in XML.

In the following DTD, a LEAF element must contain a TITLE element and may contain additional LEAF elements and PCDATA.

```
<!ELEMENT TEST (LEAF+)>
<!ELEMENT LEAF (HEADER,(LEAF|CONTENT)*)>
<!ELEMENT CONTENT (#PCDATA)>
<!ELEMENT HEADER (#PCDATA)>
```

The following document takes advantage of the LEAF structure to create several layers of LEAF elements:

```
<?xml version="1.0" standalone="no" encoding="UTF-
8"?>
<!DOCTYPE CHAPTER SYSTEM
"http://127.0.0.1/recurs.dtd">
<TEST>
<LEAF>
<HEADER>Top-layer Leaf 1</HEADER>
<CONTENT>This is a leaf.</CONTENT>
<LEAF>
```

```
<HEADER>Second-layer Leaf 1</HEADER>
<CONTENT>This is a leaf.</CONTENT>
</LEAF>
<LEAF>
<HEADER>Second-layer Leaf 2</HEADER>
<CONTENT>This is a leaf. </CONTENT>
<LEAF>
<HEADER>Third-layer Leaf 1</HEADER>
<CONTENT>This is a leaf.</CONTENT>
</LEAF>
</LEAF>
</LEAF>
<LEAF>
<HEADER>Top-layer Leaf 2</HEADER>
<CONTENT>This is a leaf.</CONTENT>
</LEAF>
</TEST>
```

Parsing this document reveals its layers of structure.

```
C:\msxml>java msxml -d  -i http://127.0.0.1/recurs.xml
<?XML VERSION="1.0" ENCODING="UTF-8"?>
<!DOCTYPE CHAPTER SYSTEM
"http://127.0.0.1/recurs.dtd">
<TEST>
    <LEAF>
        <HEADER>
            Top-layer Leaf 1
        </HEADER>
        <CONTENT>
        This is a leaf.
        </CONTENT>
        <LEAF>
            <HEADER>
                Second-layer Leaf 1
            </HEADER>
```

```
            <CONTENT>
            This is a leaf.
            </CONTENT>
        </LEAF>
        <LEAF>
            <HEADER>
                Second-layer Leaf 2
            </HEADER>
            <CONTENT>
            This is a leaf.
            </CONTENT>
            <LEAF>
                <HEADER>
                    Third-layer Leaf 1
                </HEADER>
                <CONTENT>
                This is a leaf.
                </CONTENT>
            </LEAF>
        </LEAF>
    </LEAF>
    <LEAF>
        <HEADER>
            Top-layer Leaf 2
        </HEADER>
        This is a leaf.
    </LEAF>
</TEST>
```

Using this structure allows us to simplify this

```
<!ELEMENT ALEAF (TOC1A,BT,(%content-
elements;|BLEAF)*)>
<!ELEMENT BLEAF (TOC2B,BT,(%content-
elements;|CLEAF)*)>
<!ELEMENT CLEAF (C,BT,(%content-
elements;|DLEAF)*)>
<!ELEMENT DLEAF (D,BT,(%content-
elements;|ELEAF)*)>
```

```
<!ELEMENT ELEAF (E,BT,(%content-elements;)*)>
<!ELEMENT TOC1A (#PCDATA)>
<!ELEMENT TOC2B (#PCDATA)>
<!ELEMENT C (#PCDATA)>
<!ELEMENT D (#PCDATA)>
<!ELEMENT E (#PCDATA)>
```

to this

```
<!ELEMENT LEAF (HEADER,BT,( %content-elements;|
LEAF)*)>
<!ELEMENT HEADER (#PCDATA)>
```

The LEAF element replaces all its predecessor leaf structures, and the HEADER element replaces TOC1A, TOC2B, and C, D, and E. Whenever an author creates a new leaf, it is assumed to be a subsection of the document. The level at which it appears (like A, B, C, D, or E) is determined purely by context. This may be disorienting at first, at least until the tools catch up to the possibilities.

This approach also creates some difficulties for style sheets, requiring some minor changes in the styles presented previously. The CSS specification allows for contextual selectors, which allow you to define styles based on the element type and also on the elements in which the element you're styling is nested. In our case, because all the subleaves (below the AHEAD) use the same padding value, the new style for the LEAF element is reasonably simple.

```
LEAF {
     display:block;
     padding-top:12pt
}
LEAF LEAF {
     display:block;
```

```
     padding-top:9pt
}
```

This style definition states that all LEAF elements will start out with a default padding of 12 points on top. However, all LEAF elements that are enclosed by other LEAF elements (which includes all layers below the top) will have 9 points of padding on top. The headers are more difficult, but they use the same rule.

```
LEAF HEADER {
     display:block;
     padding-bottom:6pt;
     font-size:18pt;
    font-weight:bold
}
LEAF LEAF HEADER {
     display:block;
     padding-bottom:6pt;
     font-size:14pt;
     font-weight:bold }
LEAF LEAF LEAF HEADER {
     display:block;
     font-size:14pt;
     font-weight:bold;
     font-style:italic
}
LEAF LEAF LEAF LEAF HEADER {
     display:block;
     font-size:12pt;
     font-weight:bold;
     font-style:italic
}
```

```
LEAF LEAF LEAF LEAF LEAF HEADER {
      display:block;
      font-size:14pt;
      font-style:italic
}
```

The top line of these style settings is the old TOC1A header—a header inside one layer of LEAF elements. The second line is TOC2B, and so forth. Instead of being tied to a specific named element, the style of the headline is dependent upon its position in the hierarchy of LEAF elements.

The other area that could stand significant improvement is the lists. For compatibility, we created three elements: BL, NL, and UL. These could be combined into a single LIST element with an attribute identifying the type of list.

```
<!ELEMENT LIST (LINE+)>
<!ATTLIST LINE
      TYPE CDATA (BULLETED|NUMBERED|UNORDERED)>
```

Even though this is tempting, for now it must depend on the ability of the processing application to keep up with the attribute. Cascading Style Sheets, for example, can respond to element context, but can react to the CLASS attribute only. (This could of course be solved by renaming TYPE to CLASS, but a CLASS attribute might need to reflect more than the type of list.) When XSL and other more context-sensitive style systems come into more general use, it may or may not be time for this change, depending to a large extent on the preferences of those using the tools.

At present, the list items all have their own elements—NLINE, BLINE, and ULINE. These could be combined into one LINE element as long as the processing software can keep up with it. This should not be as difficult as moving the announcement of the type of list it is from element to attribute status. The resulting declarations are

```
<!ELEMENT BL (LINE+)>
<!ELEMENT NL (LINE+)>
<!ELEMENT UL (LINE+)>
<!ELEMENT LINE (%textual-elements;)>
```

This should make converting from one list type to another far more convenient. The BL, NL, and UL elements keep their previous style definitions, and the line element uses a style declaration very similar to its predecessors.

```
LINE {display:list-item}
```

The ICON structure as it currently stands is a stretched attempt at maintaining compatibility with the previous style. ICON elements in the preceding DTD don't really represent icons—they represent callout paragraphs that start with icons. A more accurate representation of these paragraphs, including their icons, would use an attribute (instead of the empty elements) on a CALLOUT element, which would then include a different kind of ICON element, representing the actual graphic. The definitions might look like

```
<!ELEMENT CALLOUT (ICON?, BT+)>
<!ELEMENT % callout-types
("NOTE|WARNING|SHORTCUT|TIP*"))>
<!ATTLIST CALLOUT TYPE %callout-types; #REQUIRED>
<!ELEMENT ICON EMPTY>
<!ATTLIST ICON
     SRC CDATA #REQUIRED
     TYPE NOTATION (tiff|bmp|eps) "tiff">
```

The CALLOUT element would use a style similar to the one defined previously for ICON.

```
CALLOUT {
      display:block;
      text:indent:1in;
      padding-top:9pt;
      padding-bottom:9pt;
      line-height:18pt
}
```

The last improvement I would suggest is using longer names for most of the styles. XML doesn't offer a SHORTREF declaration like SGML to provide for abbreviated versions of full names, so this will results in more markup and longer files. Still, if anyone must read the actual files, they'll have a much easier time figuring out what's going where.

In the next chapter, we'll move from simple documents for print to more complex documents intended to enhance commercial document interchage. We'll be using many of the same tools but expanding on XML's ability to create machine-readable documents.

CHAPTER 7

XML for Commerce

Perhaps the most important advantage of XML is that it allows people and companies to exchange information more clearly and completely than previous formats have allowed. Although this can improve the average home page as well as the efficiency of paper-document creation, it has its greatest return on investment in more businesslike fields. XML promises to capitalize on two key trends in the electronic world: the growing use of Web sites as stores and the increasing use of electronic ordering and invoicing. XML can make Web sites more effective by making them more easily searchable, while easing the difficult transition to business-to-business communication by providing intelligible standards for data interchange.

The examples provided in this chapter explore some of the possible ways to use XML to create commerce-enabled DTDs. While the prospect of creating your own DTDs for these functions may seem exciting, you should always check to make sure that an industry standard DTD isn't already available. Creating your own DTD can give you a well-tailored solution to your systems and your particular needs, but it may also cut you off from the rest of your industry. XML markup is most useful when the same DTD is used by a number of people and tools. Commerce applications have the most at stake in standardization because search engines and other applications must be able to count on the same elements having the same meaning no matter what the source. Compatibility will be more important than a perfect solution in most cases involving multiple organizations.

Who (and What) Will Be Reading My XML?

The documents in the previous chapter were meant, in the end, for humans to read. XML makes the documents easier for machines to manipulate, providing a good way to apply formatting and possibly store the data, but in the longer term, all those documents will be read by people, whether on paper or on a screen.

The applications in this chapter take advantage of several additional advantages of XML. First, it allows developers to create documents that both humans and machines can read. Markup tags may look like information in English (or another language) to the developer, but to the computer they're simply labels that help it reach the data it needs for processing, stored neatly in nested structures. Second, XML offers considerably more flexibility than the other options currently available for data interchange between systems. XML can be used to represent the contents of a relational database, or it can represent the contents of an old hierarchical database or even the latest object-oriented database. At the same time, XML can easily represent document information, grouping information, or simple lists. Finally, XML provides a structure that is easy for programmers to manipulate using recursive structures that are widely available in most programming tools. Writing an XML parser isn't that difficult, especially if the parser foregoes validation and checks for well-formedness only.

These strengths give XML a range of capabilities far broader than those of other interchange formats. Although thousands of systems are already available for trading data between computers, none of them offers this much flexibility in a structure that is so easy to program. XML obviously won't solve all the problems of data interchange because not every program can handle every data structure XML can represent, but it still represents a major step forward. XML is definitely a generalist's tool. Given enough time and money, there will always be a more efficient or more beautiful way to perform the tasks described later with customized database connections, exquisitely hand-crafted Web sites, or specially coded distributed components.

XML's combination of flexibility and structure suit it well to a group of applications that seek out information. Search engines and agents can both consider the information available in the DTDs and the tags of these documents when they try to categorize or index them. Making full use of these capabilities will require some standardization of tags—programs will have a hard time making sense of elements like <TODAYSSPECIALPRICE> and <SALETODAYONLY> (<PRICE> probably makes considerably more sense).

Search engines have an especially difficult task gathering and sorting information in its current amorphous Web forms; adding meaningful standardized tags should make search engines better at finding relevant information. Agents usually operate on a smaller scale, typically seeking out choice bits of information for particular users, but they stand to gain in the same way, possibly achieving the status computers scientists have claimed for them for so long.

Automated search tools bring up an additional issue—the dangers of letting programs surf the Web. If your site generates XML documents from databases and could strain (or collapse) under the load created by these automated tools, you should definitely consider creating a robots.txt file for your site. When an agent or search engine visits a site, it should examine the robots.txt file to find out where on the site it is welcome and avoid all proscribed areas. Details are available at http://info.Webcrawler.com/mak/projects/robots/norobots.html. Although robots.txt is not an "official" standard, it is widely accepted by search engine developers and should keep programs from crawling all over your site, slowing it down and possibly (in the worst case) crashing it.

Developing documents for computers to read really isn't that much more difficult than developing documents for people. Computers are at least predictable, and the strong structures of XML should make it easier to create information that can be used by multiple processing applications, even processing applications of extremely different kinds.

A Better Electronic Catalog

Even though the HTML catalog in the previous chapter may have been acceptable as a way to present information on a page, and its XML transformation may have added some searchability, it can still stand some significant improvement. The main competitor to Joe's Catalog, Jane's Catalog, is embarking on this more difficult course. Building a new catalog format from the ground up may cost Jane some effort and adjustment, but it should create a more automatable catalog that is easier to manage.

As long as orders were coming in exclusively over the telephone, Jane was comfortable having a Web catalog that simply recreated her paper catalog. As the costs of her 800-number have risen, she's begun to wonder whether she shouldn't revise her system and allow Web users to order over her cheaper Internet connection. At the same time, she's moving her catalog from the ragtag group of desktop publishing files they've used into a new database system capable of holding her items and all their associated data—even pictures! Because Jane doesn't spend much on advertising, she would like automated tools to be able to understand her catalog easily, making it easier for users to find the items they want. XML sounds like it might give her a boost in that direction, and it should be a good fit for the database systems she's installing as well. The challenge is to create a catalog application that can present her data attractively to customers while easing the demands on her order-entry department.

Instead of working from the catalog as it is currently presented on the Web, we'll start by examining Jane's methods of assembling the catalog and processing orders. When Jane's computer receives an order (from a telephone operator at the moment), it processes payment, typically a credit card, and prints out a packing slip in the warehouse. Workers in the warehouse find the items and ship them out immediately. The order-entry department would like to see the Web application feed their computer a simple set of information: payment information, shipping information, and the list of products to be ordered (by item number) and quantities. This is a fairly easy set of data to deliver with existing Web tools. On the customer side, eventually, Jane would like the application to display a full invoice to the customer, complete with shipping costs. Part of the motivation for moving to XML has to do with an interest in making the user's Web browser do as much work as possible, sparing her servers the trouble of processing information that client machines could handle as easily. This saves her expensive bandwidth and processing effort. Even though XML may not be able to achieve this today, several other standards under development will make this much easier soon, as we'll see later in the chapter.

XML has several drawbacks at this point for Web application development. Adding the necessary links for JavaScript code to read the XML information may complicate the clean structures Jane would like to produce. The DTD must provide support for scripting on some level without becoming too complex. Fortunately, Jane has already planned her application to take advantage of frames, which will allow her to place code in another frame, safely outside the XML document. All the XML document needs to do is pass information about which item the user wants to a script in another frame, which will then store in a shopping basket and handle all the sales infrastructure Jane needs. The fact that Jane's computers will be generating static XML from a database will also ease the difficulties by allowing some repetitive information to appear in the XML markup.

Jane's Catalog is currently organized loosely into pages that group related products. The groups are determined informally by the team that builds the paper catalog. The electronic catalog should preserve these groupings, making it easy for customers to flip back and forth between the two versions. All the grouping information is stored in the database as well, making it much easier for a script to churn out pages based on a set of queries. Jane just needs a set of elements that can present the catalog data elegantly, with minimal processing overhead, and that can easily adapt to the upcoming improvements in scripting and document object models while still accommodating the needs of the present.

The top level of this DTD is the group—all members of a group will be presented in the same document.

```
<!ELEMENT GROUP (GROUPNAME, ITEM+,LEGALNOTICE)>
<!ATTLIST GROUP

      GROUPLINK CDATA #IMPLIED>
```

The GROUPLINK attribute holds a key value that will make it easy for a parser at Jane's to link to the original database record for troubleshooting or other information gathering. The GROUP element begins with a GROUPNAME element, which is effectively a headline for the page, and ends with a LEGALNOTICE element, which will just contain the usual warnings about typos and pricing. It is probably unlikely that a search engine or agent would look for LEGALNOTICE as an element, but it does make formatting the fine print easier.

```
<!ELEMENT GROUPNAME (#PCDATA)>
<!ELEMENT LEGALNOTICE (#PCDATA)>
```

Under this headline are catalog ITEM elements. ITEM elements contain a variety of other elements, including ITEM subelements that represent products affiliated with their parent ITEM. Like the GROUP element, the ITEM element may have an attribute that connects it to its database entry.

```
<!ELEMENT ITEM (PRODUCTNAME, DESCRIPTION?,PRICING,
ITEM*)>
```

```
<!ATTLIST ITEM
      ITEMLINK CDATA #IMPLIED>
```

The PRODUCTNAME element, like the GROUPNAME element, is really just a headline. Because the elements receive different formatting and may need to be addressed differently through scripts, the two elements are created separately.

```
<!ELEMENT PRODUCTNAME (#PCDATA)>
```

The DESCRIPTION element must be able to handle a variety of content. (Remember that the DESCRIPTION element is optional—it won't get used for subitems.) Catalog entries don't often include italic or bold text, but periodically they do, mostly for book titles. Most product descriptions are just one paragraph, but occasionally an entry can go on for several paragraphs. Many descriptions even include pictures. As a result, the DESCRIPTION element must contain PARAGRAPH elements, which themselves contain a motley assortment of other elements, and IMG elements, modeled after the HTML version.

```
<!ELEMENT DESCRIPTION (PARAGRAPH | IMG)*>
<!ELEMENT IMG EMPTY>
<!ATTLIST IMG
     SRC CDATA #REQUIRED
     HEIGHT CDATA #REQUIRED
     WIDTH CDATA #REQUIRED>
<!ELEMENT PARAGRAPH (#PCDATA | CITATION | EMPHASIS
| HIGHLIGHT)*>
<!ELEMENT CITATION (#PCDATA)>
<!ELEMENT EMPHASIS (#PCDATA)>
<!ELEMENT HIGHLIGHT (#PCDATA)>
```

This simple set of markup tags should allow them to recreate the descriptions for all the items in the catalog. Although this is exciting to the design staff, it doesn't have nearly the effect on the ordering processing as the contents of the PRICING element. The PRICING element contains all the price, shipping weight, delivery, availability, and warranty information, as well as the button that executes the script that adds the item to the shopping cart.

```
<!ELEMENT PRICING (PRODNUM,MARKER?,PRICE, MARKER?,
SHIPPING, MARKER?, DELIVERY, MARKER?, AVAIL,
MARKER?, WARRANTY, PURCHASE)>
<!ELEMENT PRODNUM (#PCDATA)>
<!ATTLIST PRODNUM
      ID      id      #REQUIRED>
<!ELEMENT MARKER(#PCDATA)>
<!ELEMENT PRICE(#PCDATA)>
<!ATTLIST PRICE
      ID      id      #REQUIRED>
<!ELEMENT SHIPPING (#PCDATA)>
<!ATTLIST SHIPPING
      ID      id      #REQUIRED>
<!ELEMENT DELIVERY (#PCDATA)>
<!ATTLIST DELIVERY
      ID      id      #REQUIRED>
<!ELEMENT AVAIL (#PCDATA)>
<!ATTLIST AVAIL
      ID      id      #REQUIRED>
<!ELEMENT WARRANTY (#PCDATA)>
<!ELEMENT PURCHASE (#PCDATA)>
<!ATTLIST PURCHASE

      onclick     CDATA      #REQUIRED>
```

Jane is reasonably confident that her warehouse will have the items listed in stock and uses the AVAIL element mostly to indicate when items are upcoming but haven't yet arrived in the warehouse, generating advance orders. A company that ran out of stock more frequently would probably need to generate its pages dynamically and reflect its current stock situation with more precise tags, like ONHAND for the number available or ONORDER to indicate when the item should arrive. Keep in mind, however, that you don't want to reveal your entire inventory to your competition.

Because this section's contents must be addressed by a script, it's picked up a lot of baggage. The following section on scripting with XML will provide more detail on techniques for adding scripts and hooks for script to valid XML.

The PRICING element is a list of the parts required for order processing, including all of the noncustomer information needed to build a packing list. Optional MARKER elements are interspersed to allow descriptions like Price: to appear without cluttering the PRICE element. (When XSL appears in force, this may no longer be necessary.) The MARKER information is really just formatting and must be kept separate from the content of the other elements.

For now, all elements that may need to contribute information to a shopping cart are assigned ID values. The ID value in this case will be created using a naming convention that includes the product number (so as to avoid having duplicate ID values on the same page). This ID value allows scripts to "find" the element and extract its contents for processing. The PURCHASE element receives an onclick attribute, which will allow it to call a script to add this item to the shopping basket. An actual PURCHASE element will look something like:

```
<PURCHASE onclick=
"javascript:parent.cart.add('12323')"> Add to
Cart</PURCHASE>
```

Using the event-handling attributes of HTML 4.0, this script will respond to clicks by calling the add method of the FRAME with the NAME attribute "cart". (This EVENT model is supported by Internet Explorer 4.0 and will be supported in some version by future versions of Netscape browsers as well.)

Combining all this information produces a DTD that encapsulates the information required for Jane's Catalog to present its information to the customer and return that data to the order department:

```
<!ELEMENT GROUP (GROUPNAME, ITEM+,LEGALNOTICE)>
<!ATTLIST GROUP
      GROUPLINK CDATA #IMPLIED>
<!ELEMENT GROUPNAME (#PCDATA)>
<!ELEMENT LEGALNOTICE (#PCDATA)>
<!ELEMENT ITEM (PRODUCTNAME, DESCRIPTION?,PRICING,
ITEM*)>
<!ATTLIST ITEM
      ITEMLINK CDATA #IMPLIED>
<!ELEMENT PRODUCTNAME (#PCDATA)>
<!ELEMENT DESCRIPTION (PARAGRAPH | IMG)*>
<!ELEMENT IMG EMPTY>
<!ATTLIST IMG
      SRC CDATA #REQUIRED
     HEIGHT CDATA #REQUIRED
     WIDTH CDATA #REQUIRED>
<!ELEMENT PARAGRAPH (#PCDATA | CITATION | EMPHASIS
| HIGHLIGHT)*>
<!ELEMENT CITATION (#PCDATA)>
<!ELEMENT EMPHASIS (#PCDATA)>
<!ELEMENT HIGHLIGHT (#PCDATA)>
```

```
<!ELEMENT PRICING (PRODNUM,MARKER?,PRICE, MARKER?,
SHIPPING, MARKER?, DELIVERY, MARKER?, AVAIL,
MARKER?, WARRANTY, PURCHASE)>
<!ELEMENT PRODNUM (#PCDATA)>
<!ATTLIST PRODNUM
      ID      ID      #REQUIRED>
<!ELEMENT MARKER(#PCDATA)>
<!ELEMENT PRICE(#PCDATA)>
<!ATTLIST PRICE
      ID      ID      #REQUIRED>
<!ELEMENT SHIPPING (#PCDATA)>
<!ATTLIST SHIPPING
      ID      ID      #REQUIRED>
<!ELEMENT DELIVERY (#PCDATA)>
<!ATTLIST DELIVERY
      ID      ID      #REQUIRED>
<!ELEMENT AVAIL (#PCDATA)>
<!ATTLIST AVAIL
      ID      ID      #REQUIRED>
<!ELEMENT WARRANTY (#PCDATA)>
<!ELEMENT PURCHASE (#PCDATA)>
<!ATTLIST PURCHASE

      onclick     CDATA      #REQUIRED>
```

The end result of this process is a structure Jane's Catalog can use both for transmitting information to users and processing it to send orders back to the ordering system. (Those orders could be sent in an XML format, but that's the subject of the next system. The preceding DTD includes just the information that a client-side processor would need to build a full packing list and invoice of ordered goods).

A sample page from Jane's Catalog, generated by her database system, might look like:

```
<?xml version="1.0" standalone="no" encoding="UTF-
8"?>
<!DOCTYPE GROUP SYSTEM "janes.dtd">
<GROUP GROUPLINK="23AA34FAB1">
<GROUPNAME>Pocket Calculating Devices</GROUPNAME>
<ITEM>
<PRODUCTNAME>Mortgage Calculator</PRODUCTNAME>
<DESCRIPTION><PARAGRAPH>Ever want to know
precisely how much of your house you own?  What
your monthly payments would be if you refinanced?
Mortgage-lovers will appreciate this handy gadget.
This calculator allows comparisons between owning
and renting, explores the impact of inflation on
your bank's profit margin, and makes it easy to
plan ahead.</PARAGRAPH></DESCRIPTION>
<PRICING><PRODNUM ID="I1024">1024</PRODNUM>
<MARKER>Price: $</MARKER>
<PRICE ID="I1024P">20.00</PRICE>
<MARKER>Shipping: $</MARKER>
<SHIPPING ID="I1024S">3.00</SHIPPING>
<MARKER>Delivery: </MARKER>
<DELIVERY ID="I1024D">Overnight</DELIVERY>
<MARKER>In Stock?: </MARKER>
<AVAIL ID="I1024A">Yes</AVAIL>
<MARKER>Warranty: </MARKER>
<WARRANTY>30 years</WARRANTY>
<PURCHASE
onclick="javascript:parent.cart.add('1024')">Add
to Cart</PURCHASE>
```

```
</PRICING>
<ITEM>
<PRODUCTNAME>Carrying Case</PRODUCTNAME>
<PRICING><PRODNUM ID="I1028">1028</PRODNUM>
<MARKER>Price: $</MARKER>
<PRICE ID="I1028P">2.00</PRICE>
<MARKER>Shipping: $</MARKER>
<SHIPPING ID="I1028S">1.00</SHIPPING>
<MARKER>Delivery: </MARKER>
<DELIVERY ID="I1028D">Overnight</DELIVERY>
<MARKER>In Stock?: </MARKER>
<AVAIL ID="I1028A">Yes</AVAIL>
<MARKER>Warranty: </MARKER>
<WARRANTY>2 years</WARRANTY>
<PURCHASE
onclick="javascript:parent.cart.add('1024')">Add
to Cart</PURCHASE>
</PRICING>
</ITEM>
</ITEM>
<LEGALNOTICE>Jane's Catalog is not responsible for
typographical errors.  Prices and availability may
change at any time.</LEGALNOTICE>
</GROUP>
```

As you can see, nesting ITEM elements is simple. There is no need for the SUBITEM element we used in the last chapter, allowing for a more consistent structure. The ID elements duplicate information available elsewhere (the product number), but this evil is necessary only for the moment, as the next section will explain.

Adding Scripts to XML

SGML was developed at a time when "good computing practice" still suggested strong separation between programming logic and the data on which they worked. SGML does an excellent job of storing data in a structured format that programs can interpret, but it doesn't provide a mechanism for the kinds of "live" content that is rapidly spreading across the Web. XML's SGML inheritance in this field is something of a hindrance. Even tasks that are basic to HTML practice—like creating SCRIPT tags to hold the code needed to manipulate the pages—are frequently difficult in XML. JavaScript (a.k.a. the newly standardized ECMAScript) and VBScript both use the symbols &, <, and > for programming purposes. To either of these scripting languages, < means less than, not start a new markup tag here. A close examination of the HTML DTD (4.0 Working Draft, September 1997) reveals that scripts could even cause problems with XML pages that use the HTML DTD for validation checking:

```
<!ELEMENT SCRIPT - - CDATA  -- script statements -
->
 <!ATTLIST SCRIPT
   type         CDATA      #IMPLIED  -- Internet
content type for script language --
   language     CDATA      #IMPLIED  -- predefined
script language name --
   src          %URL;      #IMPLIED  -- URL for an
external script --
   >
```

Because of assorted problems with SGML's implementation of it, XML doesn't offer the CDATA type for elements (as of the November 1997 Working Draft)—only #PCDATA is available. If SCRIPT contents are actually PCDATA, a parser will explode when it hits any code that uses &, <, or >. Developers must create a

SCRIPT element that uses PCDATA and then converts that PCDATA space to CDATA by hand with a marked section: <![CDATA[...*script*...]]>. The SCRIPT element declaration will look similar to the preceding HTML DTD:

```
<!ELEMENT SCRIPT (#PCDATA)>
<!ATTLIST SCRIPT

      type      CDATA      #IMPLIED

      language      CDATA      #IMPLIED

      src      CDATA      #IMPLIED>
```

Then, in all documents that use script, developers must convert

```
<SCRIPT LANGUAGE="JavaScript">
var x,y; x=1; y=2;
if x<y {alert ("X is less than Y!")}
</SCRIPT>
```

to

```
<SCRIPT LANGUAGE="JavaScript"><![CDATA[
var x,y; x=1; y=2;
if x<y {alert ("X is less than Y!")}
]]></SCRIPT>
```

Although it is possible that the XML Working Group will add a CDATA type for elements, this solution will work for the present. Another solution developers can turn to is the SRC attribute, which allows a page to load a separate file containing scripts. All the offending code can be stored in a separate file, avoiding the XML parser entirely. There's still a small hassle—you must use a full closing tag at the end of your SCRIPT element:

```
<SCRIPT LANGUAGE="JavaScript" SRC="jslib.js">
</SCRIPT>
```

Because SCRIPT has been declared as #PCDATA, using an empty tag (<SCRIPT/>) will prevent the document from being valid. Using a closing tag should prevent this.

The latest Dynamic HTML tool from Microsoft, scriptlets, may also provide a place for scripts to hide, although at present they work only with Internet Explorer 4.0. Scriptlets use the OBJECT tag to import another file, which can then be used as an interface component. This might be useful to handle the shopping cart or cash register for an electronic catalog, but it remains to be seen how popular they will prove. A scriptlet OBJECT element might look like:

```
<OBJECT width=100 height=300 TYPE="text/x-
scriptlet" DATA="jsscriptlet.htm"></OBJECT>
```

The other enormous problem in scripting for XML is addressing the elements to determine their contents. This task will become much easier when the W3C finishes work on the Document Object Model (DOM). For now, the ID solution presented in the preceding DTD will meet the needs of Microsoft's Internet Explorer Document Object Model. The NAME attribute performs functions similar to ID in Netscape browsers, although ID appears to work in Netscape Navigator and Communicator 4.0. When the DOM is complete, it should allow scripts to access elements through the document structure as well as by NAME or ID. Unfortunately, producing that model will take a very long time—the path is strewn with technical and political landmines. In the meantime, Microsoft and Netscape will no doubt continue to produce functional, but thoroughly incompatible document and event models.

Direct Connections: Business-to-Business Transactions

Electronic commerce over the Internet is only getting started, but it's rapidly becoming clear that retail sales over the Internet face security hazards and consumer skepticism. Instead of developing enormous systems for processing credit cards and handling customer inquiries, many Internet entrepreneurs have turned to the safer world of business-to-business transactions. Frequently, all parties involved in a deal already know and perhaps even trust each other, avoiding the anonymity issues associated with Internet commerce. Accounting systems already provide sales on credit to known customers, and shipping terms are already established. As we'll see in the next section, not all transactions are financial, either; many systems out there use similar connections for securely sharing private information.

Electronic data interchange (EDI) systems so far have tended to use structures from the database world—fixed-length or delimited fields ordered neatly into tables for processing. Transmission of this information has improved dramatically—companies used to mail tapes to each other regularly, but they now more frequently connect over data networks—but the form of the information hasn't yet changed greatly. XML offers businesses more flexibility than their current systems can offer, along with an opportunity to create simple standards that can be extended to cover additional data structures as necessary.

The examples presented in this section provide only a very basic outline of what is necessary to create a full-fledged commercial interchange system. The standards proposed here will probably be superceded by recommendations from standards bodies and industry organizations.

EDI for commercial transactions has been expanding wildly for the last twenty years, and the structures it has created still have much to offer our XML examples. XML is not the answer to every aspect of electronic order placement. The businesses may trust each other enough to ship each other goods, but the orders must still be placed over a secure channel. This could be as simple as encrypting the XML document with public-key encryption tools and sending it via e-mail or as complex as sending it over a specially built private network. XML documents could also be sent on magnetic tape by private courier to companies uninterested in making network connections to their financial systems.

After that channel has been established, the businesses can begin considering the format for their orders. All orders still need ship-to and bill-to information, as well as contact information that can be used reach a human if the computers fail. Dates are also critical, to give the recipient some idea of when the order was created and when it arrived. A priority level for the order might be useful in some situations, although there might be separate priorities for the order as a whole and for parts of the order. A listing of the items to be ordered will follow, concluding with an expected total number of items and total bill. The conclusion is a critical piece for making certain that items haven't been lost during processing. XML developers should probably look over their shoulder at the older forms of data interchange, if only to make certain that they haven't left out any key pieces that the older structures provided.

Our initial DTD for XML transactions, which provides a shell for the order, is deliberately abstract. At this level, it doesn't matter what kinds of items are being ordered—apples, tractors, and concrete beams are all just items to be transferred between companies. The second DTD, which defines the items, will be much more focused on the goods in question.

We'll start by defining the ORDER element, which encompasses the entire document:

```
<!ELEMENT ORDER (BILLTO, SHIPTO, CONTACT,
PRIORITY, ITEM+,TOTALS)>
```

The BILLTO and SHIPTO elements have similar contents:

```
<!ELEMENT BILLTO (REFERENCE | FULLADDRESS)>
<!ELEMENT SHIPTO ((REFERENCE |FULLADDRESS),
SHIPVIA)>
<!ELEMENT SHIPVIA (REFERENCE | FULLADDRESS)>
<!ELEMENT REFERENCE (#PCDATA)>
<!ELEMENT FULLADDRESS (COMPANY, ADDRESSLINE+,
CITY, STATE, POSTALCODE, COUNTRY, CONTACT, PHONE,
FAX?)>
<!ELEMENT COMPANY (#PCDATA)>
<!ELEMENT ADDRESSLINE (#PCDATA)>
<!ELEMENT CITY (#PCDATA)>
<!ELEMENT STATE (#PCDATA)>
<!ELEMENT POSTALCODE (#PCDATA)>
<!ELEMENT COUNTRY (#PCDATA)>
<!ELEMENT CONTACT (#PCDATA | REFERENCE)*>
<!ELEMENT PHONE (#PCDATA)>
<!ELEMENT FAX (#PCDATA)>
<!ELEMENT PRIORITY (#PCDATA)>
```

Most of this information is basic text, although the key REFERENCE element will probably be used for most transactions. By using a REFERENCE, an ordering company is announcing that it already has a record in the recipient's system. The processing application that receives this data will pass orders that use REFERENCE to the order system immediately—a relationship already exists. (If it's a bad relationship, because the company ordering doesn't pay the bills, or doesn't exist in the system, the order system can still reject the order.) Orders that arrive with full addresses will need further verification. Contacts will be called, credit checks run if necessary, and the new buyer will be entered into the order system and given its own REFERENCE information for future use.

The TOTALS element contains a summary that can be used to check the order.

```
<!ELEMENT TOTALS (TOTALITEMS, TOTALQUANTITY,
TOTALCOST)>
<!--NOTE TOTALS ARE FOR CHECKING DATA ONLY AND DO
NOT REFLECT FINAL COSTS OR QUANTITIES -->
<!ELEMENT TOTALITEMS (#PCDATA)>
<!ELEMENT TOTALQUANTITY (#PCDATA)>
<!ELEMENT TOTALCOST (#PCDATA)>
```

This basic shell could be useful to a variety of businesses, even though they will probably want to customize it to some extent to reflect their needs. The most important feature of this shell, however, is what's left out. Because the ITEM element is never defined, this DTD is incomplete and needs a companion DTD to actually handle orders.

For this example, we'll use the publishing industry, the only industry in which I've encountered electronic ordering and all its associated benefits and costs. (Searching for hundreds of missing line items on thousands of orders of thousands of books each is not an experience I care to repeat, either.) The ITEM definition for this relatively simple industry will include only three pieces: BOOK,which carries the title information; QUANTITY, which specifies how many copies they want; PRIORITY, which allows the customer to request higher-priority treatment of certain titles; and EXTENDEDCOST, which provides the total cost the purchaser expects to pay if the other information is correct. EXTENDEDCOST in this case acts like a checksum, making sure that the purchaser's information makes sense. (If they have the wrong price, they'll be billed for the correct amount, of course.)

```
<!ELEMENT ITEM (BOOK, QUANTITY, PRIORITY?,
DISCOUNT, EXTENDEDCOST)>
<!ELEMENT DISCOUNT (#PCDATA)>
<!ELEMENT EXTENDEDCOST (#PCDATA)>
```

The book industry standardized early on a notation for its products: the International Standard Book Number (ISBN). The ISBN for *XML: A Primer*, for instance, is 155828592X. The 1 indicates that the book is in English, and the next five digits indicate that the book was published by MIS:Press. The next three digits (592) uniquely identify the title for MIS:Press, and the X (which could also be a digit from 0–9) is a checksum. XML won't process the ISBN to make sure the checksum is correct; that is the responsibility of the processing application. ISBNs uniquely identify books or book-related products, like boxed sets of books and other packages that range from books with stuffed animals to paper-making kits. Each ISBN is technically allowed to refer to only one item packaged as a unit for sale, although the contents of that package may include other items with their own ISBNs. (It's really a barcode standard that makes it easy for stores to order and sell books.) In theory at least, our DTD shouldn't even need to include title or pricing information because that should all connect to the ISBN. In reality, titles and prices change regularly, and customers aren't always notified. Adding titles and prices to the information transmitted also provides some extra insurance that the order will be processed correctly and can be used to generate warnings to customers that the information they have is outdated without stopping the order completely or requiring human intervention.

The BOOK element will include ISBN, title, and price. For most previous examples I've avoided using any element names that conflict with HTML. Although none of these orders should be going anywhere near a browser, this model could eventually be extended to retail, so it's probably best to rename the TITLE element.

```
<!ELEMENT BOOK (ISBN, BOOKTITLE, PRICE)>
<!ELEMENT ISBN (#PCDATA)>
<!ELEMENT BOOKTITLE (#PCDATA)>
<!ELEMENT PRICE (#PCDATA)>
```

The other critical part of a line item is the quantity. More than likely, the company placing the order wants more than one copy of the book. Some large wholesalers and distributors want to receive books only in whole, unopened cartons. Because books come in all kinds of shapes and sizes, the number of books to a box varies from book to book. The same title can even come in different carton quantities when it is reprinted by a printer who uses a different size box! In any case, we must provide options for customers to specify whether they want whole cartons, the size of the carton they are expecting, and rough instructions for how to adjust to any differences in carton quantities. Most small customers won't care about cartons, since they'll be receiving repackaged boxes of mixed books from the warehouse.

```
<!ELEMENT QUANTITY (NUMBER, CARTON?)>
<!ATTLIST QUANTITY
      SHIPCQ     (NO | ROUNDUP | ROUNDDOWN |
ROUNDCLOSEST) "NO">
<!ELEMENT NUMBER (#PCDATA)>
<!ELEMENT CARTON (#PCDATA)>
```

Now that we have two complete DTDs, we can begin to create some orders. The first complete DTD provides the shell we'll use:

```
<!ELEMENT ORDER (BILLTO, SHIPTO, CONTACT,
PRIORITY, ITEM+,TOTALS)>
<!ELEMENT BILLTO (REFERENCE | FULLADDRESS)>
<!ELEMENT SHIPTO ((REFERENCE |FULLADDRESS),
SHIPVIA)>
```

```
<!ELEMENT SHIPVIA (REFERENCE | FULLADDRESS)>
<!ELEMENT REFERENCE (#PCDATA)>
<!ELEMENT FULLADDRESS (COMPANY, ADDRESSLINE+,
CITY, STATE, POSTALCODE, COUNTRY, CONTACT, PHONE,
FAX?)>
<!ELEMENT COMPANY (#PCDATA)>
<!ELEMENT ADDRESSLINE (#PCDATA)>
<!ELEMENT CITY (#PCDATA)>
<!ELEMENT STATE (#PCDATA)>
<!ELEMENT POSTALCODE (#PCDATA)>
<!ELEMENT COUNTRY (#PCDATA)>
<!ELEMENT CONTACT (#PCDATA | REFERENCE)>
<!ELEMENT PHONE (#PCDATA)>
<!ELEMENT FAX (#PCDATA)>
<!ELEMENT PRIORITY (#PCDATA)>
<!ELEMENT TOTALS (TOTALITEMS, TOTALQUANTITY,
TOTALCOST)>
<!--NOTE TOTALS ARE FOR CHECKING DATA ONLY AND DO
NOT REFLECT FINAL COSTS OR QUANTITIES -->
<!ELEMENT TOTALITEMS (#PCDATA)>
<!ELEMENT TOTALQUANTITY (#PCDATA)>
<!ELEMENT TOTALCOST (#PCDATA)>
```

The second DTD includes the first through a parameter entity and provides the information for the actual line items.

```
<!ENTITY % ORDER SYSTEM "order.dtd">
%ORDER;
<!ELEMENT ITEM (BOOK, QUANTITY, PRIORITY?,
DISCOUNT, EXTENDEDCOST)>
<!ELEMENT DISCOUNT (#PCDATA)>
<!ELEMENT EXTENDEDCOST (#PCDATA)>
```

```
<!ELEMENT BOOK (ISBN, BOOKTITLE, PRICE)>
<!ELEMENT ISBN (#PCDATA)>
<!ELEMENT BOOKTITLE (#PCDATA)>
<!ELEMENT PRICE (#PCDATA)>
<!ELEMENT QUANTITY (NUMBER, CARTON?)>
<!ATTLIST QUANTITY
      SHIPCQ     (NO | ROUNDUP | ROUNDDOWN |
ROUNDCLOSEST) "NO">
<!ELEMENT NUMBER (#PCDATA)>
<!ELEMENT CARTON (#PCDATA)>
```

Now that we have a framework, it's time to show how to use it. Our order document calls only the book DTD directly. The order DTD is treated as a part of the book DTD and doesn't need to be called directly.

```
<?xml version="1.0" standalone="no" encoding="UTF-
8"?>
<!DOCTYPE ORDER SYSTEM "book.dtd">
<ORDER>
<BILLTO>
<REFERENCE>8345A</REFERENCE>
</BILLTO>
<SHIPTO>
<REFERENCE>8345A</REFERENCE>
<SHIPVIA><REFERENCE>2A</REFERENCE></SHIPVIA>
</SHIPTO>
<CONTACT>Burnie Orange</CONTACT>
<PRIORITY>Normal</PRIORITY>
<ITEM>
<BOOK><ISBN>155828592X</ISBN><BOOKTITLE>XML:A
Primer</BOOKTITLE><PRICE>$24.95</PRICE></BOOK>
```

```
<QUANTITY
SHIPCQ="ROUNDDOWN"><NUMBER>100</NUMBER><CARTON>20<
/CARTON></QUANTITY>
<DISCOUNT>.42</DISCOUNT>
<EXTENDEDCOST>$1447.10</EXTENDEDCOST>
</ITEM>
<ITEM>
<BOOK><ISBN>1558285288</ISBN><BOOKTITLE>MIME,
UUNENCODE, &amp;
ZIP</BOOKTITLE><PRICE>$24.95</PRICE></BOOK>
<QUANTITY
SHIPCQ="ROUNDDOWN"><NUMBER>100</NUMBER><CARTON>20<
/CARTON></QUANTITY>
<DISCOUNT>.42</DISCOUNT>
<EXTENDEDCOST>$1447.10</EXTENDEDCOST>
</ITEM>
<ITEM>
<BOOK><ISBN>1558514716</ISBN><BOOKTITLE>Graphical
Applications with Tcl &amp;
Tk</BOOKTITLE><PRICE>$39.95</PRICE></BOOK>
<QUANTITY><NUMBER>16</NUMBER><CARTON>16</CARTON></
QUANTITY>
<DISCOUNT>.42</DISCOUNT>
<EXTENDEDCOST>$370.74</EXTENDEDCOST>
</ITEM>
<ITEM>
<BOOK><ISBN>155828480X</ISBN><BOOKTITLE>World Wide
Web Bible</BOOKTITLE><PRICE>$29.95</PRICE></BOOK>
<QUANTITY><NUMBER>10</NUMBER><CARTON>10</CARTON></
QUANTITY>
<DISCOUNT>.42</DISCOUNT>
<EXTENDEDCOST>173.71</EXTENDEDCOST>
```

```
</ITEM>
<ITEM>
<BOOK><ISBN>1558284783</ISBN><BOOKTITLE>Introducti
on to
CGI/Perl</BOOKTITLE><PRICE>$19.95</PRICE></BOOK>
<QUANTITY
SHIPCQ="ROUNDDOWN"><NUMBER>24</NUMBER><CARTON>24</
CARTON></QUANTITY>
<DISCOUNT>.42</DISCOUNT>
<EXTENDEDCOST>277.70</EXTENDEDCOST>
</ITEM>
<TOTALS><TOTALITEMS>5</TOTALITEMS><TOTALQUANTITY>3
20</TOTALQUANTITY>
<TOTALCOST>$3716.35</TOTALCOST>
</TOTALS>
</ORDER>
```

Although this may not be as compact as the previous fixed-length or the more flexible delimited files, it's certainly more readable by humans. Its extra flexibility also gives it a significant advantage because it doesn't require that all information be present all the time. The spread of networks has lowered the costs of transmission, making this kind of verbosity acceptable. Building a processing application around this DTD and connecting it to the order system will take some effort, but hopefully the extra work will pay off in added flexibility, allowing customers to use any variety of XML processor they choose.

Direct Connections: Information Interchange

Even though orders are often the most important form of information exchanged between companies, other forms of information that aren't directly revenue-generating may also need to be shared, even among competitors. Situations where multiple firms must organize multiple parts provide fertile ground for information interchange systems. Establishing this interchange may be difficult because some companies may feel that they have much to lose by revealing their proprietary information, but often there is more to be gained than lost by sharing. Even though much of the work involved in creating these interchange systems is similar to that put into the documents described in the previous chapter, sharing documents between multiple companies creates additional challenges. This section of the chapter won't build any DTDs, which are likely to be even more industry-bound than the ordering processes already described. Instead, we'll explore some of the data-sharing applications that have already appeared in SGML, pointing out resources that may be useful to XML developers.

To see a more comprehensive list of government, military, and heavy industry SGML projects, visit http://www.sil.org/sgml/gov-apps.html.

One of the most widely cited successes of SGML's commercial use is the Pinnacles Electronic Component Information Exchange (ECIX) Group. Begun as a consortium of Hitachi, Intel, National Semiconductor, Phillips Semiconductors, and Texas Instruments, it is now part of CFI (http://www.cfi.org). ECIX began as a standard for electronic databooks, the documentation that accompanies electronic components. As the integration of multiple components on to chips progressed, the size of the average component grew rapidly, and documentation for electronic components exploded. Engineers trying to build new components were spending their time searching through documentation and recreating components in their CAD (computer-assisted design) software instead of building new chips. The semiconductor companies united to make exchanging electronic information about components easier. They built two separate pieces of the standard: the Pinnacles Component Information Standard (PCIS) and the Component Information Dictionary Standard (CIDS). PCIS provides component information in electronic format that can be read by engineers or imported easily into a CAD system. CIDS provides a dictionary of component terms and definitions for easy lookup and standardization.

PCIS source documents provide detailed information about components including packages, functional descriptions, pin outs, soldering and mounting, instruction sets, register sets, and memory maps. The PCIS source doucments refer extensively to the CIDS dictionary, using a central, standardized source for definitions. As a result, engineers can query PCIS documents instead of endlessly flipping through pages in a databook. All definitions are standardized, making it much simpler for engineers to include components from other firms in their designs. By opening up their data to electronic search and manipulation, the industry has made it easier for competing firms to sell their goods—to each other. Designers can find and use parts already suited to the task at hand and apply them immediately instead of redesigning them.

For more information on ECIX, see http://www.cfi.org/ecix/.

Other industries are attempting similar projects. The Air Transport Association of America has produced a series of specifications for aircraft maintenance manuals and practices for exchanging information. The Railroad Industry Forum is building a standard for improving the exchange of electronic parts catalogs—an updated version of the work the Master Car Builders' Association performed for a century, setting standards and exchanging information to keep railcars at work, even when they were hundreds or thousands of miles from their owners.

The largest user of SGML remains the U.S. government. For the past few years, any time an HTML programmer wanted to fire a slingshot at SGML, all they've had to do is cite the extensive use the federal government makes of SGML, especially at the Department of Defense and the IRS. Even though these two institutions present a stereotypical image of bureacracy run amok, their use of SGML has had some positive side effects. Defense contractors, especially aerospace contractors like Lockheed Martin and Boeing, have been using SGML for years. The government's insistence on SGML has spread throughout the industry, making it easier for fims to share information and exchange specifications. Many contractors use SGML and several standard DTDs as the lingua franca for internal documents, exchanging information on a regular basis without the disruptions of file conversion.

What does this mean for XML? It gives XML a strong background on which to build. Although XML doesn't have all the features of SGML, it's capable of nearly as much and is easier to write. Even though HTML developers have often seen SGML as an impassable wall, XML has received a warmer reception. Hopefully, the companies that now have a strong base of HTML knowledge will be able to apply that knowledge to the new world of XML and to apply the lessons learned from these large-scale SGML projects to smaller scale XML projects. Ideally, they'll even build large-scale XML projects.

CHAPTER 8

XML for Document Management

XML promises much more than data interchange between readers and writers or buyers and sellers. XML documents carry with them the information needed to build document systems, organized collections of information that had previously been left to wither away in filing cabinets or trash cans. Traditional file structures and even the Web have provided a minimum level of storage and accessibility, but more comprehensive systems are starting to become standard equipment in offices.

Document management systems store documents, keep track of document contents, control access to them, and allow users to locate key information quickly. Many document systems are really enormous electronic filing cabinets, storing documents with only a few keywords and a date provided for quick searching. Even though full-text search is available (and is indeed an exploding industry), it consumes enormous quantities of computing resources. By giving document management systems a clearer picture of the contents of documents, XML may make it possible for document-management systems to control larger sets of documents more efficiently. Searches can be limited to individual elements, reducing the amount of processing required to get to a document and reducing the number of false matches. Document management systems will need to adapt, although SGML-based systems shouldn't have too much difficulty moving into the XML market.

A key piece of this document management dream lies in the tools used to create the documents. If the XML tools are as clunky as the hand-coding we've done throughout this book, no one will want to use them. Even though XML tools may require significant interface changes, many WYSIWYG tools are already preparing for the transition. Corel's WordPerfect 8 already includes SGML tools, including a Visual DTD Builder. Several add-on tools are available for Microsoft Word, and Microsoft has announced future support for XML as a Word file format. Although the examples that follow are hand-coded, most of the people using them will not be entering tags directly.

XML allows document management systems to store documents as parts rather than as large clumps of often indecipherable information. Removing formatting information from the core of a document makes it far easier for search engines and similar tools to parse text without having to ponder formatting codes. A document management tool written for XML from the ground up might even store documents as sets of elements within hierarchically organized databases. The object-relational tools available with database systems from Informix, IBM, and oracle allow for the creation of a wide variety of data types, some of which are rich enough to store XML documents in a manner reflecting the structure of the document—a set of small pieces that can be manipulated, rather than a chunk of text that requires a full parsing every time it is accessed.

Building document management applications is well beyond the scope of this book. The remainder of this chapter will explore ways to create DTDs that consider real business needs, creating centrally stored documents that can be easily searched and that meet the needs of more than one part of a company. The first example standardizes the memo, perhaps the most commonly used business document type of all. The second creates a custom solution to a problem common in larger companies, that of keeping track of completed projects.

Small Steps Toward the Paperless Office

Our first management DTD will address one of the largest paper-wasters in business environments: the memos that perpetually fill in-boxes. Many companies produce small weekly newsletters in a memo format, and this DTD will disseminate chatty pieces of information as well as the boss' announcement that the company is cutting off the supply of free donuts. Although many people might question the wisdom of saving and managing memos, memos and other small-scale communications have grown dramatically in importance with the rise of litigation and the need to document processes. The Freedom of Information Act (FOIA), for example, requires that the federal government must maintain records of its activities and release them (in some form) to the public. At present, an FOIA request can take weeks or months as agencies contact their warehouses to gather old files. With a system like this, the time needed to locate documents could be greatly reduced. This DTD can be reused easily for a number of other tasks (e.g., e-mail is usually formatted on a similar model).

Virtually no one will want to hand-code their memos in XML. In the case of the memo, with its very simple structure, a program might even be able to read the memo DTD and use it as a template. XML parsers can use the information in a wide variety of ways, not just as document presentation information. An advanced XML processor might create the memo through an interview process rather than the usual clicking in fields in a document.

The first step in creating the memo DTD is interviewing people and collecting memos—lots of them—to examine how they are assembled. Most companies use a fairly standard format, with a letterhead of some kind at the top, followed by a distribution list, the source of the memo, a brief headline, and then the contents. In some cases, the typist is indicated at the bottom of the memo if the typist was someone other than the original author. For our example, we'll use a very imaginary company—Jimmy's Delectable Car Parts Design (JDCPD). JDCPD is a successful firm that sells after-market high-performance parts for all kinds of cars and trucks. A typical memo might look like that shown in Figure 8.1.

Jimmy's Delectable Car Parts Design

To: Accounts Payable
Cc: All Employees
From: Jimmy
Re: Donut payments prohibited
Date: October 10, 1997

Please note that all requests for donut reimbursement should be rejected in the future. Our health insurance company is protesting about the ever-growing size of the average employee. Given the difficult choice between getting our designers to exercise and denying them donuts, management has found it considerably simpler to end the donut reimbursement program.

All protesting employees should be directed to my office, where rice cakes and herbal tea will be available.

JD:tgk

Figure 8.1 A typical memo.

Some memos are more complex. Jimmy's Delectable Car Parts Design has a public relations office, which also puts out an internal weekly newsletter. The newsletter has short items of interest to JDCPD employees, presented in a friendly, informal style.

Jimmy's Delectable Car Parts Design

To: Jimmy
Cc: All Employees
From: Lois Turpin, PR Department
Re: JDCPD Today
Date: October 10, 1997

Design Contest Winner—Frank Kravitz of the fuel injection division has won the September award for best car part drawing. Frank's masterpiece, On to the Spark Plug II, will be on display in the lobby through November 12. Frank also won the award in January and July.

Donut Reimbursement Ends—To avoid a threatened doubling of health insurance premiums, JDCPD has ended its donut reimbursement program. "We are extremely sad to have to take such unpleasant measures," said Jimmy, but we hope our employees will understand the difficult situation we face."

Rice Cakes Available—For a limited time, rice cakes and a variety of herbal teas will be available in Jimmy's office. Employees needing a quick snack to get them charged up for a hard day of parts designing are welcome to stop by.

Remember—"Parts is parts!" Take pride in your work. The annual award for best design will be announced in December.

LT

Figure 8.2 A more complex memo.

The public relations department would like to be able to use the memo format for other presentations as well, although they haven't planned anything specific quite yet. They know that in future editions of the newsletter, especially the upcoming Intranet newsletter, they would like to include thumbnails of the award winning drawings and dress up the page a bit with more logos. Press releases are also distributed in a similar format, although they probably won't be included in this project.

The human resources department has a few requests to make of the memo DTD project. Because all of these memos will eventually be going into a document management system, the human resources director would like to be able to search the memo files for information by particular employees and about specified employees and projects. This feature could come in handy in case of a lawsuit, saving a tremendous amount of time and money spent searching through piles of memos for anything incriminating. They obviously don't have time to read every memo throughout the firm, but this could give them a step up in building an early warning system.

The mailroom is another critical customer for memos because they must distribute them. The mailroom's primary concern is that the distribution list receive a standard format, preferably one that can be switched over to e-mail painlessly so that they can get back to shipping packages instead of handing out memos. The rest of the company, including upper management, firmly believes that "memos is memos," although some of the designers would like to be able to add their drawings within memos to provide a point of reference.

The humble memo apparently handles a variety of tasks, even though it does not need to carry much information. These tasks aren't all compatible, nor are they all likely to be accomplished on the first pass. Building a workable DTD will take some experimentation and approval from many people who do not wholly support electronic memos.

The best place to start on a document type definition is usually that area of a document that already has the most structure. In this case, that's the header area. The header always contains a distribution list, a source (the From: field), a topic, and a date. The distribution list at present can be anything the mail room understands, but the prospect of using e-mail for all memos looms in the not-so-distant future. Initially, we'll create a memo DTD that includes very little detail:

```
<!ELEMENT MEMO (HEADER, MAIN)>
<!-- MEMO DTD Version 0.1 - Experimental Use Only
-->
<!ELEMENT HEADER (DISTRIBUTION, SUBJECT, DATE)>
<!ELEMENT DISTRIBUTION (TO+, CC?, FROM+)>
<!ELEMENT TO (#PCDATA)>
<!ELEMENT CC (#PCDATA)>
<!ELEMENT FROM (#PCDATA)>
<!ELEMENT SUBJECT (#PCDATA)>
<!ELEMENT DATE (#PCDATA)>
<!ELEMENT AUTHOR (#PCDATA)>
<!ELEMENT TYPIST (#PCDATA)>
<!ELEMENT MAIN (#PCDATA,(AUTHOR | TYPIST)*)>
```

This is enough of a DTD for a simple demonstration of what's possible. To show what it can do, we parse a sample document:

```
<?xml version="1.0" standalone="no" encoding="UTF-
8"?>
<!DOCTYPE MEMO SYSTEM "http://127.0.0.1/memo.dtd">
<MEMO>
<HEADER>
<DISTRIBUTION>
<TO>To: Jimmy</TO>
<FROM>From: Simon</FROM>
</DISTRIBUTION>
<SUBJECT>Re: Sample Document Created with Memo
DTD</SUBJECT>
<DATE>Date: 10/11/1997</DATE>
</HEADER>
<MAIN>
```

```
I just thought you might like to see what a memo
in XML looks like.  Thanks for the vote of
confidence at the last meeting.  With any luck,
this will make our transition to electronic
documents reasonably painless.
<AUTHOR>SSL</AUTHOR>
</MAIN>
</MEMO>
```

Even though this parses well, it has some problems:

```
C:\msxml>java msxml -d -i http://127.0.0.1/memo1.xml
<?XML VERSION="1.0" ENCODING="UTF-8"?>
<!DOCTYPE MEMO SYSTEM "http://127.0.0.1/memo.dtd">
<MEMO>
    <HEADER>
        <DISTRIBUTION>
            <TO>
                To: Jimmy
            </TO>
            <FROM>
                From: Simon
            </FROM>
        </DISTRIBUTION>
        <SUBJECT>
            Re: Sample Document Created with Memo DTD
        </SUBJECT>
        <DATE>
            Date: 10/11/1997
        </DATE>
    </HEADER>
    <MAIN>
        I just thought you might like to see what a
memo in XML looks like. Thanks for the vote of
confidence at the last meeting. With any luck, this
will make our transition to electronic documents
reasonably painless.
        <AUTHOR>
           SSL
        </AUTHOR>
```

```
    </MAIN>
</MEMO>
```

The distribution fields are the main problem. Because they must include the "To:", "CC:", and "From:" headers, they don't quite make sense. This may be acceptable for paper documents, where humans can make sense out of the list just by reading it, but it will keep e-mail programs from working properly and make it difficult for the soon-to-arrive document management system to keep track of senders and recipients. These fields all need to be broken down some more. Fortunately, they all use the same kind of information, referring to individuals or organizations within the company. Our solution clearly requires an extra element to identify senders and recipients. Because the two groups are composed of the same set of addresses of people and groups, they can share an element:

```
<!ELEMENT IDENTITY (#PCDATA)>
```

For now, it's not completely certain what the address will be. The #PCDATA type lets us accept this uncertainty for the present, although JDCPD will probably want to move to a more specific model after they work out a directory structure. If they just need to combine name and e-mail address, they could use:

```
<!ELEMENT IDENTITY (NAME, EMAIL?)>
<!NAME (#PCDATA)>
<!ELEMENT EMAIL (#PCDATA)>
```

Better yet, if they start using some real directory management tools, they might be able to use:

```
<!ELEMENT IDENTITY (#PCDATA)>
<!ATTLIST IDENTITY NAMEID CDATA #REQUIRED>
```

The information contained in the IDENTITY element could be a description ordinary humans can understand, whereas the

NAMEID attribute of the IDENTITY element would provide a unique identifier for an individual that corresponds to a listing in a central directory system. People distributing memos on paper could read the IDENTITY element text easily, whereas e-mail and document management systems could pick up the NAMEID attribute. This combination of human and machine-readable data would ideally suit the needs discussed earlier by the human resources department, because IDENTITY elements could be used elsewhere in a document to identify individuals and company divisions.

Including the IDENTITY element also requires a reworking of the elements in the DTD for the header. Even though they could be mixed declarations and just include addresses with other data, this wouldn't require addresses in the format that the document management system would like. (The content of the address element will still be PCDATA, but a list of acceptable attributes could force the NAMEID, if one existed, to be meaningful.) Enforcing these requirements requires creating another layer of elements. The "To:", "CC:", and "From:" headers and the information can remain in PCDATA. These items could also be made into entities, although they're short enough that it's probably overkill. It might also be smart to convert the author/typist material at the bottom to IDENTITY elements.

XSL will be capable of handling the issue of text headers for a list of elements without needing extra text. E-mail systems won't be interested because they tend to provide that information automatically, and the document management system won't need that extra text. Still, for now, the documents will probably need to include the text. Later systems can ignore it, but current systems will look better.

The last part of our document that may require significant improvement is the date. Dates have given programmers immense difficulty (e.g., the year 2000 bug) over the years because there isn't a single system for formatting them. 10/11/97 means October 11,

1997, to an American, but could mean November 10, 1997, to someone elsewhere in the world. Because the century (1900) isn't included, a computer will have difficulty determining the century when we finally hit the year 2000. To make sure that our system handles dates reliably, we need to separate year, month, day, and possibly hour, minute, and second to create date fields that can be easily sorted and interpreted. The program in which the memos are written and read must recombine the dates in a way that people find acceptable, but that task is generally trivial compared to building code that handles multiple date formats interspersed throughout a collection of data.

Depending on the processing application, it may be smarter to use a date field of some type rather than atomizing the year, month, and day information. This solution is presented to enhance compatibility with the widest number of document viewers, including viewers that will present only a styled version of the content. Recombining the atoms is generally easier than interpreting a date in an unfamiliar format. Given a smart enough processing application, date information can also be stored as attributes of the memo document rather than as subelements.

After taking all these considerations into account, our DTD looks like this:

```
<!ELEMENT MEMO (HEADER, MAIN)>
<!--MEMO DTD Version 0.2 - Experimental Use Only--
>
<!ELEMENT HEADER (DISTRIBUTION, SUBJECT, DATE)>
<!ELEMENT DISTRIBUTION (TO, CC?, FROM)>
<!ELEMENT TO (#PCDATA |IDENTITY)*>
<!ELEMENT CC (#PCDATA |IDENTITY)*>
<!ELEMENT FROM (#PCDATA |IDENTITY)*>
<!ELEMENT IDENTITY (#PCDATA)>
<!--May add NAMEID attribute for easier connection
to directory structures later -->
```

```
<!ELEMENT SUBJECT (#PCDATA | DESCRIP)*>
<!ELEMENT DESCRIP (#PCDATA)>
<!ELEMENT DATE(YEAR, MONTH, DAY,
(HOUR,MINUTE,SECOND)?)>
<!ELEMENT YEAR (#PCDATA)>
<!ELEMENT MONTH (#PCDATA)>
<!ELEMENT DAY (#PCDATA)>
<!ELEMENT HOUR (#PCDATA)>
<!ELEMENT MINUTE (#PCDATA)>
<!ELEMENT SECOND (#PCDATA)>
<!ELEMENT AUTHOR (IDENTITY+)>
<!ELEMENT TYPIST (IDENTITY+)>
<!ELEMENT MAIN (#PCDATA | AUTHOR | TYPIST)*>
```

The new document is considerably more marked-up:

```
<?xml version="1.0" standalone="no" encoding="UTF-
8"?>
<!DOCTYPE MEMO SYSTEM "memo.dtd">
<MEMO>
<HEADER>
<DISTRIBUTION>
<TO>To: <IDENTITY>Jimmy</IDENTITY></TO>
<FROM>From: <IDENTITY>Simon</IDENTITY></FROM>
</DISTRIBUTION>
<SUBJECT>Re: <DESCRIP>Sample Document Created with
Memo DTD</DESCRIP></SUBJECT>
<DATE>
<YEAR>1997</YEAR><MONTH>10</MONTH><DAY>11</DAY></D
ATE>
</HEADER>
<MAIN>
```

```
I just thought you might like to see what a memo
in XML looks like.  Thanks for the vote of
confidence at the last meeting.  With any luck,
this will make our transition to electronic
documents reasonably painless.
<AUTHOR><IDENTITY>SSL</IDENTITY></AUTHOR>
</MAIN>
</MEMO>
```

This parses well, although you can see that it has a few more layers:

```
C:\msxml>java msxml -d -i http://127.0.0.1/memo2.xml
<?XML VERSION="1.0" ENCODING="UTF-8"?>
<!DOCTYPE MEMO SYSTEM "http://127.0.0.1/memo2.dtd">
<MEMO>
    <HEADER>
        <DISTRIBUTION>
            <TO>
                To:
                <IDENTITY>
                    Jimmy
                </IDENTITY>
            </TO>
            <FROM>
                From:
                <IDENTITY>
                    Simon
                </IDENTITY>
            </FROM>
        </DISTRIBUTION>
        <SUBJECT>
            Re:
            <DESCRIP>
                Sample Document Created with Memo DTD
            </DESCRIP>
        </SUBJECT>
        <DATE>
            <YEAR>
                1997
            </YEAR>
```

```
                <MONTH>
                    10
                </MONTH>
                <DAY>
                    11
                </DAY>
            </DATE>
        </HEADER>
        <MAIN>
            I just thought you might like to see what a
    memo in XML looks like. Thanks for the vote of
    confidence at the last meeting. With any luck, this
    will make our transition to electronic documents
    reasonably painless.
            <AUTHOR>
                <IDENTITY>
                    SSL
                </IDENTITY>
            </AUTHOR>
        </MAIN>
    </MEMO>
```

This model should work for most simple documents. The header will keep the memos filed properly, making it easy for a document management system to track documents based on author, recipient, or title. The body content model remains a blank, however. The only kind of content that users can apply in the MAIN element right now is plain text. The body of the document needs some simple formatting elements to break up the text and provide a few options for breaking up the tedium of the ordinary memo. JDCPD needs only three options to produce the memos they have now: PARAGRAPH, HIGHLIGHT (to give extra emphasis to important material), and HEADLINE.

```
<!ELEMENT PARAGRAPH (#PCDATA|HIGHLIGHT|IDENTITY)*>
<!ELEMENT HIGHLIGHT (#PCDATA)>
<!ELEMENT HEADLINE (#PCDATA)>
```

Note that the paragraph element allows writers to include IDENTITY information. Sorting out IDENTITY information from regular text is normally difficult, especially in informal documents. Encouraging the regular use of IDENTITY information will make it far simpler. All of these elements make it much easier for styles to connect to the users' documents. While we're at it, it's probably a good idea to add some style sheet linking information. The easiest way to connect to a style sheet (i.e., the one that causes the least damage to your DTD) is with the LINK element in the HEAD element. Re-creating the elements you'll need to make this work in XML is not very difficult:

```
<!ELEMENT HEAD (LINK)>
<!ELEMENT LINK (EMPTY)>
<!ATTLIST LINK
     REL CDATA #REQUIRED
     HREF CDATA #REQUIRED
     TYPE CDATA #REQUIRED>
```

If you use style sheets with several DTDs, you may want to create this as a separate DTD and link it into your main DTD with a parameter entitity. Also remember that this is not a "true" XML link, just a temporary measure to connect a style sheet in HTML browsers. See Chapter 10 for more on XML links.

The entire DTD now looks like this:

```
<!--MEMO DTD Version 0.3 - Experimental Use Only--
>
<!ELEMENT MEMO (HEAD?,HEADER, MAIN)>
<!--CSS HEAD information for HTML compatibility-->
<!ELEMENT HEAD (LINK)>
<!ELEMENT LINK (EMPTY)>
```

```
<!ATTLIST LINK
     REL CDATA #REQUIRED
     HREF CDATA #REQUIRED
     TYPE CDATA "text/css">
<!--HEADER information for addressing -->
<!ELEMENT HEADER (DISTRIBUTION, SUBJECT, DATE)>
<!ELEMENT DISTRIBUTION (TO, CC?, FROM)>
<!ELEMENT TO (#PCDATA | IDENTITY)*>
<!ELEMENT CC (#PCDATA | IDENTITY)*>
<!ELEMENT FROM (#PCDATA| IDENTITY)*>
<!ELEMENT IDENTITY (#PCDATA)>
<!--May add NAMEID attribute for easier connection
to directory structures later -->
<!ELEMENT SUBJECT (#PCDATA | DESCRIP)*>
<!ELEMENT DESCRIP (#PCDATA)>
<!ELEMENT DATE(YEAR, MONTH, DAY,
(HOUR,MINUTE,SECOND)?)>
<!ELEMENT YEAR (#PCDATA)>
<!ELEMENT MONTH (#PCDATA)>
<!ELEMENT DAY (#PCDATA)>
<!ELEMENT HOUR (#PCDATA)>
<!ELEMENT MINUTE (#PCDATA)>
<!ELEMENT SECOND (#PCDATA)>
<!ELEMENT AUTHOR (IDENTITY+)>
<!ELEMENT TYPIST (IDENTITY+)>
<!ELEMENT PARAGRAPH (#PCDATA|HIGHLIGHT|IDENTITY)*>
<!ELEMENT HIGHLIGHT (#PCDATA)>
<!ELEMENT HEADLINE (#PCDATA)>
<!ELEMENT MAIN ((PARAGRAPH | HIGHLIGHT |
HEADLINE)*, AUTHOR?, TYPIST?)>
```

This will work well for most memos, but it might be useful to allow content outside the confines of textual memo data to use the memo DTD. The public relations department, for example, would also like to use the memo DTD for its newsletters. Even though they could use PARAGRAPH, HIGHLIGHT, and HEADLINE, they would prefer to have something more specific for their newsletter, which would show up separately in the document management system. More importantly, they would like to be able to modify their DTD later without creating repercussions throughout the company. The best solution for their situation appears to be a separate DTD that includes their elements, which can be combined with the main memo DTD when necessary. Their newsletter DTD will look like

```
<!ELEMENT NEWSLETTER (STORY+)>
<!ELEMENT STORY (LEAD, PARAGRAPH*)>
<!ELEMENT LEAD (#PCDATA)>
```

Combining this with the memo DTD may be a bit of a problem. The easiest way to allow the NEWSLETTER element to replace the MAIN element in the memo is to change the MEMO element:

```
<!ELEMENT MEMO (HEAD?, HEADER, (MAIN |
NEWSLETTER))>
```

Alternately, the MAIN element could be changed to include NEWSLETTER elements

```
<!ELEMENT MAIN (((PARAGRAPH | HIGHLIGHT |
HEADLINE)*, AUTHOR?, TYPIST?) | NEWSLETTER))>
```

If it turns out, however, that another part of the company also wants to repurpose the memo DTD, these declarations will grow incredibly unwieldy. If XML allowed a document to declare an element more than once (as it does with attributes), the solution would be simple: override MAIN in the newsletters by making a new MAIN declaration in another DTD. This is isn't possible—declaring elements more than once is an error in XML that prevents the document from being valid. The easiest way to make this work is similar to our first attempt:

```
<!ELEMENT MEMO (HEAD?, HEADER, (MAIN |
ALTERNATE))>
```

By using ALTERNATE, we've made it possible for multiple other users to take advantage of our DTD and repurpose the memo for other applications. (ALTERNATE isn't a keyword—any element name, as long as the element is left undefined in that DTD, will do.) The public relations department can now create a DTD that uses the memo DTD and expands it:

```
<!ENTITY % memo SYSTEM "memo.dtd">
%memo;
<!ELEMENT NEWSLETTER (STORY+)>
<!ELEMENT STORY (LEAD, PARAGRAPH*)>
<!ELEMENT LEAD (#PCDATA)>
```

The newsletter shown previously can be converted to XML in a fairly straightforward way:

```
<?xml version="1.0" standalone="no" encoding="UTF-
8"?>
<!DOCTYPE MEMO SYSTEM
"http://127.0.0.1/newslet2/news.dtd">
<MEMO>
<HEADER>
<DISTRIBUTION>
<TO>To: <IDENTITY>Jimmy</IDENTITY></TO>
<CC>CC: <IDENTITY>All Employees</IDENTITY></CC>
```

```
<FROM>From: <IDENTITY>Lois Turpin, PR
Department</IDENTITY></FROM>
</DISTRIBUTION>
<SUBJECT>Re: <DESCRIP>JDCPD Today  - Sample
Newsletter Created with Memo
DTD</DESCRIP></SUBJECT>
<DATE>
<YEAR>1997</YEAR><MONTH>10</MONTH><DAY>10</DAY></D
ATE>
</HEADER>
<ALTERNATE><!--BEGIN ALTERNATE CONTENT TO REPLACE
MAIN -->
<NEWSLETTER>
<STORY><LEAD>Design Contest Winner -
</LEAD><PARAGRAPH>Frank Kravitz of the fuel
injection division has won the September award for
best car part drawing.  Frank's masterpiece,
<HIGHLIGHT>On to the Spark Plug II</HIGHLIGHT>,
will be on display in the lobby through November
12.  Frank also won the award in January and
July.</PARAGRAPH></STORY>
<STORY><LEAD>Donut Reimbursement Ends -
</LEAD><PARAGRAPH>To avoid a threatened doubling
of health insurance premiums, JDCPD has ended its
donut reimbursement program.  "We are extremely
sad to have to take such unpleasant measures,"
said Jimmy, "but we hope our employees will
understand the difficult situation we
face."</PARAGRAPH></STORY>
<STORY><LEAD>Rice Cakes Available -
</LEAD><PARAGRAPH>For a limited time, rice cakes
and a variety of herbal teas will be available in
Jimmy's office.  Employees needing a quick snack
to get them charged up for a hard day of parts
```

```
designing are welcome to stop
by.</PARAGRAPH></STORY>
<STORY><LEAD>Remember - </LEAD><PARAGRAPH>"Parts
is parts!"  Take pride in your work. The annual
award for best design will be announced in
December.</PARAGRAPH>
</STORY>
</NEWSLETTER></ALTERNATE>
</MEMO>
```

This newsletter XML file parses quite happily using the news DTD in combination with the memo DTD:

```
C:\msxml>java msxml -d -i http://127.0.0.1/newslet.xml
<?XML VERSION="1.0" ENCODING="UTF-8"?>
<!DOCTYPE MEMO SYSTEM
"http://127.0.0.1/newslet2/news.dtd">
<MEMO>
    <HEADER>
        <DISTRIBUTION>
            <TO>
                To:
                <IDENTITY>
                    Jimmy
                </IDENTITY>
            </TO>
            <CC>
                CC:
                <IDENTITY>
                    All Employees
                </IDENTITY>
            </CC>
            <FROM>
                From:
                <IDENTITY>
                    Lois Turpin, PR Department
                </IDENTITY>
            </FROM>
        </DISTRIBUTION>
```

```
        <SUBJECT>
            Re:
            <DESCRIP>
                JDCPD Today - Sample Newsletter
Created with Memo DTD
            </DESCRIP>
        </SUBJECT>
        <DATE>
            <YEAR>
                1997
            </YEAR>
            <MONTH>
                10
            </MONTH>
            <DAY>
                10
            </DAY>
        </DATE>
    </HEADER>
    <ALTERNATE>
      <!-- BEGIN ALTERNATE CONTENT TO REPLACE MAIN  -->
        <NEWSLETTER>
            <STORY>
                <LEAD>
                    Design Contest Winner -
                </LEAD>
                <PARAGRAPH>
                    <IDENTITY>
                       Frank Kravitz
                    </IDENTITY>
                    of the fuel injection division has
won the September award for best car part drawing.
Frank's masterpiece,
                    <HIGHLIGHT>
                        On to the Spark Plug II
                    </HIGHLIGHT>
                    , will be on display in the lobby
through November 12. Frank also won the award in
January and July.
                </PARAGRAPH>
            </STORY>
```

```
            <STORY>
                <LEAD>
                    Donut Reimbursement Ends -
                </LEAD>
                <PARAGRAPH>
                    To avoid a threatened doubling of
health insurance premiums, JDCPD has ended its donut
reimbursement program. "We are extremely sad to have
to take such unpleasant measures," said Jimmy, "but we
hope our employees will understand the difficult
situation we face."
                </PARAGRAPH>
            </STORY>
            <STORY>
                <LEAD>
                    Rice Cakes Available -
                </LEAD>
                <PARAGRAPH>
                    For a limited time, rice cakes and
a variety of herbal teas will be available in Jimmy's
office. Employees needing a quick snack to get them
charged up for a hard day of parts designing are
welcome to stop by.
                </PARAGRAPH>
            </STORY>
            <STORY>
                <LEAD>
                    Remember -
                </LEAD>
                <PARAGRAPH>
                    "Parts is parts!" Take pride in
your work. The annual award for best design will be
announced in December.
                </PARAGRAPH>
            </STORY>
        </NEWSLETTER>
    </ALTERNATE>
</MEMO>
```

Using this model, other divisions can create their own ALTERNATE content models. The designers, for example, could develop a design brief that included NOTATION elements that allowed them to include all kinds of drawings and additional information. The public relations department could do the same to include their extra logos and perhaps even create an electronic version of the company letterhead. Although the memo model won't be able to cope with everything, XML offers it a chance to expand into new fields without becoming completely overloaded.

This is by no means the only way to accomplish this task. Instead of using an ALTERNATE element to allow expansion, it might be more useful to move the entire MAIN element definition out of the main DTD and into another file. The memo's core functionality is primarily the header and its distribution mechanism, so this might make sense. In this case, because approximately 90% of the documents created with this DTD are simple memos, and because the newletter DTD reuses parts of the DTD under the MAIN element (e.g., PARAGRAPH), it seems simplest to keep the DTD for a simple memo in the memo DTD. Yet another option would be to move the distribution information out of the memo DTD, making it easier to reuse with other DTDs. Choosing between these options is frequently difficult and very dependent upon the particular needs of your document structures and management systems.

Even though the document management system won't care directly about the style sheets, it can keep track of which style sheet was used where. After all, style sheets are just another link. Placing your style information into a document management tool makes it easy to foresee the impact of significant changes because the tool can warn designers which documents are about to receive the new style. Best of all, the document management system may to able to support some kind of versioning. Older documents can stay with their older style sheet, whereas newer documents receive a facelift. The capabilities of the management system, of course, may vary.

It's probably best to create a separate style sheet for each DTD, even if you combine DTDs on a regular basis. In that way, the user's machine doesn't waste cycles parsing style information it won't be using, and developers don't waste time searching through an enormous collection of styles. Choose a naming convention and stick with it. I tend to name my DTD files *name*.dtd and the corresponding CSS files *name*.css. You can keep them in separate directories if you like but try to maintain as much parallelism as possible between the two structures so parts don't disappear. When it's time to modify a DTD, create a new DTD file (and associated CSS or other style sheet file) so that older documents don't suddenly become invalid. Document management systems require humans to behave systematically—changing a DTD significantly could leave the document system stranded with files of documents it can't parse. Although writing conversion programs is possible, it is rarely fun, and changing a significant library of documents by hand is even more tedious.

Building Histories: A DTD for Corporate Memory

History is rarely a favorite corporate subject. The future is always in sharp focus: companies strive to make the next quarter, the next year, or even the next decade their best one yet. Yesterday's sales figures may have paid for a new car or cost a promised bonus, but today's holdings and tomorrow's profits are of greater concern. As a result, companies often let their history slide. Memos and reports may accumulate in file cabinets, but periodically they get emptied or shipped to far-off storage, and key employees leave the company or retire. As employees have become more mobile, the odds of losing the person "who knows where all the bodies are buried" greatly increase. Most companies lack strategies for debriefing employees and organizing the information, costing wasted hours spent trying to determine what happened when a legal battle or a customer inquiry requires a reexamination of past activity.

The document structures we'll build in this example are designed expressly to keep some of that history alive and available at the end of a project or when an employee changes positions. Combined with a document management system, the information stored in that structure will make producing quick, comprehensive answers to questions about past projects easier. Large corporations that write proposals for large projects are often required to present past performance references; the information contained in this system will make it far easier for companies to describe their previous work, saving expensive resources for use on developing the forward-looking parts of the proposal.

This project and its associated DTDs could grow to be gigantic, especially if it expanded from project history into project management. This discussion will explore only some of the basic needs of the project and develop some of the core document types.

This project needs a considerable amount of political work before DTD design can even begin. Structured documents are useless if they aren't applied consistently. Even though it's easy to require that a particular element appear in a document, it's difficult to require that individuals who are already on their way out the door fill out a few acres of paperwork. Building this document database successfully requires adding it to the process as a standard business procedure. The needs of that process will probably have direct effects on the nature of the DTD and the level of flexibility required. If this system is likely to be used on a regular basis, it might even be worthwhile to build a custom interview application to collect the information.

Each project will probably have a set of data associated with it, representing interviews and other documents collected over the life of the projects. Projects that last for years could end up with sizable quantities of information under a single header. Even though it would be conceivable for all this information to be assembled in a single document, large projects will quickly amass too much information even for a document management system. Although a single document approach makes great sense for small projects, a larger system will function more smoothly if information is broken into more manageable chunks. Even though the use of elements makes finding relevant information easier, documents with thousands or hundreds of thousands of elements have probably outgrown a single-document file structure. Our example will reflect that need by building several document types, each of which can connect to a central project record.

We'll return to the need for compound documents, and to this example in particular, in Chapter 10 when we explore XML linking. For now, consider the links described as connections to information on a directory or database server, both of which are handled by the application, not the XML parser.

This project requires a set of DTDs, not just a single all-encompassing DTD. Because it is possible that all the DTDs will be combined in a single document, designers must take care not to use the same element name twice. We'll begin by creating a set of common elements that may be used throughout all the documents in the set. IDENTITY is an even more important element in this situation than it was in the previous example because the participants on the project and their positions need to be clearly defined. IDENTITY in this case will carry an attribute value linking it to a centralized directory of employees, as well as providing space for the person's name, current title, and position:

```
<!ELEMENT IDENTITY (NAME,TITLE?,POSITION?)>
<!ATTLIST IDENTITY
     IDLINK CDATA #REQUIRED>
<!ELEMENT NAME (#PCDATA)>
<!ELEMENT TITLE (#PCDATA)>
<!ELEMENT POSITION (#PCDATA)>
```

Even though breaking the NAME element into first name and last name might be useful, it isn't really necessary because of the required IDLINK attribute of the IDENTITY element. IDLINK will connect the identity back to a directory, which includes a full set of information. IDENTITY isn't restricted to individuals; it could also refer to departments or even companies. The link to the directory will produce some extra overhead because all people and groups referenced through IDENTITY must be entered in the directory. Not all organizations store customer information in their directories, although it's become more popular as the computer encroaches on the turf of the Rolodex.

XML includes no way to check the value of the IDLINK. It can require that it appear, but the parser will not itself check the value of IDLINK against the directory. That kind of logic must be placed in the application that processes the information returned by the parser. (The application could be the document management system or another application preparing the information for display.) It should also be implemented in the program used to create the documents. Ideally, a simple lookup procedure would allow authors to select IDENTITY values from a list of names provided by the directory.

LOCATION elements are similar to IDENTITY elements—they refer to individual units and can be looked up in a directory server, probably the same server that stores identities. However, because companies may briefly use locations all over the world for only a brief visit, it doesn't seem as worthwhile to require that all LOCATION elements have a link in the directory. Key locations, like company offices and places of work, should definitely be listed, but hotels may not be as important.

```
<!ELEMENT LOCATION (#PCDATA)>
<!ATTLIST LOCATION
     IDLINK CDATA #IMPLIED>
```

The next key element is the date. The documents themselves will be marked with the date they were written, and using a standard format for the date will make searching for information inside other elements much easier. The DATE element is the same as the date element used previously in the memo application, although it lacks the initial #PCDATA information:

```
<!ELEMENT DATE(YEAR, MONTH, DAY,
(HOUR,MINUTE,SECOND)?)>
<!ELEMENT YEAR (#PCDATA)>
<!ELEMENT MONTH (#PCDATA)>
<!ELEMENT DAY (#PCDATA)>
<!ELEMENT HOUR (#PCDATA)>
<!ELEMENT MINUTE (#PCDATA)>
<!ELEMENT SECOND (#PCDATA)>
```

This DTD will undoubtedly explode with additional elements for formatting and notation, but we'll start simple. The four elements we'll include at first for content are EMPHASIS, RUMOR, QUOTE, and PARAGRAPH. EMPHASIS will allow authors to hit certain points harder; RUMOR will allow authors to include content that isn't certain, but may be useful (and which probably should not be repeated); and QUOTE allows them to include material from customers and others. PARAGRAPH just provides a basic grammatical structure. These elements may all contain mixed content, including their counterparts, represented by the parameter entity %TEXTELEMENTS;:

```
<!ENTITY % TEXTELEMENTS "(#PCDATA | EMPHASIS |
RUMOR | QUOTE | IDENTITY | LOCATION | DATE)*">
<!ELEMENT EMPHASIS (%TEXTELEMENTS;)>
<!ELEMENT RUMOR (%TEXTELEMENTS;)>
<!ELEMENT QUOTE (%TEXTELEMENTS;)>
<!ELEMENT PARAGRAPH (%TEXTELEMENTS;)>
```

Now that we have a set of elements we can use within the text, let's define some document-level structures. The information in this dataset will be stored in several different kinds of documents.

Project managers will have different information to report than field technicians or accountants, reflected by a wide range of different document structures. For our example, we'll use a project completion report, which provides a general report from the project manager on the work performed after a project is finished. Our root element is FINALREPORT, which contains elements identifying the project, the author, the date of the report, and the classification of the document and provides elements in which the author can add an overview of the project, financial information, schedule information, detailed information about the work done, and list any commendations from the customer.

```
<!ELEMENT FINALREPORT (PROJECT, IDENTITY, DATE,
CLASSIFICATION, OVERVIEW, FINANCIALS, SCHEDULE,
DETAIL, COMMENDATIONS?)>
```

The PROJECT element, like the IDENTITY and LOCATION elements, links to other sources of information. This saves the author the effort of redescribing the project, the customer, the type of contract, and other stable information like the start date of the project. (Start dates are not always stable, but they should be pinned down by the time the project is completed.) As a result, the PROJECT element can stay very simple, storing the name of the project in #PCDATA and linking to more detailed information through the PROJLINK attribute:

```
<!ELEMENT PROJECT (#PCDATA)>
<!ATTLIST PROJECT
     PROJLINK CDATA #REQUIRED>
```

The IDENTITY and DATE elements that follow the project indicate the author of this document and the date of its writing, respectively. Their position in the PROJECT element is all that identifies them as such; developers who want to make this more explicit (e.g., to help out weaker search tools) could create wrappers for them:

```
<!ELEMENT AUTHOR (IDENTITY)>
<!ELEMENT REPORTDATE (DATE)>
```

This would require a small change in the FINALREPORT element:

```
<!ELEMENT FINALREPORT (PROJECT, AUTHOR,
REPORTDATE, CLASSIFICATION, OVERVIEW,
FINANCIALS,SCHEDULE, DETAIL, COMMENDATIONS?)>
```

CLASSIFICATION is designed to help the document management control access to the document. Some documents may be OPEN, available to the public without restriction (which means they're handy for the public relations office), others may be PROPRIETARY (for use only within the company), some may even be SECRET (which should limit access to particular readers within the company), and others may be SPECIAL. SPECIAL could be a classification above SECRET, or it could just be a general classification that requires the application to check the identity of the reader against a list someplace else.

No matter how this element is created, remember that the application, not the parser, must enforce security. XML has no built-in tools for providing security; document management systems and other tools must take on this responsibility, locking users out of documents completely until their identity and permissions have been validated.

Implementing this kind of element requires making some choices. The easiest way to implement this is by making CLASSIFICATION an element that uses #PCDATA as its data type. In this way, new types can be added easily, but the parser won't check the type. An adventurous author could add "GOOFY" as a security classification.

```
<!ELEMENT CLASSIFICATION (#PCDATA)>
```

Another way to implement this element would be to make CLASSIFICATION an empty element with attributes that indicate the level of security:

```
<!ELEMENT CLASSIFICATION EMPTY>
<!ATTLIST CLASSIFICATION
      SECLEVEL (OPEN | PROPRIETARY | SECRET |
SPECIAL) "SPECIAL"
      SECLINK CDATA #IMPLIED>
```

The SECLEVEL attribute indicates the level of security, whereas SECLINK makes linking to an outside security directory for "SPECIAL" situations easy. (Depending on the type of application, the developer might want to set the default to a different value, or simply to #REQUIRED.)

We've finally reached the meat of the document: what was actually accomplished on this project, how much it cost, and how long it took. Because this document is a summary document, all this information can be stored quite simply. Heavy-duty accounting and schedule information can be stored in other documents (or even databases) and linked to the project through a centralized system, in much the same way that the PROJECT element is connected by the PROJLINK attribute. The FINALREPORT document is here for quick reference, not a line-by-line accounting of every widget purchased and sold. The overview section begins the summary:

```
<!ELEMENT OVERVIEW (PARAGRAPH+)>
```

The FINANCIALS element is a little more broken down but still presents only a general explanation of the project's costs:

```
<!ELEMENT FINANCIALS (ORIGINALQUOTE, FINALCOST,
EXPLANATION?)>
<!ELEMENT ORIGINALQUOTE (#PCDATA)>
<!ELEMENT FINALCOST (#PCDATA)>
```

```
<!ELEMENT EXPLANATION (PARAGRAPH+)>
```

The SCHEDULE element provides a similar broad description of the project schedule and uses the EXPLANATION element created for FINANCIALS:

```
<!ELEMENT SCHEDULE
(ORIGINALSCHEDULE,ACTUALSCHEDULE, EXPLANATION?)>
<!ELEMENT ORIGINALSCHEDULE (STARTDATE, ENDDATE?)>
<!ELEMENT ACTUALSCHEDULE (STARTDATE, ENDDATE?)>
<!ELEMENT STARTDATE (DATE)>
<!ELEMENT ENDDATE (DATE)>
```

In many cases DTDs can be simplified by using elements in more than one context, but this can create large problems for simple processing applications. If someone wants a list of all the explanations for financial transactions, they need a processor smart enough to separate EXPLANATION elements nested inside of FINANCIALS elements from those nested inside of SCHEDULE elements. Developers should find out the limitations of the planned processing application early. That way, creating separate FINEXPLANATION and SCHEDEXPLANATION elements is easy, if necessary.

Despite its name, the DETAIL element receives a very simple XML declaration. DETAIL is the area wherein the project manager enters detailed information, but from the perspective of the parser, all that information uses PARAGRAPH elements, which can contain all the elements listed in the %TEXTELEMENTS; parameter entity. The COMMENDATIONS element is likewise a container for text elements:

```
<!ELEMENT DETAIL (PARAGRAPH+)>
<!ELEMENT COMMENDATIONS (PARAGRAPH+)>
```

Now that we have all the parts defined, it's time to combine them into DTDs. Our first DTD contains all the text elements needed through documents in this system, providing basic text content types:

```
<!--TEXT CONTENT ELEMENT INFORMATION -->
<!--IDENTITY INFORMATION -->
<!ELEMENT IDENTITY (NAME,TITLE?,POSITION?)>
<!ATTLIST IDENTITY
     IDLINK CDATA #REQUIRED>
<!ELEMENT NAME (#PCDATA)>
<!ELEMENT TITLE (#PCDATA)>
<!ELEMENT POSITION (#PCDATA)>
<!--LOCATION INFORMATION -->
<!ELEMENT LOCATION (#PCDATA)>
<!ATTLIST LOCATION
     IDLINK CDATA #IMPLIED>
<!--DATE INFORMATION -->
<!ELEMENT DATE(YEAR, MONTH, DAY,
(HOUR,MINUTE,SECOND)?)>
<!ELEMENT YEAR (#PCDATA)>
<!ELEMENT MONTH (#PCDATA)>
<!ELEMENT DAY (#PCDATA)>
<!ELEMENT HOUR (#PCDATA)>
<!ELEMENT MINUTE (#PCDATA)>
<!ELEMENT SECOND (#PCDATA)>
<!--OTHER TEXT CONTENT -->
<!ELEMENT EMPHASIS (%TEXTELEMENTS;)>
<!ELEMENT RUMOR (%TEXTELEMENTS;)>
<!ELEMENT QUOTE (%TEXTELEMENTS;)>
<!ELEMENT PARAGRAPH (%TEXTELEMENTS;)>
```

```
<!ENTITY % TEXTELEMENTS "(#PCDATA | EMPHASIS |
RUMOR | QUOTE | IDENTITY | LOCATION | DATE)*">
```

The second piece, which actually defines our project report, includes the preceding DTD through a parameter entity:

```
<!--DTD for Final Project Reports -->
<!ELEMENT FINALREPORT (PROJECT, AUTHOR,
REPORTDATE, CLASSIFICATION, OVERVIEW,
FINANCIALS,SCHEDULE, DETAIL, COMMENDATIONS?)>
<!--Link to text content declarations -->
<!ENTITY % TEXTDECLARATION SYSTEM "textelem.dtd">
%TEXTDECLARATION;
<!--Project Identification -->
<!ELEMENT PROJECT (#PCDATA)>
<!ATTLIST PROJECT
     PROJLINK CDATA #REQUIRED>
<!--AUTHOR AND REPORT DATE WRAPPERS, FOR EASIER
SEARCHING -->
<!ELEMENT AUTHOR (IDENTITY)>
<!ELEMENT REPORTDATE (DATE)>
<!--CLASSIFICATION.  ENFORCED BY DOCUMENT
MANAGEMENT SYSTEM -->
<!ELEMENT CLASSIFICATION EMPTY>
<!ATTLIST CLASSIFICATION
     SECLEVEL (OPEN | PROPRIETARY | SECRET |
SPECIAL) "SPECIAL"
     SECLINK CDATA #IMPLIED>
<!--REPORT ELEMENTS -->
<!ELEMENT OVERVIEW (PARAGRAPH+)>
<!ELEMENT FINANCIALS (ORIGINALQUOTE, FINALCOST,
EXPLANATION?)>
```

```
<!ELEMENT ORIGINALQUOTE (#PCDATA)>
<!ELEMENT FINALCOST (#PCDATA)>
<!ELEMENT EXPLANATION (PARAGRAPH+)>
<!ELEMENT SCHEDULE
(ORIGINALSCHEDULE,ACTUALSCHEDULE, EXPLANATION?)>
<!ELEMENT ORIGINALSCHEDULE (STARTDATE, ENDDATE?)>
<!ELEMENT ACTUALSCHEDULE (STARTDATE, ENDDATE?)>
<!ELEMENT STARTDATE (DATE)>
<!ELEMENT ENDDATE (DATE)>
<!ELEMENT DETAIL (PARAGRAPH+)>
<!ELEMENT COMMENDATIONS (PARAGRAPH+)>
```

This DTD is only a possible beginning for a much larger and more elaborate structure. With a well-built document management system, multiple document types could be constructed around a database of PROJECT information. Document types for drawings, detailed reports of tasks carried out, customer orders, time spent on projects, status reports, and even project management information could be kept in the same system, allowing secure but easy access and cross-reference. These systems have yet to appear, and most of them will undoubtedly need a considerable amount of customization, but they will probably be the most efficient keepers of XML information. With any luck, document management systems will replace the file cabinets and file systems of today, keeping track of large numbers of documents and their components and making them readily accessible.

CHAPTER 9

XML for Data-Driven Applications

The documents in the preceding chapters all corresponded to real paper documents, the kind of documents that people can pick up and read. XML isn't limited to this kind of information; indeed, many of its earliest applications supplied information in forms not readily presentable to humans. The field in which XML may make the greatest strides is communication between computers and between computers and other devices, which has been a difficult affair so far. The DTDs and other examples in this chapter provide solutions for what I call nontraditional documents—data structures for which XML is very appropriate but that aren't documents humans would normally read.

Data Documents

Our first example applies XML to a rather different computing field—device control. Given a system that responds to a small set of inputs without requiring processing of return values, it is possible to write a "program" purely in data. For starters, we'll build a DTD that could be used to control a set of light switches (or other electrical devices). Light switches are an extremely simple example, but there are many situations with hundreds or thousands of lights that need to be controlled. Our example will begin with the lighting in a typical house, but it could be extended to cover display lights or even stage lights.

My parents used to receive the DAK catalog every few months; it was crammed with odd and unusual stereo equipment and gadgetry. One of the weirdest items they carried was the X-10 system, which let you control electrical devices by remote control. Originally it came with a controller unit and modules that plugged in between the electrical socket and the plug of a lamp or other electrical device. The controller unit sends signals over the electrical wires to the individual boxes (up to 256 of them) telling them to turn on and off or dim to a particular level. Eventually it sprouted a serial computer interface, which made it easy to program devices to turn on and off at various times of day—effectively, a more expensive, but more accurate device timer than the boxes with the dials on them. At this point, it's grown considerably more elaborate (see http://www.x10.com for details). Remote controls that can run a house rather than a TV make it easy for the ultimate couch potatoes to run significant portions of their houses without getting up.

Although the DTD we'll develop isn't designed expressly for the X-10 interface, it wouldn't be too difficult to build an interface that converted the data in these documents into the signals controlling electrical devices. The X-10 system actually uses a limited set of commands to control its devices, but our DTD doesn't need to worry about particular commands. It will just define particular states that the control system should achieve. A processing application would take the information returned by the parser and determine which commands are needed to achieve the state desired. Instead of giving the controller a sequence of steps, our document will give it a desired result and allow the controller to figure out how best to get there.

We'll be controlling two different categories of equipment: lights and appliances. Lights can be turned on and off and dimmed, whereas appliances can be turned on and off. (If someone wants to extend this to controlling appliances via remote controls and not just their power, extending the DTD shouldn't be too difficult.) Lights and appliances are identified by addresses that effectively represent hexadecimal numbers. The address begins with a house code, A–P.

General practice is to set up an entire system on one letter, limiting users to 16 devices but avoiding conflicts with neighbors. Users without gadget-minded neighbors can use more than one house code. The unit code identifies the controlling module. It's a number from 1 to 16. Device modules can be set to the same address; all device modules with the same address will respond simultaneously to commands. A set of three lamps on address B10 will all turn on or off or dim as requested in response to commands sent to B10.

Our DTD will allow users to create documents to give orders to this system. All these documents will be processed by a computer, but we'll keep them human-readable for easy editing. To help with this, our documents may include a description of all the modules on the system, followed by the states desired and the conditions that set them off.

```
<!ELEMENT CONTROLSCHEDULE (MODULE*, STATE*,
TRIGGER*)>
```

Our modules need several identifiers. For now we'll stick with the system that X-10 uses to build an address, adding two pieces that provide additional information to the processing application and human editors:

```
<!ELEMENT MODULE (ADDRESS, TYPE?, DESCRIPTION?)>
<!ELEMENT ADDRESS (HOUSE, UNIT)>
<!ELEMENT HOUSE (#PCDATA)>
<!ELEMENT UNIT (#PCDATA)>
<!ELEMENT TYPE (#PCDATA)>
<!ELEMENT DESCRIPTION (#PCDATA)>
```

We give the MODULE element a little bit of extra flexibility by allowing it to contain ADDRESS and TYPE elements. We could require the user or the program creating these files to keep track of whether the module at a particular address is a light module or an appliance module and to identify the modules purely through addresses. Adding TYPE adds some extra flexibility and makes these documents more portable. A processing application that doesn't care about TYPE can strip it out, whereas a new application that's being set up for the first time might use the TYPE element to import more complete information about the control modules. TYPE also adds a bit of flexibility in case new varieties of a module appear because commands may vary depending on the kind of module receiving them. (At present, the X-10 system doesn't, but a more advanced future system might.) DESCRIPTION is provided to give the humans programming these devices a description of the device and its location.

The ADDRESS element allows us to identify modules uniquely (or in sets, as described previously.) A developer impatient with the A–P, 1–16 identifiers of the X-10 system could convert them to their hex equivalents easily and represent them in the DTD like this:

```
<!ELEMENT ADDRESS (HEXADDRESS | (HOUSE, UNIT))>
<!ELEMENT HEXADDRESS (#PCDATA)>
```

For now, we'll stick to using the HOUSE and UNIT identifiers.

Even though the MODULE element includes ADDRESS elements, it won't be that useful for issuing commands because multiple modules can share a single address. ADDRESS will be the key element for issuing commands. After a document's initial MODULE declarations, a series of STATE declarations may follow. STATE declarations define a final position rather than a means of getting there. We'll provide names for our STATEs, as well as a description and a list of component parts:

```
<!ELEMENT STATE (NAME, DESCRIPTION?, COMPONENT+)>
```

The NAME element provides a reference our programs will use to find and implement this STATE. The DESCRIPTION element is the same one we used previously for modules, providing descriptions to human users. The COMPONENT element defines the final position for the devices on modules at a single address:

```
<!ELEMENT COMPONENT (DESCRIPTION?, ADDRESS,
POSITION)>
<!ELEMENT POSITION (#PCDATA)>
```

ADDRESS elements are the same elements defined previously for identifying modules. POSITION holds the data defining the position to which the module should be set. For appliance modules, it could be ON or OFF; for the lamp module, it could be ON, OFF, or a dimmer position defined by a percentage. If new modules came on the market, the POSITION element could hold new values as necessary, because only the processing application interprets the meaning of this element.

Telling the system to move to one of these states is a little trickier because a user might want to select a particular state for several different reasons. Many of the home automation uses for these modules are just controlled by timers. Lights can turn on and off depending on the time of day. This can make a house look like it is occupied while the owners are away, or it can just make sure that the lights are on when people come home from work. Users may also want to be able to select a state by flipping a (specially wired) light switch. Motion detectors and remote consoles can also select a state. This requirement makes constructing our TRIGGER element a little tricky.

```
<!ELEMENT TRIGGER (STATENAME, TIMED*, SWITCH*)>
<!ELEMENT STATENAME (#PCDATA)>
```

STATENAME is just a reference to a previously defined STATE element. TIME elements define a time at which the chosen STATE should be implemented. Because users may need a variety of timing mechanisms, several options are available for daily events, weekly events, and events that should take place on a particular day:

```
<!ELEMENT TIMED ((DAILY | WEEKLY | DATE), TIME)>
<!ELEMENT DAILY EMPTY>
<!ELEMENT WEEKLY (WEEKDAY*)>
<!ELEMENT WEEKDAY (#PCDATA)>
<!ELEMENT DATE (DAY,MONTH, YEAR)>
<!ELEMENT DAY (#PCDATA)>
<!ELEMENT MONTH (#PCDATA)>
<!ELEMENT YEAR (#PCDATA)>
<!ELEMENT TIME (HOUR, MINUTE, SECOND?)>
<!ELEMENT HOUR (#PCDATA)>
<!ELEMENT MINUTE (#PCDATA)>
<!ELEMENT SECOND (#PCDATA)>
```

As mentioned in the previous chapter, many date formats are available that don't require atomizing the day, month, year, etc. For an application like this one, those formats might well be preferable.

The SWITCH element contains a *description*—a name or address understood by the processing application—of the switch triggering the implementation of the state:

```
<!ELEMENT SWITCH (#PCDATA)>
```

The processing application for this document must parse the document and set up an internal timer as well as the serial connection to the modules and switches. When any of the trigger conditions are met, it will send out the appropriate commands to the control modules, setting the lights and other devices to their appropriate positions.

Most wall and remote switches in these systems are hard-coded to particular modules. Users who need to connect only one switch to one device could still use direct calls to the module and bypass this processing system directly. The system that makes a later call to a module will simply override whatever previous commands were issued. Of course, if someone turns a light off or leaves it unplugged, nothing will visibly happen.

Assembling our DTD produces the following:

```
<!ELEMENT CONTROLSCHEDULE (MODULE*, STATE*,
TRIGGER*)>
<!ELEMENT MODULE (ADDRESS, TYPE?, DESCRIPTION?)>
<!ELEMENT ADDRESS (HOUSE, UNIT)>
<!ELEMENT HOUSE (#PCDATA)>
<!ELEMENT UNIT (#PCDATA)>
<!ELEMENT TYPE (#PCDATA)>
<!ELEMENT DESCRIPTION (#PCDATA)>
<!ELEMENT STATE (NAME, DESCRIPTION?, COMPONENT+)>
<!ELEMENT COMPONENT (DESCRIPTION?,ADDRESS,
POSITION)>
<!ELEMENT POSITION (#PCDATA)>
<!ELEMENT TRIGGER (STATENAME, TIMED*, SWITCH*)>
<!ELEMENT STATENAME (#PCDATA)>
<!ELEMENT TIMED ((DAILY | WEEKLY | DATE), TIME)>
<!ELEMENT DAILY EMPTY>
<!ELEMENT WEEKLY (WEEKDAY*)>
<!ELEMENT WEEKDAY (#PCDATA)>
<!ELEMENT DATE (DAY,MONTH, YEAR)>
<!ELEMENT DAY (#PCDATA)>
<!ELEMENT MONTH (#PCDATA)>
```

```
<!ELEMENT YEAR (#PCDATA)>
<!ELEMENT TIME (HOUR, MINUTE, SECOND?)>
<!ELEMENT HOUR (#PCDATA)>
<!ELEMENT MINUTE (#PCDATA)>
<!ELEMENT SECOND (#PCDATA)>
<!ELEMENT SWITCH (#PCDATA)>
```

We can use this DTD to create files that a processing application could use to control a small set of lamps and a radio:

```
<?xml version="1.0" encoding="UTF-8"?>
<!DOCTYPE CONTROLSCHEDULE SYSTEM "controller.dtd">
<CONTROLSCHEDULE>
<MODULE>
<ADDRESS><HOUSE>B</HOUSE><UNIT>2</UNIT></ADDRESS>
<TYPE>APPLIANCE</TYPE>
<DESCRIPTION>Radio in livingroom</DESCRIPTION>
</MODULE>
<MODULE>
<ADDRESS><HOUSE>B</HOUSE><UNIT>10</UNIT></ADDRESS>
<TYPE>LAMP</TYPE>
<DESCRIPTION>Lamp in entryway</DESCRIPTION>
</MODULE>
<MODULE>
<ADDRESS><HOUSE>B</HOUSE><UNIT>10</UNIT></ADDRESS>
<TYPE>LAMP</TYPE>
<DESCRIPTION>Light outside front
door</DESCRIPTION>
</MODULE>
<MODULE>
<ADDRESS><HOUSE>B</HOUSE><UNIT>11</UNIT></ADDRESS>
```

```
<TYPE>LAMP</TYPE>
<DESCRIPTION>Lamp in livingroom</DESCRIPTION>
</MODULE>
<STATE>
<NAME>AFTWORK</NAME><DESCRIPTION>Come home to a
friendly house.</DESCRIPTION>
<COMPONENT>
<DESCRIPTION>Turn the radio on</DESCRIPTION>
<ADDRESS><HOUSE>B</HOUSE><UNIT>2</UNIT></ADDRESS>
<POSITION>ON</POSITION>
</COMPONENT>
<COMPONENT>
<DESCRIPTION>Turn on the living room
light</DESCRIPTION>
<ADDRESS><HOUSE>B</HOUSE><UNIT>11</UNIT></ADDRESS>
<POSITION>ON</POSITION>
</COMPONENT>
</STATE>
<STATE>
<NAME>AFTDINNER</NAME><DESCRIPTION>turn on front
light, dim lights</DESCRIPTION>
<COMPONENT>
<DESCRIPTION>Turn on porch, front
lights</DESCRIPTION>
<ADDRESS><HOUSE>B</HOUSE><UNIT>10</UNIT></ADDRESS>
<POSITION>ON</POSITION>
</COMPONENT>
<COMPONENT>
<DESCRIPTION>Dim livingroom</DESCRIPTION>
<ADDRESS><HOUSE>B</HOUSE><UNIT>10</UNIT></ADDRESS>
<POSITION>80%</POSITION>
```

```
</COMPONENT>
</STATE>
<STATE>
<NAME>POWERSAVE</NAME><DESCRIPTION>Dim front
lights</DESCRIPTION>
<ADDRESS><HOUSE>B</HOUSE><UNIT>10</UNIT></ADDRESS>
<POSITION>40%</POSITION>
</STATE>
<STATE>
<NAME>MORNING</NAME><DESCRIPTION>Turn off front
lights</DESCRIPTION>
<ADDRESS><HOUSE>B</HOUSE><UNIT>10</UNIT></ADDRESS>
<POSITION>OFF</POSITION>
</STATE>
<TRIGGER>
<STATENAME>AFTWORK</STATENAME>
<TIMED>
<WEEKLY><WEEKDAY>MON</WEEKDAY><WEEKDAY>TUES</WEEKD
AY><WEEKDAY>WED</WEEKDAY><WEEKDAY>THURS</WEEKDAY><
WEEKDAY>FRI</WEEKDAY></WEEKLY>
<TIME><HOUR>17</HOUR><MINUTE>00</MINUTE></TIME>
</TIMED>
</TRIGGER>
<TRIGGER>
<STATENAME>AFTDINNER</STATENAME>
<TIMED>
<DAILY/><TIME><HOUR>20</HOUR><MINUTE>00</MINUTE></
TIME>
</TIMED>
</TRIGGER>
<TRIGGER>
```

```
<STATENAME POWERSAVE</STATENAME>
<TIMED>
<DAILY/><TIME><HOUR>23</HOUR><MINUTE>00</MINUTE></
TIME>
</TIMED>
</TRIGGER>
<TRIGGER>
<STATENAME>MORNING</STATENAME>
<TIMED>
<DAILY/><TIME><HOUR>7</HOUR><MINUTE>00</MINUTE></T
IME>
</TIMED>
</TRIGGER>
<TRIGGER>
<STATENAME>AFTWORK</STATENAME>
<SWITCH>RMT01 - ON</SWITCH><!--Remote Control in
case we get home early -->
</TRIGGER>
<TRIGGER>
<STATENAME>MORNING</STATENAME>
<SWITCH>LT01 - OFF</SWITCH><!--If you don't want
to leave lights on all night -->
</TRIGGER>
</CONTROLSCHEDULE>
```

This document would tell the controller of the existence of several modules controlling some lights and a radio. At 5 P.M., or when someone pushed a remote control button, the living room would light up, and the radio would turn on. At 8 P.M., the living room lights would dim a bit (for better television viewing, perhaps) and the front porch light would turn on to welcome visitors or frighten away thieves. At 11 P.M., the front lights would dim to save a few dollars on power. In the morning (or when someone flips a switch off), the porch lights would go off.

This is a fairly elaborate exercise for rather small results. The real power of this example, however, comes in situations where automation is more widespread. Although writing XML directly like this is tedious and error-prone, it could serve well as a file format for control data produced by a friendlier GUI application. File formats like this make it easier to exchange data written for a particular control program to a different program, without losing all the logic. Because the information is presented as a series of states rather than direct commands, it doesn't matter what mechanism underlies those states. These files could work with an X-10 system, a different system that uses radio frequencies, a manual system that printed out instruction cards for lamplighters, or a much larger system controlling hundreds or thousands of lights. XML's easy-to-parse structure makes it a reliable tool for exchanging information between systems of every size.

DTDs like this one are appropriate for simple control situations where the expected results are easily defined, and it doesn't matter very much if something fails. XML is obviously not a programming language; it is really just a delivery vehicle for data. Situations where the flow of data is essentially one-way are ideal for this application of XML, but more complex situations that produce exceptions or errors demand a much richer set of commands delivered in a more interactive fashion. XML could be used to transmit data between processing applications on different nodes on a network, where all nodes can send and receive XML responses, but the core logic must remain in the processing application. XML just provides a structured way of storing and communicating data.

Object Documents

XML's nested structure bears a strong resemblance to the hierarchies of data that appear in object-oriented programming's data structures. XML and object-oriented programming are a good fit, because both systems can store datasets within datasets within datasets. Storing the information contained in object structures has often been difficult, because the linear and tabular file types most commonly used for documents are a poor fit for this kind of hierarchical structure. This section of the chapter won't produce any specific DTDs, because they will vary radically from chapter to chapter. Instead, we'll examine general principles and a simple example that may help developers plan XML file types that mirror data structures.

Our example is an object that contains several subobjects—the Appearance object of a very simple program. This object and its properties are loaded when the program starts and saved when the program finishes, more or less like a preferences file. It keeps track of settings for menus, toolbars, and the main window's height and width. Users who leave the program can reasonably come back to find things looking much as they did when they left. As Figure 9.1 shows, the appearance object is really a container for other objects, which themselves contain additional objects and properties.

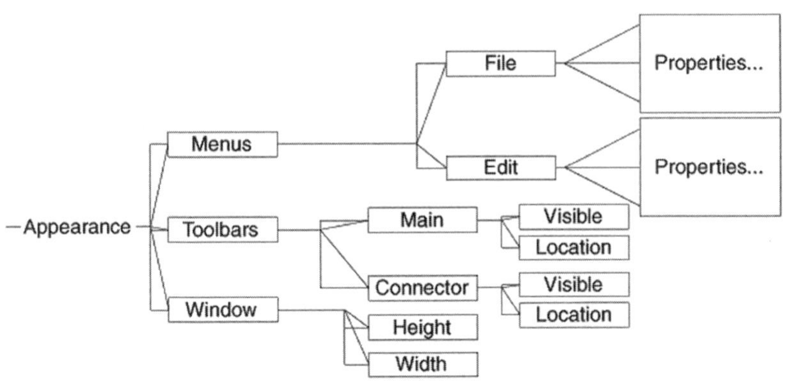

Figure 9.1 The Appearance object and its components.

The code for these objects is written into the main program, and our XML need not concern itself with any of the methods. XML can, however, provide a means for storing the property information that reflects the hierarchical structure of the objects. Implementing this structure will require adding some methods to each of the objects that can connect to a parser to read in their properties when the program starts and write out their properties as XML when the program ends.

There are several ways to structure the XML. All objects could be represented by elements, their immediate properties could be stored as attributes, and the objects they contained stored as subelements. This would produce XML that looks like

```
<APPEARANCE>
<!--Other elements -->
<TOOLBARS>
<TOOLBAR NAME="MAIN" VISIBLE="Yes" LOCATION="1"/>
<TOOLBAR NAME="CONNECTOR" VISIBLE="No"
LOCATION="2"/>
</TOOLBARS>
<WINDOW HEIGHT=450 WIDTH=400/>
</APPEARANCE>
```

Alternatively, we could give each attribute its own element. In this way, all properties would be treated the same way, regardless of whether the contents of those properties are values or other objects. The preceding code would now look like

```
<APPEARANCE>
<!--Other elements -->
<TOOLBARS>
<TOOLBAR><NAME>MAIN</NAME><VISIBLE>Yes</VISIBLE><L
OCATION>1</LOCATION>
<TOOLBAR><NAME>CONNECTOR</NAME><VISIBLE>No</VISIBL
E><LOCATION>2</LOCATION>
```

```
</TOOLBARS>
<WINDOW> <HEIGHT>450</HEIGHT>
<WIDTH>400</WIDTH></WINDOW>
</APPEARANCE>
```

Programmer's preferences will probably rule in these situation, at least until standard libraries arise to handle this coding. Both approaches will find their defenders. (I lean toward avoiding attributes because they tend to generate more verbose markup. They are more readable, but less efficient.)

Most programmers probably will not go to the trouble of validating these files. Even though a DTD might be useful for documenting the structures used by this code, and perhaps useful for debugging, a well-written parser/output program should be able to create well-formed code by itself. Another significant issue that gets in the way of creating a DTD for these files is that the sequence in which the objects write out their properties may vary from time to time, producing documents that are perfectly acceptable to the program using them but unacceptable to a strictly written DTD.

Metastructures—Emerging Standards Using XML

Even before XML has been finalized, a number of proposed standards that would use it have appeared. Microsoft's Channel Definition Format (CDF), Netscape's Meta Content Framework (MCF), Marimba and Microsoft's Open Software Description Format (OSD), and webMethods' Web Interface Definition Language (WIDL) are among the earliest proposals. The W3C is also developing a standard framework that can include many of these systems—the Resource Definition Format (RDF). Apart from a love of acronyms, these proposals share an interest in making the Web a more automated place.

Channel Definition Format

CDF is the first XML-based standard to receive anything resembling widespread use. Microsoft submitted the proposal to the W3C in March, but it looks like CDF will probably remain a Microsoft-only standard. CDF provides a standard set of tags for defining push content channels. *Channels* automate the flow of data from Web server to Web browser, providing the browser with a schedule for downloading new content from the channel's server and labeling that content with a button and some brief descriptions. CDF is based on a DTD that contains information pointing the browser to the source of the information, descriptive information (e.g., author, logo, abstract, and copyright), and a schedule for regular downloads. When the user wants to visit the channel (using the button bar shown in Figure 9.2), the information is already loaded for them—avoiding waiting for downloads and making it easy for users to reference Web information offline.

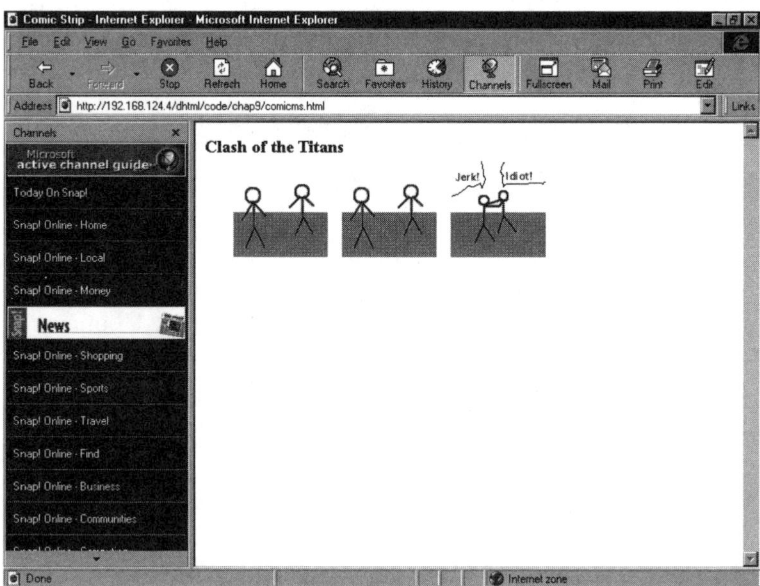

Figure 9.2 The channel bar in action in Internet Explorer 4.0.

Channel content is still (as of Internet Explorer 4.0) in HTML, not XML. XML just provides a framework that allows the browser to find and describe the content. The schedule can have odd effects on computers that use dial-up connections; since most schedules are designed to download data at off-peak times (midnight to 4 A.M.), Internet Explorer 4.0 users may wake up in the middle of the night to the cheerful sound of their modem dialing out to their Internet Service Provider.

CDF information is available from several sources. The submission to the W3C, which includes a full description of the DTD, is at http://www.w3.org/TR/NOTE-CDFsubmit.html. Microsoft has white papers and other information available through its Site Builder (http://www.microsoft.com/sitebuilder/) and Internet Explorer (http://www.microsoft.com/ie) Web sites.

Meta Content Framework

Like CDF, MCF uses XML to provide information about HTML documents. The Meta Content Framework began as Project X at Apple's Advanced Technology Group and is now under development at Netscape. Project X provided a three-dimensional interface to the Web that allowed users to navigate through a site without having to stop at every page. By presenting the layers of links in a projection that users could move around in, Project X created a new way for users to navigate indices and other sets of links. A sample image from Apple's Web site is shown in Figure 9.3; at one point the entire content of Yahoo was available in MCF.

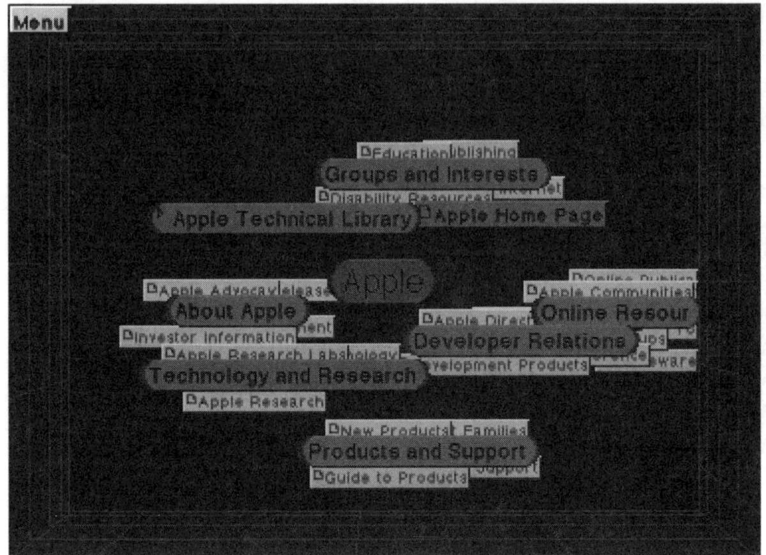

Figure 9.3 An image from Project X, created using MCF information.

Netscape took Apple's initial MCF development and moved it from its original file formats to XML. The current MCF model uses XML to create nodes of information describing pages and sites, which may include more nodes. These nodes can link across multiple files, creating a web of metadata that reflects the web of HTML underneath.

The Netscape MCF submission to the W3C is available at http://www.w3.org/TR/NOTE-MCF-XML.html. The original Apple Project X information, programs, and plug-in are available at http://www.atg.apple.com/technology/tech/projectx/.

Open Software Description Format

OSD has a more ambitious project: delivering software and software updates over the Internet, not just Web pages. Millions of programs have already been downloaded and installed via the Web, but OSD promises a much more complete solution. OSD can automatically download and install programs and packages in Java (the reasons behind Marimba's involvement) and platform-specific code (driving Microsoft's interest in the project.) OSD provides a set of information that can be used to install the same software on multiple platforms (and versions of those platforms), even when the code to be downloaded will change depending on the platform. OSD files can specify program dependencies, allowing Java programs to download their packages and Windows programs to download necessary DLLs and other files, for example. OSD significantly expands upon the current abilities of the OBJECT and APPLET tags, allowing Web documents to refer to much more complex program structures. OSD is designed to fit with CDF as well—channels that refer to OSD files can be used to update software automatically and regularly. (The security problems this project opens up, especially for platform-specific code, are obviously mammoth.)

The Open Software Description Format submission, including a complete DTD, is available at http://www.w3.org/TR/NOTE-OSD.html.

Web Interface Definition Language

WIDL provides a "service-based architecture over the document-based resources of the World Wide Web." It provides key information about available Web services to client machines, allowing them to automate many Web-based processes. Programs that use WIDL can take advantage of Web services without running a browser. A shipping clerk who needs to track thousands of FedEx, UPS, and DHL packages can use WIDL to connect their list of tracking numbers to the tracking area of the FedEx Web site, for example. WIDL may not always provide the most efficient interface to services (e.g., FedEx offers other products that can track large numbers of packages without using their Web site), but WIDL makes it easy to connect clients to back-end systems through the Web interfaces that have spread rapidly over the last few years.

WIDL addresses one of the major deficiencies of our light switch DTD; it provides return values that indicate successful completion or provide error messages. These messages can be used to retry services when necessary or give up trying after a number of failures. (The messages need to be generated by a processing application, but WIDL provides a standard way of specifying how the application should deal with them.) Web services are notorious for working the second or third time rather than the first, which may be acceptable to a human user but could break an automated process trying to interpret bad data. It also provides a framework for "reading" HTML pages using their textual information, although the WIDL documents themselves will need to be repaired any time labels on the page are changed.

WIDL offers client-server developers a new tool for connecting and automating their systems, converting light-duty Web applications into more sophisticated interfaces for accessing data. To be effective, WIDL will need considerable API and tool development, which webMethods has promised for C, C++, Java, and Visual Basic. Even though some parts of WIDL may be made obsolete if XML comes into more general use (making it easier for programs to parse Web data without the use of a separate interface), WIDL promises easy access to HTML-based documents in a much shorter timeframe.

Futures

The W3C is actively working on the RDF, a model for metadata applications that could potentially support all the preceding XML applications, except perhaps for WIDL. RDF is an effort to move the W3C ahead of the curve on XML applications and build standards that interoperate more easily. For more information, visit http://www.w3.org/Metadata/RDF/.

XML's popularity for data applications will depend heavily on how much use developers find for its combination of structure, flexibility, machine-readability, and human-readability. Unlike most documents in the previous chapters, these applications aren't intended for direct consumption by human users. Readability is maintained to make documents easier to examine and debug, but few of the documents will ever see a style sheet or be presented directly to human readers. Even though XML does incur more overhead than traditional binary files, its verbosity and its emphasis on nested structures give programmers new tools for communications between computers and applications. As XML spreads, we may see more programs based on shared parser architectures, all using a common set of file formats for wildly different projects.

CHAPTER 10

The XML Linking Specification

HTML's explosive growth probably had more to do with its linking than with any other single factor. Hundreds of people and organizations were working at the same time on hypertext systems, some even using SGML, but none of them had the simplicity of HTML's convenient linking system. <A HREF="*url*"> has strung millions of pages together and built the World Wide Web. Still, there's definitely room for improvement. Hypertext specialists and other developers complained of the limited abilities of these basic links, and at least some HTML developers looked at SGML's more complete HyTime specification and wished for some of its power. XML is a chance to do things better, and the XML working group has focused on linking early. XML linking builds on HTML's success and provides more powerful, yet more complex tools.

Simple Links

After six years of extensive use, HTML's linking systems are under mounting criticism for providing only the most basic of links. Many developers are perfectly content with the current linking syntax, and a small army of development tools and Web-mapping tools have grown up around this key standard. HTML's HREF attribute has done well enough for most developers. Why break it? XML doesn't break the previous standard, it just adds to it. It adds a lot in fact, but the basic HTML link structure is still preserved, and certain aspects of it are even grandfathered into the XML standard to make it easier for XML documents to link to HTML. We'll start by examining the kinds of links available to HTML documents, and then we'll look at how we can implement them in XML.

Links in HTML

The A element is the key to nearly all HTML linking, although the LINK element plays a limited role. A simple HTML link created with an A element is shown in Figure 10.1.

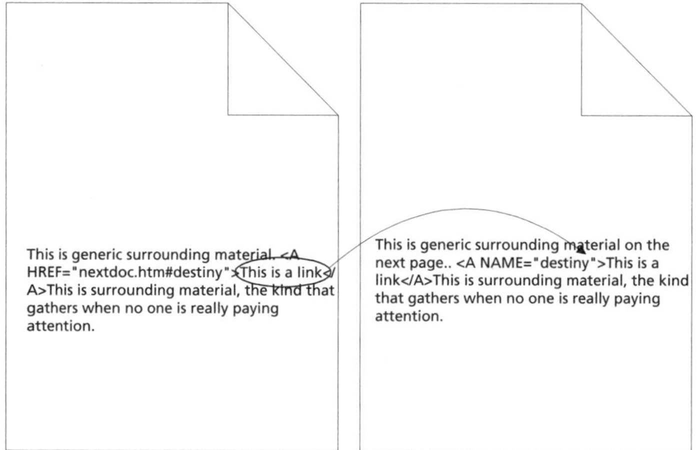

This is generic surrounding material. <A HREF="nextdoc.htm#destiny">This is a link</A>This is surrounding material, the kind that gathers when no one is really paying attention.
This is generic surrounding material on the next page.. <A NAME="destiny">This is a link</A>This is surrounding material, the kind that gathers when no one is really paying attention.

Figure 10.1 Simple unidirectional in-line link, HTML.

The A element has several attributes, only one of which gets constant use from HTML developers: the all-powerful HREF. HREF always takes a URL for its value, which represents the target of the link. URLs may be absolute or relative. Absolute URLs begin with a scheme, which describes the protocol that should be used to interpret the URL. Commonly used schemes include http:, ftp:, gopher:, mailto:, nntp:, file:, and javascript:. The information applicable to the scheme follows the scheme. In most cases, this will be a reference to a server or a file on a server, prefixed with two slashes. For example, an absolute URL using the HTTP protocol uses the following syntax:

```
http://hostcomputer:port/path?query
```

The *port* and *query* are optional. The *hostcomputer* must be a valid DNS name or IP address, and the *port* optionally specifies a port on the hostcomputer (80 is the default for http). *Path* specifies a path to a particular file on the host computer; only numbers, letters, and $, -, _, +, !, *, ‘, (,), and the period and comma are allowed in the path. Other characters may be escaped by the % sign, followed by their hexadecimal value. The optional query provides additional information to the server, allowing it to respond appropriately to form or other information. The content of query is limited to the same characters as path.

For the javascript: scheme, the value after the colon can be any valid javascript code. The javascript: scheme is on the way out—HTML 4.0 provides the onclick attribute to allow elements to activate scripts without placing javascript in the HREF attribute.

Relative URLs use the URL of the current page (or, if it exists, the URL set by the BASE element in the HEAD element of the page) as a prefix to their information. Relative URLs do not include a scheme.

The complete official syntax for URLs is defined in RFC 1738 (http://www.w3.org/Addressing/rfc1738.txt) and RFC 1808 (http://www.w3.org/Addressing/rfc1808.txt).

Both absolute and relative URLs may include a fragment identifier at the end in place of the query. Fragment identifiers in HTML include a pound sign (#) and a value that should connect to the

NAME attribute of an A element in the target document. For example, in

```
<A HREF="#laterlink">Skipping around is fun!</A>
...
...
<A NAME="laterlink">Aren't you glad you skipped
ahead?
```

clicking on "Skipping around is fun!" would scroll the document to the location of the A element with the NAME attribute "laterlink". Of course, fragment identifiers can also be used in combination with URLs.

```
<A HREF="zip.html#nothingness">
```

would take a user who clicked on it to the line in the zip.html file that contained

```
<A NAME="nothingness">
```

The A element also allows for REV and REL tags, which are intended to show the relationship between the anchor and the target URL. REL indicates the relationship of the URL to the anchor (moving forward along the link), whereas REV indicates the relationship of the anchor to the URL (moving backward along the link). Neither of these is widely used in anchor tags. The LINK element, which appears in the HEAD element of HTML documents, also supports the HREF, REL, and REV attributes. In the case of LINK (as we saw in Chapter 2), REL does get used to indicate that the target URL is a style sheet. LINK also provides a TYPE attribute to indicate the MIME type of the target URL. Unlike an A element, the LINK element doesn't take the user anywhere—it just connects outside files to the document, in much the same way that an SRC attribute does for an IMG, APPLET, SCRIPT, or OBJECT.

Simple Links in XML

In XML, all these links are called simple in-line links. Links connect resources—"anything which happens to be reachable by the use of a locator in some linking element." (Resources include documents, but they also include graphics and other files.) The locator is a URL, defined the same way as URLs for HTML, and equally capable of using fragment identifiers. For in-line links, the element defining the link counts as one of those resources, and the target is the other. The classic HTML HREF link is an in-line link because it points only one direction: from the element that provides the link to the target location. (The "Back" button doesn't count, in this example, as providing two-way linking.) The action taken when a link is actuated is called traversing, even if the link doesn't "take" the actuator (which may be a user or a program) any place new.

A simple link in XML carries all its linking information in the linking element. There is no need in a simple link for the application to search out other elements carrying information about the locators—all the locator information is provided in the HREF attribute.

Building a true XML link isn't exactly simple, however; it takes more than an HREF attribute for an element to be a link. A sample declaration for an element using simple links (taken from the 7/31/97 XML-Link Working Draft) follows:

```
<!ELEMENT SIMPLE ANY>
 <!ATTLIST SIMPLE
    XML-LINK      CDATA               #FIXED "SIMPLE"
    ROLE          CDATA               #IMPLIED
    HREF          CDATA               #REQUIRED
    TITLE         CDATA               #IMPLIED
    INLINE        (TRUE|FALSE)        "TRUE"
    CONTENT-ROLE  CDATA               #IMPLIED
```

```
    CONTENT-TITLE CDATA                    #IMPLIED
    SHOW          (EMBED|REPLACE|NEW) "REPLACE"
    ACTUATE       (AUTO|USER)              "USER"
    BEHAVIOR      CDATA                    #IMPLIED
>
```

Link elements don't have to be called SIMPLE—any element can be a link element. The SIMPLE element declaration is used, both here and in the Working Draft, only for illustration. In fact, any element can be a link—there is no need to create separate elements like the HTML A that exist solely to implement simple links.

The familiar HREF attribute is still there and works the same way as it did in HTML, although, as we'll see later, it too has been extended. The rest of the attributes are new. The first link, XML-LINK, announces to the processing application that this element is in fact a linking element and that it is a simple link. The XML-LINK attribute is required for all links; defining it with a fixed value in the DTD is usually a better solution than spelling out this attribute in every single instance of the element.

Avoid the temptation to create documents and DTDs that use an HREF attribute without declaring XML-LINK. Even though they might work in HTML browsers, XML-LINK compliant processing applications will ignore the HREF attribute if the XML-LINK attribute is missing.

The ROLE attribute is optional (as are all the attributes marked #IMPLIED or provided with a default value here), allowing the link to specify the "meaning" of the link to the application processing the link. The ROLE attribute is intended for use only by machine processors—information meant for humans to read should be kept in the TITLE attribute. The HREF attribute provides the link with a locator, a URL as already described. The TITLE attribute, also optional, includes information that could, for example, pop up as the user rolls the mouse over a link much as the ALT tags for clickable images appear during rollovers in the latest versions of the Netscape and Microsoft browsers.

The TITLE attribute in XML has nothing to do with the TITLE element in HTML; it's just an unfortunate overlap in name.

The INLINE attribute, when set to "TRUE" declares that links built on this element are in-line links. In a simple link, INLINE should be made "TRUE" by default. The Working Draft states that simple links are "usually in-line and always one-directional," but it's difficult to think of scenarios where a simple out-of-line link could be useful. Simple links will point forward to another single locator, without the use of the more complex tools needed for multidirectional or out-of-line links. Even though simple links could conceivably point to other links, XML (as we'll see later) has better mechanisms for achieving that result.

The next two attributes presented here, CONTENT-ROLE and CONTENT-TITLE, perform similar functions to ROLE and TITLE; however, they describe the content to which the locator points rather than the link. While ROLE and TITLE describe the link element as a resource, CONTENT-ROLE and CONTENT-TITLE describe the target resource.

The SHOW attribute is one of XML's greatest improvements on HTML linking. The SHOW attribute accepts EMBED, REPLACE, and NEW as values. REPLACE is the standard practice in HTML: links replace the current resource in the processing application (the browser window, for instance) with the target resource. NEW provides similar functionality to that available through HTML's TARGET attribute: the ability to open the target resource in a new context. Within a browser, that new context would probably be a new window; within a processing application, that new context could be an additional process operating in parallel. EMBED adds an entirely new dimension. When the link is traversed, the resource designated by the HREF attribute should be embedded in the body of the originating resource. In other words, it should be embedded in the element acting as the link. EMBED allows XML developers to create links that act more as if they have SRC attributes than HREF attributes. In fact, XML documents that need to use SRC attributes should probably use EMBED in combination with the automatic traversal made possible by the ACTUATE attribute.

The ACTUATE attribute accepts the values AUTO and USER. USER requires an external action (e.g., a user clicking) before the link is traversed. The user, again, may be a human viewing the document or another processing application exploring or otherwise using it. AUTO requires that the link be traversed by the processing application as soon as the resource is encountered. When combined with the SHOW attribute's EMBED value, AUTO acts like a client-side include, requiring the processing application to seek out the resource and include it in the linking element. Processing applications will need to be versatile to support this because the content of those resources is bound to be varied.

The last attribute presented, BEHAVIOR, is another place for developers to place information directing programs how to traverse this link. Unlike ROLE and CONTENT-ROLE, it isn't linked to a particular side of the connection and may be used to describe the link as a unit.

The kind of link created by the SIMPLE element is shown in Figure 10.2.

Now that we've described all these attributes, we'll create a SIMPLE element using the preceding declaration element, which uses these attributes and describes what the parts might do.

```
<SIMPLE ROLE="testlink"
HREF="http://www.webtype.com/zero/zero.html"
TITLE="link to zero" CONTENT-ROLE="emptiness"
CONTENT-TITLE="nothing at all" SHOW="REPLACE"
ACTUATE="USER" BEHAVIOR="here|zero"/>
```

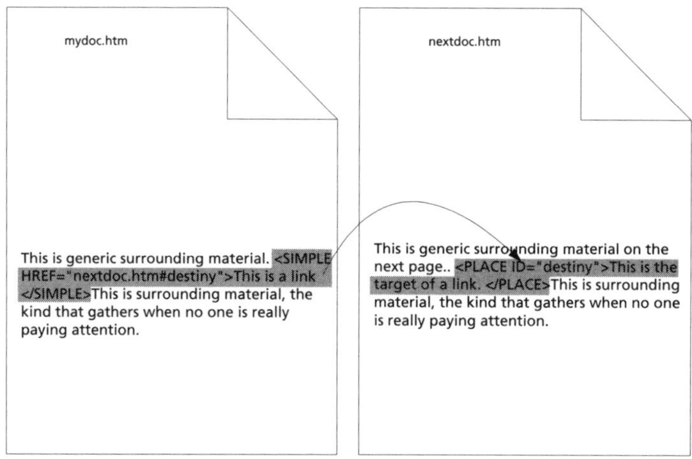
mydoc.htm
This is generic surrounding material. <SIMPLE HREF="nextdoc.htm#destiny">This is a link </SIMPLE>This is surrounding material, the kind that gathers when no one is really paying attention.
nextdoc.htm
This is generic surrounding material on the next page.. <PLACE ID="destiny">This is the target of a link. </PLACE>This is surrounding material, the kind that gathers when no one is really paying attention.

Figure 10.2 Simple in-line link, XML.

The HREF attribute identifies the targeted resource. The ROLE attribute provides our processing application with information about our SIMPLE element's position in this link—that it is a "testlink". CONTENT-ROLE provides that same processing application with information about the target resource, in this case that it is "emptiness". The BEHAVIOR attribute describes the link as a whole—a connection between this element ("here") and the target ("zero"). TITLE describes the link element as a "link to zero", whereas the CONTENT-TITLE provides users with a target description of "nothing at all".

Because the ACTUATE attribute is set to "USER", the processing application will do nothing to the link until it is directed to act on it. When the link is traversed, the target document will replace the linking resource (technically the element, but quite likely the entire document) because the SHOW attribute is set to "REPLACE".

Reconstructing HTML with XML

Now that we've gone through the entire gamut of simple link possibilities, it's time to reconstruct the A element in XML. We'll begin with a simple version and add features so that it becomes clear how XML differs from HTML. Our first version of the A element declares a minimum set of attributes:

```
<!ELEMENT A ANY>
<!ATTLIST A
      XML-LINK      CDATA      #FIXED "SIMPLE"
      HREF          CDATA      #REQUIRED
      TITLE         CDATA      #IMPLIED
      INLINE        (TRUE|FALSE)        "TRUE"
      SHOW          (EMBED|REPLACE|NEW)     "REPLACE"
      ACTUATE       (AUTO|USER)      "USER">
```

It isn't technically required to provide the options lists for the INLINE, SHOW, and ACTUATE attributes, but it is generally good practice and may save some processing application confusion down the line.

Our XML A element will now work like its predecessor in the form <A HREF="target.html"> or <A HREF="target.html" TITLE="My Link!">. The XML-LINK, INLINE, SHOW, and ACTUATE values already have default values specified and don't need to be declared explicitly. The A element is a classic example of a user-actuated, simple in-line link that by default replaces the content of the originating resource with the content of the target resource. So far, so good.

The REV and REL attributes have been replaced for the most part by ROLE and CONTENT-ROLE, respectively. Although we could plow ahead and just create REV and REL attributes for our A element (since they aren't used much anyway), it's probably a better idea to move them into XML compliance. XML provides a mechanism for remapping the XML-LINK attributes to other attribute names. This is more frequently used in situations where an element already has an attribute named ROLE or TITLE that has nothing to do with linking, but it is also useful for creating backward-compatible attributes. Using this remapping requires the addition of an XML-ATTRIBUTES attribute. The value of this attribute is a list of attribute names in pairs. The first member of a pair must be the standard name of an XML-LINK attribute; the second member is the name of the attribute to which it will be mapped. In our case, this means that the following attribute listing will need to be added to our attribute declaration for the A element:

```
XML-ATTRIBUTES      CDATA #FIXED "ROLE REV CONTENT-
ROLE REL"
REV      CDATA      #IMPLIED
REL      CDATA      #IMPLIED
```

The XML-ATTRIBUTES declaration requires that the value of the REV attribute will be treated as the value of the usual XML ROLE attribute for linking, whereas the value of the CONTENT-ROLE attribute will be made equivalent to the value of the REL attribute.

When remapping attributes, never assign attributes names beginning with XML-. These are reserved for the future use of the XML standard. The examples in the standard use XL- as an alternative prefix.

The HTML version of the A element includes one feature that cannot be carried over directly into XML. The TARGET attribute is not available, even though giving SHOW a value of “NEW” might produce similar results. In combination with the SHOW attribute, the TARGET attribute could be mapped to the BEHAVIOR attribute, but the success of that tactic will depend completely on the ability of the processing application to interpret the

BEHAVIOR. Web browsers will probably be able to cope with this problem, but XML parsers may not.

The last attribute of the HTML A element that needs to be addressed in XML is the NAME attribute, which is used to create fragment identifiers in HTML. XML-LINK takes a somewhat different approach to creating fragment identifiers, although it isn't that hard to create an A element that looks like HTML but behaves like XML. For now, you can create a NAME attribute for your A element of type ID.

```
NAME            ID      #IMPLIED
```

The XML development community frowns on calling ID-type attributes anything but ID. In the long term, you'll want to rename your NAME attributes ID.

XML, confronted with a simple *#fragmentidentifier*, will check the list of ID values in a document. The ID values include all attributes defined as type ID, not just those named ID. (Always remember to declare the ID attribute as type ID; otherwise, XML will ignore it.) In this case, XML will be able to use the NAME attribute, since it is of type ID, as a fragment identifier. The result is HTML syntax that smoothly provides XML functionality. Our (mostly) complete A element now looks like the following:

```
<!ELEMENT A ANY>
<!ATTLIST A
     XML-LINK      CDATA      #FIXED "SIMPLE"
     XML-ATTRIBUTES      CDATA #FIXED
          "ROLE REV CONTENT-ROLE REL"
     HREF            CDATA      #REQUIRED
     TITLE        CDATA      #IMPLIED
```

```
INLINE      (TRUE|FALSE)      "TRUE"
SHOW      (EMBED|REPLACE|NEW)      "REPLACE"
ACTUATE      (AUTO|USER)      "USER"
REV      CDATA      #IMPLIED
REL      CDATA      #IMPLIED
NAME      ID      #IMPLIED
TARGET      CDATA      #IMPLIED>
```

Locators and Chunks

Even though XML can use the simple fragment identifier notation of HTML, it is capable of far more interesting things. Many of the tasks it is capable of performing are quite useful even in simple links, allowing authors and developers to treat elements, rather than documents, as the primary unit involved in linking. XML's locator syntax is considerably more robust than that of HTML, providing a number of tools that can address parts of documents by structure, ID, HTML anchor, or even text content.

HTML allowed fragment identifiers to follow a URL using the following syntax for the HREF attribute:

```
HREF="url#fragmentidentifier"
```

XML allows a similar syntax but uses its more developed XPointer in place of HTML's fragment identifier:

```
HREF="url#XPointer"
```

or

```
HREF="url|XPointer"
```

In the first case, using #, the location referenced by the URL is to be fetched as a whole document by the processor (replacing the current document, if the SHOW attribute is set to "REPLACE"), and then the location referenced by the XPointer is to be located by the client. In the second, using the | connector, according to the XML-LINK standard, "no intent is signaled as to what processing model is to be used to go about accessing the designated resource." This provides a means for the server to handle the XPointer processing, cutting down on the bandwidth needed for transmission because the server can return only as much of the document as is needed.

XPointers: An Introduction

The XPointer (an abbreviation for Extended Pointer) is derived from the TEI standards described above in Chapter 4. XPointers designate resources using location terms. An XPointer may contain either one or two locators; if it contains two, they are separated by two periods (..). If the XPointer contains two locators, the XPointer refers to all content between the start of the element identified by the first locator and the end of the element identified by the second locator. We'll build some locators first and then see how XPointers work.

Locators may contain absolute, relative, or string-matching location terms. String-matching terms are the most limited, but they provide a degree of precision the other terms can't match. Relative terms allow links to refer to document content by its position within the element tree of a document or even by its content. Absolute location terms identify elements using the more conventional ID and NAME addressing schemes, as well as some other basic locations.

The default absolute keyword, which will rarely if ever be used, is ROOT( ). This specifies the root element of the document, the outermost element of the document tree. ROOT( ) effectively refers to the entire content of the document. The HERE( ) keyword refers to the linking element itself and is frequently used to provide an absolute position for subsequent relative terms. This allows an XPointer to specify content "2 paragraphs below the link element," for example. The DITTO( ) keyword may be used only as the second term of a pair, and simply duplicates the terms of the first term.

The empty parentheses following the ROOT( ), HERE( ), and DITTO( ) keywords are required.

The next two keywords will produce somewhat more familiar results. The HTML(*namevalue*) keyword takes a value that matches an HTML A element's NAME attribute, providing exactly the same service for fragment identifiers as was available in HTML. This will mostly get used in XML documents that refer to HTML documents, of course, because XML documents should use the ID attribute instead. The ID(*name*) keyword provides similar but improved functionality. Every element in a document may have an ID value; this means that any element can be quickly referenced this way. In fact, the XML-Linking documents recommend the use of this mode. By default, as noted previously, all fragment identifiers that aren't otherwise marked are treated this way. The fragment identifier "*#fragmentidentifier*" will be treated as ID(*fragmentidentifier*) automatically.

This use of the ID value makes it very easy to subdivide a document into more manageable chunks with well-structured elements. It gives the EMBED value of the SHOW attribute considerably more power because it allows a link to refer to a section of a document rather than the entire thing. A long file containing many smaller chunks can now be displayed broken down into those chunks rather than as an enormous file. This makes it easy to excerpt other documents using links—a feature known in other systems, notably Ted Nelson's Xanadu, as transclusion. For more on transclusion and Xanadu, see the article entitled "Embedded Markup Considered Harmful," in the Winter 1997 issue of *World Wide Web Journal*, available from O'Reilly and Associates.

For this to work really well, file structures will need to change to avoid making the processing application load the entire document rather than just the desired chunk. The file system itself would have to be an XML processor (perhaps even an object database), storing XML documents as elements rather than as a single file that must be parsed sequentially.

Relative location terms are more complicated, although considerably more flexible. The keywords for relative location terms are tools for navigating the document tree, as shown in Table 10.1.

Table 10.1 Pointer Keywords

Keyword	**Effect**
CHILD	Selects child elements of the location source (must be elements nested directly under the source).
DESCENDANT	Selects elements appearing in the content of the location source (may be nested more than one level).
ANCESTOR	Selects elements in whose content the location source is found (parent elements).
PRECEDING	Selects elements that appear before the location source.
PSIBLING	Selects sibling elements which appear before the location source. (Sibling elements share the same parent element.)
FOLLOWING	Selects elements appearing after the location source.
FSIBLING	Selects sibling elements that appear after the location source. (Sibling elements share the same parent element.)

All the relative keywords use the same set of arguments, enclosed in parentheses:

```
(Instance, ElType, Attr, Value)
```

Instance (which is a numeric value, or 'ALL') and ElType (element type) must always be included; Attr (attribute) and Value are optional and used only when needed to identify an element by the value of one of its attributes. The Instance value allows developers to specify elements in positions relative to the location source. ElType defines the candidate type of the location term. The location source by default will be the root element of the document referred to by the URL, although this can be changed, as we'll see.

Using Instance and ElType allows developers to specify the *n*th appearance of a certain element in the structure described by the relative location keyword, making it easy to specify relative position using position in a document. For example, CHILD(3,QUOTE) would refer to the third appearance of the QUOTE element within the location source element. CHILD(5,EXPLANATION) would refer to the fifth appearance of the EXPLANATION element within the location source element. Using negative numbers for the instance value counts backward, CHILD(-1, PRICE) refers to the last PRICE element within the location source, whereas CHILD(-3,PRICE) refers to the third-last, and so on.

Developers may not always know, or need to know, the name of the element to which they should be pointing. To accommodate this, XML allows the ElType to take three values that aren't element names. The **.** (period) value allows the location term to accept all elements as candidates for a match. CHILD(2,.) refers to the second element within the location source element. The CDATA value tells the location term to accept pseudo-elements as candidates for a match. Pseudo-elements are composed of the character data that are combined with markup in a mixed declaration. For example, in

```
<CASE>Name:<NAME>Jim</NAME>
Fish bonker:<BONKER>01234</BONKER>
Crime:<CRIME>Fishing without mowing the lawn
first</CRIME>
Status:<STATUS>Dismissed</STATUS></CASE>
```

the first pseudo-element contains the text "Name:", the second contains a newline character (remember, XML preserves whitespace) and "Fish bonker:", and so on.

The last available value for ElType is *. This ElType allows both elements and pseudo -elements to count as candidates. If applied to the previous example, using the CASE element as the location source, CHILD(1,*) would refer to "Name:", whereas CHILD(2,*) would refer to the NAME element following it.

Attribute matching allows another level of precisely specifying locations. Both the attribute and value arguments are optional. If the attribute argument appears, the value argument must follow. CHILD(1,*,TARGET,ME) would refer to the first element within the locator source that had an attribute TARGET with the value ME. CHILD(2,QUOTE,SPEAKER,ROOSEVELT) refers to the second QUOTE element with a SPEAKER attribute set to ROOSEVELT.

Both arguments will accept the value * in place of a specific argument. If * is used for the attribute argument, any attribute whose value matches the value argument is a match. If * is used for the value argument, the attribute named by the attribute argument may have any value. CHILD(1,QUOTE,SPEAKER,*) refers to the first QUOTE element that has a SPEAKER attribute declared, no matter what the value. CHILD(3,QUOTE,*,ROOSEVELT) refers to the third QUOTE element that has any attribute with a value set to ROOSEVELT. The attribute could be named PRESIDENT, SPEAKER, or Q2FD—it doesn't matter.

String matching terms are the last set of available location terms. The STRING keyword is used with the following syntax:

```
STRING(Instance, String, Offset)
```

The Instance argument works the same way it did with the relative terms. The String argument is just the string to match. (In searching for a match, the processor is supposed to ignore all markup characters, so string values can cross element boundaries.) Offset provides the precise character position identifying the location returned, measured as characters from the first character of the found string. If Offset is 0, then the location will be the position of the first character of the string when found; if it is 2, it will be the third character from the start, and so on. In the code

```
<LINE>The worms crawl in and the worms crawl
out</LINE>
<LINE>The ones that crawl in are lean and
thin</LINE>
<LINE>The ones that crawl out are fat and
stout</LINE>
```

STRING(1,worms,4) will return the location of the letter *s* in "worms" in the first appearance of the word in the first line. STRING(2,worms,3) will return the location of the letter *m* in "worms" in the second appearance of the word. STRING(1,crawl,1), STRING(2,crawl,1), and STRING(3,crawl,1), and STRING(4,crawl,1) will return the location of the letter *c* in the first, second, third, and fourth appearance of the word "crawl," respectively.

Much of the power of location terms comes when they are used in combination. Absolute location terms make it easy to specify a new default locator element instead of the default ROOT( ). Relative location terms can be combined to allow you to specify the element directly above the fifth appearance of the FRAB element whose FLIPGELLY attribute is set to "postmaster". Combining terms is simple—just list them in sequence. Terms will be evaluated from left to right. For example, given the fragment:

```
<BOOKSHELF ID="history">
<BOOK><TITLE>The Shaping of America, Volume 2:
Continental America, 1800-
1867</TITLE><AUTHOR>Meinig</AUTHOR></BOOK>
<BOOK><TITLE>That Noble Dream: The Pursuit of
Objectivity in the American Historical
Profession</TITLE><AUTHOR>Novick</AUTHOR></BOOK>
<BOOK><TITLE>The Origins of the Korean War, Vol.
II</TITLE><AUTHOR>Cumings</AUTHOR></BOOK>
```

```
<BOOK><TITLE>Nature's Metropolis: Chicago and the
Great West</TITLE><AUTHOR>Cronon</AUTHOR></BOOK>
</BOOKSHELF>
```

The locator ID(history) would select the entire BOOKSHELF element. ID(history)CHILD(3,BOOK) would select our third BOOK element. The AUTHOR element, in this case "Cumings," is selected by ID(history)CHILD(3,BOOK)CHILD(1,AUTHOR).

ID(history)CHILD(3,BOOK)PSIBLING(1,BOOK) would select the second BOOK element. Finally, both the third and fourth book elements, and their content is selected by ID(history)CHILD(3,BOOK)..ID(history)CHILD(4,BOOK). The possibilities are nearly endless, giving developers all kinds of power for creating chunks, even when the chunks don't neatly match single elements.

XML allows a shorthand notation for multiple argument lists. (This is unusual in itself because XML allows very little abbreviation.) ID(history)CHILD(3,BOOK)(1,AUTHOR) is equivalent to ID(history)CHILD(3,BOOK)CHILD(1,AUTHOR); XML understands that the keyword is repeated between steps.

At this point, we can create some rather powerful links that already surpass the powers granted developers by the HTML A element. Our links can cruise through document structures to precisely locate their targets, and our links can even embed those targets within our XML file rather than forcing us to open an entirely new file. XML has expanded the toolbox considerably already, but extended and out-of-line links will bring linking to a whole new level.

More Complex Links

Extended links give the world of linking entirely new geometries, making possible new architectures and new interfaces. Even though the "I am here—click to go there" model of the HTML A element has done an excellent job getting the Web started, it's time to move on to "I am one part of a set—treat me as such and explore." Extended links, multidirectional links, and out-of-line links will let developers build more intricate structures that make managing links easier in the long run.

Extended links allow developers to create groups of links, effectively providing the user (or a processing application) with a set of choices from a link rather than a single target. Even though the requirements for how an extended link must be treated by a processing application remain very loose in the working draft, the easiest way to picture an extended link is as set of choices that will appear on a pop-up menu (or other interface) to allow the user to select a direction. The classic application for this is a thesaurus. When the user clicks on a word, a set of synonyms will be listed on a pop-up menu. The user chooses from among the words and is taken to further information on the word chosen.

Implementing these links is a bit complex. As we did with simple links, we'll start with the DTD provided by the Working Draft:

```
<!ELEMENT EXTENDED ANY>
<!ATTLIST EXTENDED
  XML-LINK      CDATA                  #FIXED "EXTENDED"
  ROLE          CDATA                  #IMPLIED
  TITLE         CDATA                  #IMPLIED
  INLINE        (TRUE|FALSE)           "TRUE"
  CONTENT-ROLE  CDATA                  #IMPLIED
  CONTENT-TITLE CDATA                  #IMPLIED
  SHOW          (EMBED|REPLACE|NEW)    "REPLACE"
  ACTUATE       (AUTO|USER)            "USER"
  BEHAVIOR      CDATA                  #IMPLIED
  >
```

As was the case with the previous SIMPLE example, elements implementing extended links do not need to be named EXTENDED. All that is required is that the XML-LINK attribute be set to "EXTENDED".

Our EXTENDED element is very similar to the SIMPLE element, with two changes. First, the XML-LINK attribute is now "EXTENDED" instead of "SIMPLE". Second, the EXTENDED element has no HREF attribute. The EXTENDED element must rely on a set of subelements to contain its locators. The LOCATOR element described in the Working Draft DTD looks like:

```
<!ELEMENT LOCATOR  ANY>
  <!ATTLIST LOCATOR
     XML-LINK CDATA                    #FIXED "LOCATOR"
     ROLE     CDATA                    #IMPLIED
     HREF     CDATA                    #REQUIRED
     TITLE    CDATA                    #IMPLIED
     SHOW     (EMBED|REPLACE|NEW)  "REPLACE"
     ACTUATE  (AUTO|USER)              "USER"
     BEHAVIOR CDATA                    #IMPLIED
  >
```

The LOCATOR element (which, again, needn't be called LOCATOR) carries key linking information. The HREF carries the locator that will be used if the link is activated. The TITLE provides information that will be presented to human users, whereas ROLE carries information for the processing application. Every LOCATOR is allowed its own SHOW, ACTUATE, and BEHAVIOR as well. If the LOCATOR doesn't specify these attributes, it should use the attribute specified in the EXTENDED element by default. This makes creating groups of links that point to different locations but share the same behavior easier, while preserving the right of individual links to behave differently when needed.

Extended links are useful in a great number of situations and may be inline or out of line. An in-line extended link might use the DTDs presented previously and look something like this:

```
<EXTENDED>History Texts
<LOCATOR TITLE="African" HREF="african.xml"/>
<LOCATOR TITLE="Asian" HREF="asian.xml"/>
<LOCATOR TITLE="European" HREF="european.xml"/>
<LOCATOR TITLE="North American"
HREF="namerican.xml"/>
<LOCATOR TITLE="Pacific" HREF="pacific.xml"/>
<LOCATOR TITLE="South American"
HREF="samerican.xml"/>
</EXTENDED>
```

This link accomplishes several things. First, if a user encounters it in a document, this element is a live in-line link. Clicking on the words "History Texts" might bring up a menu that offered the titles of the choices listed in the LOCATOR elements. Choosing one of those titles would take the user to the referenced document. Second, because this is an extended link, it sets up links that can connect all these documents. The documents listed in the LOCATORs, if they have encountered this declaration at some point (we'll see how later), are all linked to each other at the document level. Right clicking in the margin of any of them, for example, could bring up a menu of the other documents to which the document clicked on is linked. We'll cover that again in a moment, when we reach the DOCUMENT value of the XML-LINK attribute.

Extended out-of-line links are very similar to the preceding links, except that the content of the extended link element is not itself a part of the link. Clicking on the content of an extended link element, if it has any, won't bring up a menu. Extended out-of-line links just set up the connections between other elements. For example:

```
<EXTENDED INLINE="FALSE">
<LOCATOR TITLE="Overview" HREF="#overview"/>
<LOCATOR TITLE="Architecture"
HREF="#architecture"/>
<LOCATOR TITLE="Detailed Design" HREF="#details"/>
<LOCATOR TITLE="Parts List" HREF="#parts"/>
</EXTENDED>
<SECTION ID="overview"><TITLE>Overview</TITLE>
...
</SECTION>
<SECTION
ID="architecture"><TITLE>Architecture</TITLE>
...
</SECTION>
<SECTION ID="details"><TITLE>Detailed
Design</TITLE>
...
</SECTION>
<SECTION ID="parts"><TITLE>Parts List</TITLE>
...
</SECTION>
```

The extended element in this case has no content apart from links. What it does is create links between the SECTION elements that follow. A reader who doesn't care about the Overview SECTION can click on it and get a menu of the more detailed descriptions available. Similarly, someone who stumbled into the parts list can use that same menu to return to the Overview or Architecture SECTION elements. These links are truly multidirectional because users can navigate between multiple locations without regard for moving forward or backward in the senses Web users have come to expect. These links can be traversed in either direction—clicking on the target document (or using its linking interface) will bring up a list of links that include the document from which the user came. This added flexibility will no doubt confuse many users who already get lost in the web of HTML links but gives power users a great new tool for navigation.

For comparison, an extended in-link link is shown in Figure 10.3, and its equivalent extended out-of-line link is shown in Figure 10.4. Note that all links may be traversed in either direction.

As exciting as these new tools are, they seem to make it even more difficult to manage links. It's difficult for an XML document to "know" of other documents with which it shares links, especially if those links are stored in content owned by other people. Managing the mazes of links created by the ability to include more than one location in a link is a logistical challenge that seems to call for centralization of linking information. Fortunately, XML-LINK provides some basic tools that address both of these issues. GROUP and DOCUMENT values for the XML-LINK attribute can create extended link groups—elements that help to manage links, telling documents to check each other for relevant links and allowing the creation of centralized link clearinghouses for sets of related data.

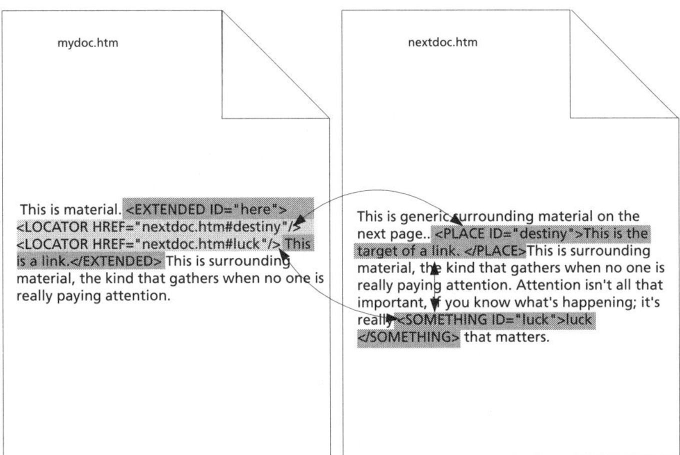

Figure 10.3 Extended in-line link, XML.

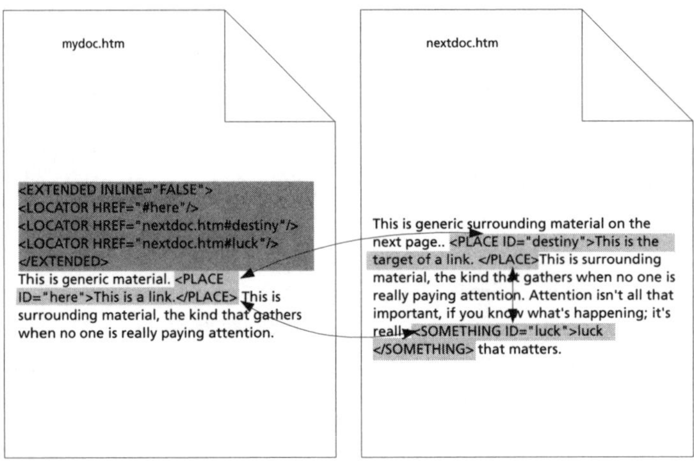

Figure 10.4 Extended out-of-line link, XML.

Using extended link grouping requires the creation of two elements—one to define a group and the other to identify the documents in the group. The declarations for those elements, as shown in the Working Draft, look like

```
<!ELEMENT GROUP (DOCUMENT*)>
  <!ATTLIST GROUP
          XML-LINK CDATA #FIXED "GROUP"
          STEPS    CDATA #IMPLIED
  >
  <!ELEMENT DOCUMENT EMPTY>
  <!ATTLIST DOCUMENT
          XML-LINK CDATA #FIXED "DOCUMENT"
          HREF     CDATA #REQUIRED
  >
```

These declarations are far simpler than their fellows. In the GROUP element, all that needs to be declared in element instances is the

STEP attribute, which tells the processing application how many layers of links it should follow before stopping its search for related links. (This keeps endlessly deep searches from tying up machines.) The DOCUMENT elements just contain HREFs that will take the processing application to the documents that need to be searched for links. When the processing application comes across one of these elements, it will load the documents specified by the HREF attributes of the DOCUMENT elements in the GROUP. It then checks those documents for links to the original document, building a table of links. The processing application will load all the documents and process the linking information in them—that counts as step 1. If the STEP attribute is greater than 1, the processing application will load documents to which the original document was linked by the first round of documents loaded. (STEP should generally be kept low to keep documents from loading in hundreds of other documents and chewing up bandwidth.)

The initial advantage of extended link groups is that they make it easy for a processing application to obtain reasonably complete information about the documents to which an initial document is linked, instead of "discovering" links only when the new documents are opened. Sets of documents can be arranged in groups, making it easy for related links to be discovered:

```
<GROUP STEPS=1>
<DOCUMENT HREF="cousin2.xml"/>
<DOCUMENT HREF="cousin3.xml"/>
<DOCUMENT HREF="cousin4.xml"/>
<DOCUMENT HREF="cousin5.xml"/>
</GROUP>
```

When the processing application reaches this group of elements in the file cousin1.xml, it will open the documents cousin2.xml, cousin3.xml, cousin4.xml, and cousin5.xml. After parsing them, it will determine whether they have any links to the cousin1.xml. If they do, it will add those links to the list of links for cousin1.xml and make them available to users. Without these declarations, a user of the cousin1.xml would have seen only those links that originated in the cousin1.xml file itself, which is probably a much more restricted set of links.

The implications of this change are profound. Extended link groups make it possible to centralize link information, replacing a maze of links (shown in Figure 10.5) with a centralized hub-and-spoke system (shown in Figure 10.6) that allows developers to examine and manage links without having to read endless documents. It also reduces the bandwidth overhead, allowing developers to require an XML document to download only one extra document (or perhaps a few) to create a complete list of links.

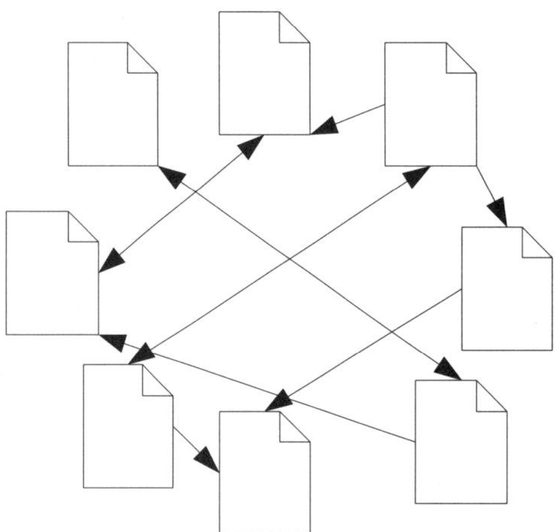

Figure 10.5 Old-style linking, connecting a set of documents through decentralized links.

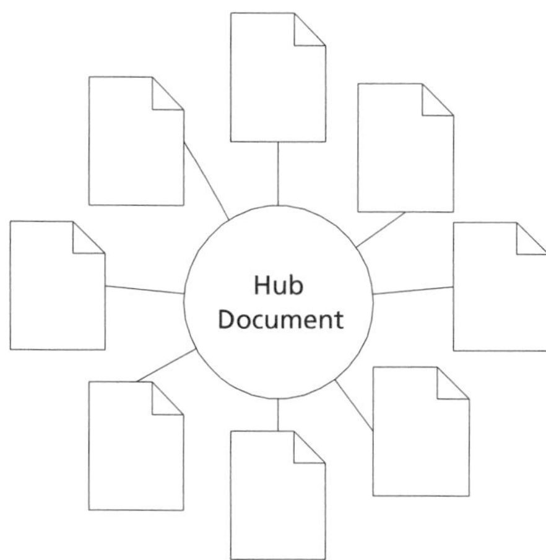

Figure 10.6 Centralized linking, providing a hub for easy management of links.

Extended link groups also make it possible to add links from other documents to your own effectively. As long as the other document is aware of your document (i.e., your document is either referenced from a DOCUMENT element or connected through a number of links no greater than the STEPS attribute will allow), links from your document to the target document will be recognized by the target document and may appear as outgoing links by it. Even if the target document isn't aware of your document, links from your document may still be "remembered" by the processing application when they are traversed, allowing documents to reference each other easily. If the processing application remembers the links from document to document, the target document will become linked to your document, although only within the context of the processing application. This makes annotating documents much simpler than it has been in the past.

XML links may seem complicated, but use will make them friendlier. As we'll see in the following chapters, the implications of these linking schemes are nearly as great as the implications of XML itself.

CHAPTER 11

Processing XML: Applications, Servers, Browsers

Even though most of this book covered how to write XML documents and create XML DTDs, creating documents and DTDs is only a part of what developers need to do to take full advantage of XML. All the examples so far have, to some extent, lamented the lack of processing applications. A full-scale treatment of parsing and processing applications would take another book (or, more likely, a set of books), but a basic understanding of how these applications will work is critical to creating usable XML. Many of the teams working on XML development will have separate groups building document types and creating processor applications because the two kinds of work demand different skillsets. Still, both groups need to share a common vocabulary. In this chapter, we'll examine the new vocabularies and architectures that XML is creating and some of the implications of XML for data processing.

Programming for XML

Although we've taken as much advantage as possible of XML's ability to keep documents human-readable, the real reasons that make XML exciting have to do with machine-readability. Markup is designed to be easy to program, using a nested structure that works well with both recursive functions and object-oriented programming. Although parsing valid XML documents is not a light task, neither does it present the enormous challenges faced by programs that must parse other formats.

The developers of the XML specification have made XML programming much easier by tightening the rules for XML document structure syntax, while at the same time loosening many of the constraints by adding the well-formedness option. XML's firm requirement that all elements have complete start- and end-tags, or indicate that they are empty by closing the tag with />, makes it far easier to write a parser. Both SGML and HTML allowed elements to skip the end tags, which required significant code effort to determine where exactly the end of an element was supposed to be. SGML also allowed abbreviated element names, adding an extra level of lookup to the parsing process. XML's basic structures, expressed in the criteria for well-formed documents, ensure that parsers can be reasonably simple programs that won't add incredible amounts of processing overhead to document processing.

Validating XML documents, as opposed to checking them for well-formedness, remains something of a challenge, thanks to parameter entities and the need to check element structures against the DTD. DTDs can be incredibly complex documents to interpret, especially DTDs that extend back through several files because of multiple parameter entities and DOCTYPE declarations. Applying large DTDs to small files can waste processor cycles while the parser interprets extra information it will never apply and adds overhead to every element lookup. Still, validating documents is a critical part of XML development. As we'll see later, validation may occur at several different points in the lifetime of a document, from its initial construction to its final presentation.

Many XML applications are probably going to end up using parts of XML, creating parsers that straddle the well-formed and the valid. Applications that can handle XML linking will probably need to do some validating, unless programmers want to present the attributes needed to create links in every single element instance.

Documents that use entities extensively might not need a DTD that defines their elements and attributes, but they do need a parser that can expand their entity references. How far practice will diverge from the twin standards of valid and well-formed remains to be seen, but more levels are likely to appear. Murmurings have appeared in XML-DEV, the XML development mailing list, of situations for which full DTDs may not be appropriate. Combining the extreme flexibility of well-formed documents with the more powerful tools available in valid documents will likely cause some problems.

The XML-DEV mailing list is a key forum for developers creating parsers and other XML applications. The archives for the list and information on joining are available at http://www.lists.ic.ac.uk/hypermail/xml-dev/. When communicating on this list, keep in mind that it is a mailing list aimed at high-level development, not XML tutorials.

Tools for Programming XML

At this point, the leading contender for XML development appears to be Java. Java has a significant advantage over other languages and development tools for a very simple reason: like XML, it was built for Unicode from the ground up. The requirement that parsers be able to handle the full 2-byte Unicode canonical encoding causes problems for C++ (although there are detours), Perl (where a key part of the language will need an upgrade), and all other development tools that expect characters to occupy a single byte. As a result, much of the work currently under way in XML development is being done in Java.

Java's structures are also a good match for XML, with hierarchies that are easily compatible with XML. Java also provides easy interfaces between classes and objects, making it very simple to add a generic parser to a data processing application. Even though Java's facilities for handling text are not the most advanced, they are more than a match for the level of processing required by XML parsing.

Java applets, as we'll see in the next chapter, also fit well with several of the Web-based possibilities for XML.

C++ is also a very viable environment for XML development. Like Java, its object structures can embrace nested element structures quite easily. Even though adding classes to a C++ project is somewhat more complex than it is with Java, there is no lack of powerful C++ tools. C++ is already in use for a wide variety of data processing projects, including markup processing, and libraries are available. Unfortunately, most of the C++ world still expects to see single-byte characters, making it fairly difficult to work with Unicode. Documents encoded in UTF-8 should work well with C++, and tools for C++ Unicode development are starting to appear.

Perl has been the text hacker's choice for years, helping developers blast through seemingly impossible barriers with a few lines of code. Perl's rich support for regular expressions has helped thousands of programmers create CGI scripts, writing HTML and interpreting the data sent back by forms. At the same time, Perl has helped developers implement changes across entire sites, addressing challenges like changing all the legal notices on a site overnight with elegance and ease. Perl use is hardly limited to HTML: SGML developers have used Perl to find problems in their documents and fix them as automatically as possible. Unfortunately, Perl has (at present) no support for Unicode. Although workarounds are possible, the regular expressions engine that drives much of Perl will need a thorough rebuilding before it will be capable of handling Unicode XML.

A Unicode module for Perl is available at http://www.perl.com/CPAN-local/modules/modules/by-module/Unicode/. It doesn't provide full Unicode support, but it may be a good place to start.

Also, even though Perl is an excellent choice for utility programs, Perl might not be the best choice for creating reusable validating parsers. It's certainly possible, and someone out there may be able to do it in ten lines of code; it just probably isn't the best solution for complex projects. For a good exploration of the issues surrounding Perl and XML, read Michael Leventhal's excellent article entitled "XML: Can the Desperate Perl Hacker Do It?" in *XML: Principles, Tools, and Techniques*, the Winter 1997 issue of the *World Wide Web Journal.* Similar problems haunt most of the popular UNIX scripting languages.

Does Unicode matter anyway? The answer is probably not yet. Unicode has been slow to take off because of limited application support. However, both XML and Java require support for processing Unicode characters (not necessarily displaying them, which is more a matter of the operating system and the available font sets) at their foundations. Unicode has begun picking up steam, however, with native support available in both Microsoft's Windows NT and Sun Solaris 2.6 operating systems. Java and XML are two key components for the future of document processing, so expect to see more action in the Unicode field.

Architecture for XML Processing Applications

Designing an XML application requires far more than coding a DTD, borrowing a generic parser, and writing some code that interprets documents. XML is one piece in a very complex environment that requires analysis of authoring, validation, storage, transmission, parsing, processing, and rendering. Not every application will involve all those parts, but most large applications will need to include all of them, as shown in Figure 11.1.

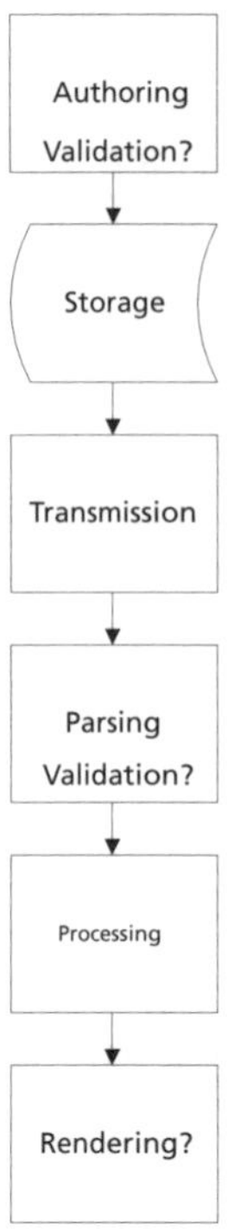

Figure 11.1 The life of an XML document.

Validation (or at least well-formedness checks) may take place at nearly any point in the process. Some developers may want to validate documents as they're being authored, others may wait until they've been stored, allowing bulk processing, and others may validate at the receiving processor. A few may even validate at all of these steps. Given the complications that linking can introduce, validating at more than one stage in the processing of an XML documents may be a good idea, or even a requirement in some cases.

Authoring tools are as much a part of efficient XML development as parsers. As we've already discussed in several previous examples, hand-coding XML is not fun for most people. Finding or building useful XML authoring tools is critical to the success of any project that involves more than a few die-hard coders. SGML and HTML tools are available, and XML tools are on the horizon. Even though word processors have demonstrated their flexibility as general-purpose creators of a wide variety of documents over the last few years, XML developers may want to consider turning against this general-purpose model and focus on creating applications that zero in on particular documents. A well-written DTD can provide the basis for an interview-driven application, which walks authors through the required elements and doesn't let them complete their documents until all required parts are present. Effectively, this kind of authoring tool performs validation even while the document is being written, ensuring that documents are complete.

Storage and transmission are two more fronts that XML may transform. XML can be stored easily as files, but its structure also lends itself to storage as elements or chunks. Storage facilities that break XML into components smaller than files can perform validation as the document enters and exits storage, providing another layer of security that documents are properly constructed and allowing users and programs to request smaller chunks of documents. As we'll see later, this may change the architecture of the familiar Web server.

Parsing, of course, is at the core of any XML application. In Figure 11.1, the parsing being performed is on the client side, interpreting the file and preparing it for processing. Parsing can in fact take place at any level of this structure, although client applications will probably continue to need text file parsers for a long time. (Files will probably remain a key unit of transmission for a number of years to come, even if improvements in standards reduce the size of those files.)

The processing application is the recipient of all this effort. We've explored several different operations that could be performed here. The processing application could just be passing information to a rendering engine, the last stage shown in Figure 11.1, which will present the information in some format (screen, paper, CD-ROM, etc.). The processing application could also be a search application used to retrieve document information for storage in a database, a statistical package converting document data into mathematical results, a data mining application searching for trends in stored documents, or even a document checker (which could check for spelling, style, or anything else a computer can interpret) that can examine documents, flag problems, and return them to the server for intervention. The processing application more or less generates the results of all this work, whereas the rendering engine does its best to present those results in an acceptable form.

Now that we've examined all these steps, we'll look more closely at the implications they hold for the two most ubiquitous Web tools—servers and browsers.

Extending the Server

Although Web servers have grown considerably more ornate since the Web first appeared, the basic concepts underlying Web page distribution remain quite simple. A Web server receives information over a network from a Web browser, interprets that information, and sends back a reply. In most cases, the browser is just requesting a particular file, which the server locates in its file structure and sends back to the browser with appropriate header information that informs the browser of what it's getting. Although servers have sprouted extensions that allow these files to be generated by database interfaces, parsed includes, scripts, and other processors, the venerable HyperText Transfer Protocol (HTTP) still carries a high proportion of traffic that is generated only by simple file requests. Other protocols, like those that allow Java applets to communicate with the server directly, are growing, but simple file requests remain a key part of the basic Web infrastructure.

XML threatens to break this fundamental file request structure by making much heavier demands for files in order to fulfill its validation and linking requirements. Although DTDs and style sheets may not hit the ceiling of the current capabilities of file-based Web servers (they can be easily cached and used for multiple documents in most cases), the new linking features may. The new EMBED functionality will encourage developers to create documents that include parts of other documents. XPointers make selecting chunks of documents easy. If all the XPointer processing takes place on the client, servers will spend considerable amounts of effort sending files to clients that can be used only in part. Documents that link to multiple documents this way could increase the load dramatically—especially if the processing applications are other programs voraciously seeking out key bits of information. While extended link groups may provide delightful functionality to the client by creating true multidirectional links, they promise an enormous traffic jam at the server, especially if developers keep their links distributed across multiple files rather than consolidating them in centralized link clearinghouse files.

The solution to all these problems is simple, even though it will take considerable work to implement: servers need to able to distribute chunks as well as files. XPointers provide one syntax for specifying chunks of data that can be passed to the server as a URL. If the server interprets the XPointers before returning the data, the transmission of a great deal of unnecessary information may be ignored. Extended link groups will work well in this structure, taking advantage of the ALL value for the instance argument. Using these structures, the client can send the server a very precise description of exactly the document parts it needs.

Creating servers that can efficiently handle these requests will require a significant change in the way documents are stored. Traditional file systems keep XML serially (e.g., retrieving the content of the second-last element of a document requires retrieving the entire document, parsing it, and extracting the second -last element). This produces enough overhead that the administrators of many busy servers might prefer to just let the client application handle the processing—until, of course, they run short of bandwidth because their server is transmitting excessive amounts of lightly used information.

Fortunately, a more efficient solution has recently reached commercial viability, with Informix, IBM, and others offering products. Although still complex, carrying a steep learning curve, object-relational databases are capable of handling precisely these kinds of requests efficiently. Object-relational databases provide hierarchical structures (i.e., they correspond neatly to XML's nested elements) that can be retrieved, searched, and processed quite easily. If you haven't worked with object-relational databases before, it's probably not worth your effort to run out and buy one for your server. It will take much coding to make the translations between XML documents and the database smooth, and it's probably a task better left to vendors. XPointer-enabled servers that can process requests for chunks efficiently are probably not too far off. Several firms in the SGML and HTML worlds already provide object-relational tools. Inso, a participant in the XSL proposal and DOM working group, uses an object-relational database as the foundation for its DynaBase HTML site management tool, for example.

Pure object databases, like POET and Jasmine, offer developers more appropriate—though perhaps more difficult—object databases.

Extending the Browser

XML has so far seen only limited application in browsers. CDF files are valid XML documents, and Microsoft has included two XML parsers (one written in Java, one in C++) with Internet Explorer, but so far the focus of the browser vendors has been strictly on XML for use by metadata applications. The SGML community has embraced XML for documents more throughly, although with some reservations about the simplifications it has made. Whether or not XML is a replacement for HTML, it seems likely that browsers will soon be able to present XML documents using at least the CSS toolkit already available for HTML. The continuing efforts of the W3C to create a DOM for both HTML and XML will eventually lead to the development of highly scriptable pages that combine content and function, giving XML another boost into the browser. In this chapter we'll examine the place the browsers may hold in the XML world, and the possibilities XML holds for making the browser model entirely obsolete.

This chapter is fairly abstract and not critical to XML implementation. Developers who need to make sites work but aren't especially interested in how the underlying architecture works are welcome to skip to the next chapter.

Anatomy of a Browser

Throughout this book, I've had to use XML parsers to demonstrate the structure of XML documents. Although they may seem primitive, these parsers are in fact at the foundations of browsers. Grossly simplified, browsers consist of four key parts: a communications engine that can send requests and receive information using HTTP and other network protocols, a parser that interprets that information, a presentation engine that displays the elements found by the parser, and an interface that controls user interaction with the information provided. A simple model of how a browser processes HTML documents appears in Figure 11.2.

The communications engine gets HTML files from Web servers and passes them to the parser, which breaks them down into a tree of discrete elements. The presentation engine examines the contents of those elements and formats them properly for the screen, downloading additional materials as necessary. The interface provides the browser window in which the document is displayed, with its menus, navigation aids, scroll bars, and other features. It handles user actions and opens new pages when necessary, which go through the same communications—parsing and processing.

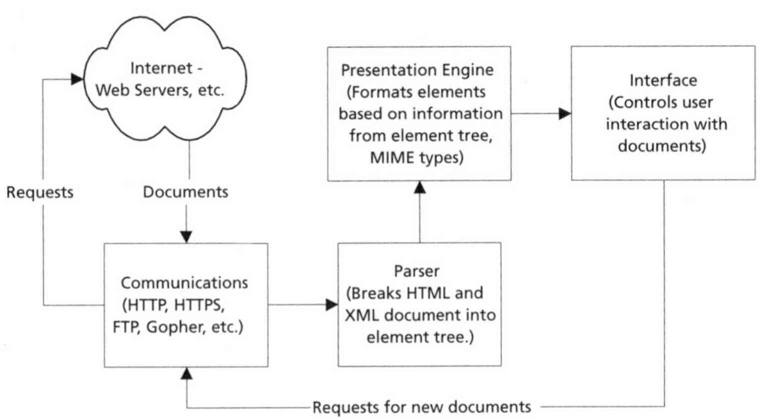

Figure 11.2 Basic browser structure.

Browsers right now are far more complicated than this simple model. They include scripting engines, style sheet interpreters, Java Virtual Machines, plug-in interfaces, and all kinds of graphics engines, along with an ever-growing number of attachments to provide mail, news, groupware, HTML editing, and other integrated features. The channel features described in Chapter 9 have added some extra overhead, as do the two separate parsers for XML that are available in Internet Explorer 4.0. Handling all those parts has exploded the browser out from its origins as a very small, simple program. Browsers now are growing as large as full-scale office applications, eating up more hard drive space and consuming more download time with every new version release.

Competition between the browser vendors has also changed the rules for parser, presentation, and interface: documents are becoming dynamic. We touched on this in Chapter 7, but its impact on the browser deserves more attention. Documents are no longer static entities incapable of changing after they've reached the browser. Scripts can add and remove elements, change their appearance, modify their contents, and move them around the screen. The parsing engine still reads in code as it arrives, but the resulting tree it produces is now open to manipulation and modification. Effectively, scripts have been given read and write access to the document tree, making possible a whole new category of browser-based interfaces.

For more information on early developments in dynamic documents, see my book *Dynamic HTML: A Primer* (MIS:Press, 1997).

The W3C is currently in the process of standardizing the competing approaches to this technique. The Document Object Model Working Group presented their first Level 1 Working Draft on October 9, 1997. Their abstract presents neatly the impact the Document Object Model will have on the simplified model presented in Figure 11.2:

> The Document Object Model (DOM) level one provides a mechanism for software developers and Web script authors to access and manipulate parsed HTML and XML content. All markup as well as any document type declarations are made available. Level one also allows creation "from scratch" of entire Web documents in memory; saving those documents persistently is left to the programmer. DOM Level one is intentionally limited in scope to content representation and manipulation; rendering, validation, externalization, etc. are deferred to higher levels of the DOM.

Our all-powerful parser serves to create only an initial state for the browser, after which the element tree it creates may be modified, reorganized, or even rebuilt. Our XML documents, and even their document type declarations, may change shape (which may cause problems, at least until higher levels of the DOM appear to clarify validation).

These developments are the latest stimulus for the continuing expansion of the browser. Netscape's long-held dream of creating a browser that provides a complete interface is on the verge of being realized, although Microsoft seems to have stolen the lead with Internet Explorer 4.0. The implications of this extreme new flexibility are enormous. The browser environment is reaching the point where it is rich enough to handle a variety of data presentation and processing jobs, most of which used to be the field of applications built with specialized client-server tools. Although it remains to be seen if the DOM will provide enough flexibility for developers to write a word processor in a browser, it certainly promises enough flexibility to make it possible to create far more powerful client interfaces than the forms we have at present.

XML in the Browser: Architectural Implications

All the tools described previously in the browser anatomy section are available today, if not in forms that fulfill the standards committees' specifications. Style sheets and dynamic documents are available in both Netscape and Microsoft browsers, although in different and incomplete implementations. Microsoft is using XML in its browser as well, although in a very limited way. Microsoft includes two scriptable parsers in Internet Explorer, but it still can't display XML directly on the screen, or style it with CSS. The preliminary steps they have taken are promising but don't nearly take advantage of XML's potential.

We'll start by looking at one of the first XML browsers, written by Peter Murray-Rust , a Java applet named Jumbo. Jumbo is the Java Universal Molecular (or Markup) Browser for Objects. Jumbo was written to handle Chemical Markup Language, an application of XML that uses markup to provide information on various molecules. Jumbo is written as a Java applet, making it a browser within a browser. Jumbo's main screen is quite simple, using drop-down boxes for menus and providing a visual representation of the element tree for users to navigate, as shown in Figure 11.3.

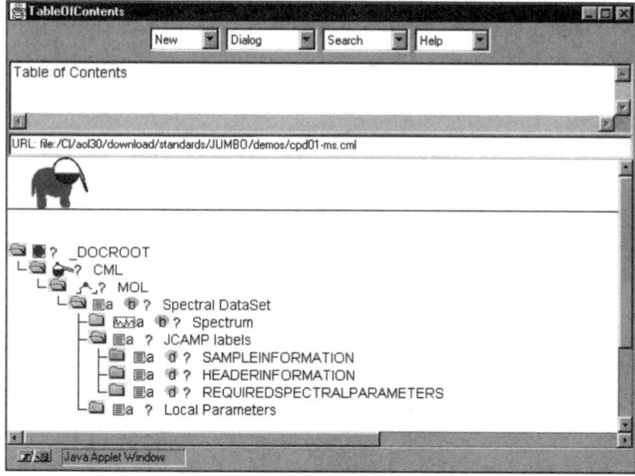

Figure 11.3 A CML file containing information about a molecular spectrum.

Clicking on the graph icon next to the word *Spectrum* fires up another window, a Java applet that displays a mass spectrum chart, as shown in Figure 11.4.

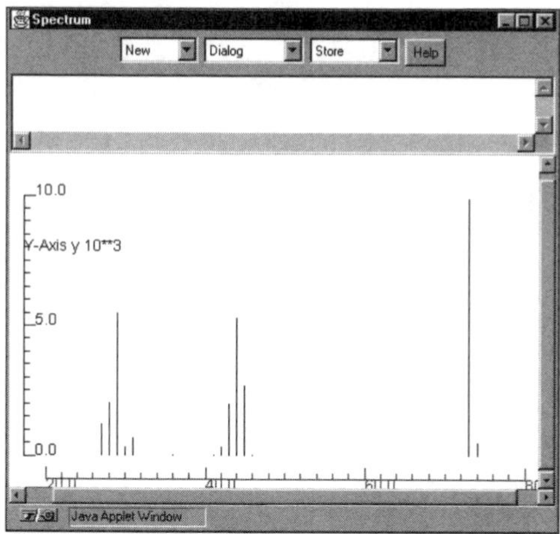

Figure 11.4 Mass spectrum chart displayed by Jumbo.

Other information is available in the same file; a graph displaying mass information, created by another Java applet, is shown in Figure 11.5.

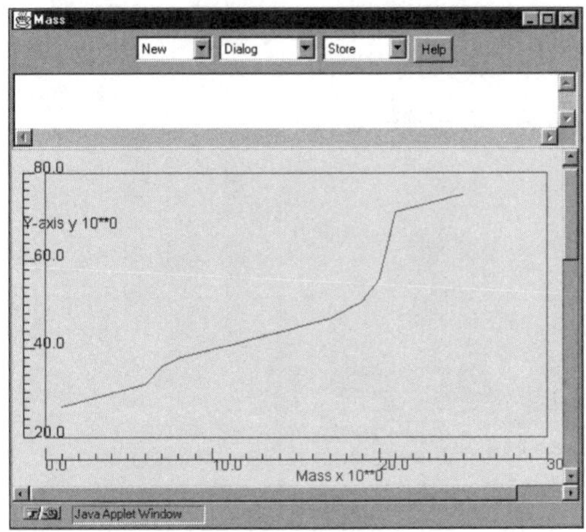

Figure 11.5 Mass chart displayed by Jumbo.

Although Jumbo was built to display chemical information, it is also quite capable of displaying other marked-up information. In Figure 11.6, Jumbo is displaying a small portion of the first scene of *Julius Caesar*.

Although Jumbo's interface isn't comparable to its HTML competitors, it's still an impressive achievement. Jumbo uses a relatively small set of core classes to process chemical information stored as markup and presents different views of those elements with small Java applets for graphs and other displays. The architecture is fairly simple: a parser, a tree display (the table of contents), and a set of Java applets that can present particular elements and sets of elements.

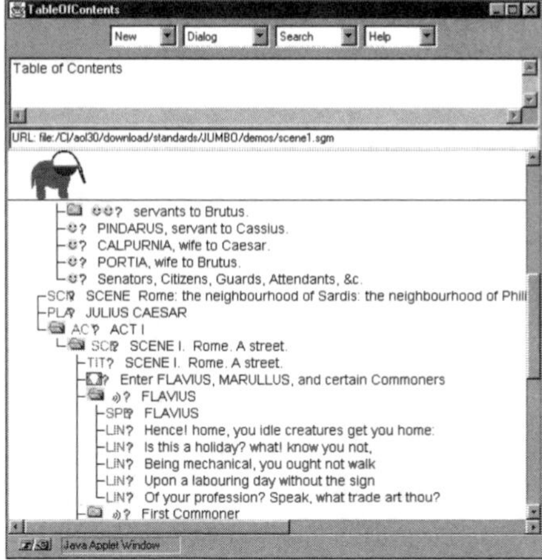

Figure 11.6 Shakespeare in XML, displayed by Jumbo.

Jumbo's architecture strongly suggests ways that XML could be used with current architectures to supplement the existing plug-in and object mechanisms for displaying content. Right now, all content that isn't images or markup must be declared using special tags—EMBED, APPLET, or OBJECT. Adding plug-ins to a browser isn't as smooth a process as it should be, and all these methods (with the possible exception of applets) expose users to the risk of damage from poorly written or malicious code. A more flexible architecture might allow users or documents to associate applets (or similar programs) with XML elements, providing element-specific processing either in the browser window or in separate pop-up windows. In this way, elements that just contain text can be displayed with the tools available for handling markup, while elements meant for further processing can receive it using tools they specify.

Implementing this architecture in the current browsers will undoubtedly create yet another arena in which the competing browser developers can built incompatible standards, APIs that refuse to interoperate, and code that works only with a particular browser. Still, XML itself includes a few features that could be useful for parts of this, like the NOTATION declaration. Even though using NOTATION to specify external viewers is rather obsolete in the age of the integrated browser, it may still have some use for XML as a mean of specifying external processing. A NOTATION declaration that links to a Java applet could be connected to an element with a #FIXED attribute, announcing to the browser that this element needs its own specified processing tool. In combination with other attributes specifying whether the element needs its own window or should be presented in-line, this could significantly ease the first steps of XML integration. The hard part will come in developing an API that allows the developers of those in-line presentation vehicles to negotiate size and location and to redraw with the browser.

Jumbo even goes so far as to allow users to pick their parsing engine! This kind of modularity promises enormous flexibility.

Breaking Down the Browser

Adding this kind of support for XML processors may have an unexpected side effect on the browser. Opening the browser to external, in-line applications like this is a much more dramatic move than the earlier additions of plug-in architectures or even applets. The browser would be able to become much less integrated, reversing the trend of piling more and more applications into the same "browser" space. In this scenario, the browser is reduced to a communications engine and a parser, along with a framework that allows different applications to communicate and modify the element tree. The browser could still provide the interface services, if needed, and a basic set of tools for displaying text, but even those could be "outsourced" to other applications. Branding this browser and selling it would be a far harder task than marketing the current batch of integrated browsers, but it may be the logical final destination of browser development.

In this possible browser future, the presentation and interface aspects of the browser would be taken over by other applications (even miniapplications) that process elements. They would have their own presentation and interface structures, which the "browser" might continue to coordinate. Figure 11.7 provides a rough sketch of this possible browser architecture.

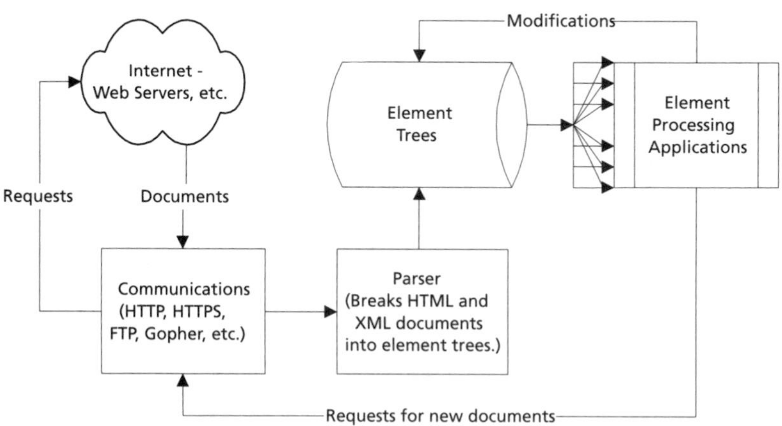

Figure 11.7 Multiapplication processing of parsed information.

In this model, much of the functionality that used to be in the browser is distributed across applications devoted to the processing of particular elements. They can all share a parser, a communications engine, and the same element tree, but the browser as a unit is unnecessary. The parser, engines, and element tree interface become browser services, rather than a distinct unit.

At this level, the much-discussed integration of operating system and browser is possible, although both disintegrate to a certain extent. An operating system is still needed to provide an environment for running these services, and several parts of the browser become even more important than they had been previously, but the element processing applications and the services for keeping them in sync provide a new area for applications and API development. The applications could be Java applets, ActiveX controls, or even COBOL programs—it doesn't really matter, as long as they can communicate with the element trees and with each other. The processing applications could use Java's Abstract Windowing Toolkit or the upcoming Java Foundation Classes, Microsoft's Win32, or the Mac OS Toolbox. The model could work as well in any of those systems, or even an entirely new system, provided it allowed for the communication and coordination between the growing number of parts.

Why would anyone want this Hydra-headed replacement for the friendly browser? It offers a number of advantages. First, although it is actually built out of a large number of different parts, it doesn't need to look any different to the user. A single browser window could still coordinate all these parts (and provide a nice home for a company logo). Second, it provides parsing services to a large number of potential processing applications without requiring every application to include its own parser. It provides a single interface for parsing services, allowing developers to build to a browser services API rather than choosing a parser, licensing it, and writing code that fits the parser.

This may muddy the operating systems/graphical user interface/browser waters even more than Microsoft already has, but their systems work on a somewhat different model. At present, Windows programs can use Internet Explorer as an Active X control, and Internet Explorer can provide a home for Active X controls and their data. This could, if developed further by Microsoft, develop into the shared browser services model described previously, but for now Internet Explorer remains in practice a collection of programs that communicate internally with each other as pieces but communicate to external programs as a unit. Microsoft certainly seems intent on piling as much of its browser into the operating system as possible, so this may change rapidly. Microsoft's clients grow ever larger, demanding more resources by the year.

Browser services, as defined in this abstract model, are in my mind better suited to a less overgrown environment than Windows, an environment built on a set of standard set of shared and manipulable class libraries rather than a set of APIs. As Jon Bosak of Sun Microsystems has stated in his white paper *XML, Java, and the Future of the Web* (available at http://sunsite.unc.edu/pub/sun-info/standards/xml/why/xmlapps.htm), "XML gives Java something to do." Java is already built on a standard set of class libraries, complete with network interfaces that already provide the functionality of the communications engine shown previously. The JavaBeans standard that arrived with Java Developer's Kit 1.1 provides mechanisms for applications and applets to communicate, providing direct channels of communication between large numbers of objects.

Although not a JavaBean, Microsoft's validating Java XML parser provides (ironically) an example of how easy it is to create parser components in Java and to make them accessible to other Java programs as well. All the parsing examples demonstrated so far have only called MSXML from the command line and accepted its output as text. Java applications can use MSXML as an all-purpose parser, reading elements through an object structure created by the parser. Despite its lack of interest in following Sun's direction on Java, Microsoft has produced a parser that Java developers can use as the foundation of an XML toolkit. (As of October 1997, the source code is available and the licensing is not too restrictive.) Perhaps in a few years the Network Computers (NCs) proposed by Sun, Oracle, IBM, and others will still be running Microsoft code—but as a parser, not as an operating system.

XML and the Future of the Browser

The scenario portrayed here is only one of many possibilities for the browser. Centralized browser services may never come to pass because the XML standard is simple enough that the extra work of building (or just including) a parser isn't that heavy. XML applications and HTML may well stay in their own compartments, occupying different parts of the programming world. HTML may continue to dominate the presentation side of the Web, whereas XML will provide infrastructure for data transfer services only.

Even though many HTML developers might prefer that XML stay in a separate world of Web services (if only to avoid yet another learning curve), it doesn't seem likely. XML is a drastic change from the HTML model, but it remains close enough to seem familiar. HTML developers who have spent years trying to interpret the latest tags from Netscape and Microsoft can now focus on creating their own tag systems and accompanying style sheets without needing to be as tightly bound to a single set of rules. Client-server developers who have struggled with complex tools but haven't been able to make the Web do what they need may see XML with the accompanying document object model as their best option. XML, style sheets, and Java all have their own sets of rules (of course), but the additional flexibility they allow should convince several different groups to converge on this new standard for data interchange. With any luck, the new standard in data interchange will drive changes in the tools we use to read, write, process, and share that data as well.

CHAPTER 12

XML and the Future: Site Architectures

Even though it's clear that XML's adoption will require some significant changes to the basic infrastructure of the Web, its impact on the structures of sites remains less clear. The W3C's positioning of XML in the Architecture Domain leaves open many questions about what XML is really for. So far, XML has mostly seen use as a standard used to define other standards—MCF, CDF, RDF, and WIDL, among others, which in turn define other files. XML's eventual position in the world of the Web is not yet clear. Concluding our exploration of XML's potential, we'll survey its implications for the development of Web sites.

Current Web Site Architectures

When the Web first appeared, sites had extremely simple structures, modeled after the hierarchical models of its predecessors, FTP and Gopher. All requests for files referred to actual files, stored in the file system of the server. URLs corresponded to a subset of the file structure on the server, and answering requests was a matter of finding the right file, adding an appropriate header, and sending it back to the browser that requested it. Hyperlinks contained the URL information, allowing developers to create crazy quilts of HTML without having create crazy quilt file structures. Directory structures were the most commonly used organizational tool in the early days, allowing developers to create somewhat structured sites.

As the demand for more up-to-date information has exploded across the Web, many sites have turned to database-driven sites. Tools like CGI, Cold Fusion, Active Server Pages (ASP), and LiveWire put attractive front ends on information stored in relational database systems and even legacy mainframes. Database-generated pages make sites like the FedEx tracking page possible, but are also used for many pages that seem like ordinary HTML. Visitors to the Microsoft site, for example, will encounter many pages created with ASP. Microsoft uses a database system in the background to manage data used on many of its pages, allowing it to make changes quickly.

Database-driven sites power many intranets as well, allowing employees to tap into data sources once locked in cold rooms guarded by protective MIS staff. Groupware and communications software have metamorphosed into Web applications. Lotus Domino's transition from Notes server to Web server was a notable change, providing instant translation of Notes-formatted documents into Web pages. The complex data structures behind Notes have applications on the public as well as the private Web, and Domino has moved out from behind the corporate firewall to power a few Internet servers.

There are several problems with database-driven sites, however. First, they tend to require more horsepower to overcome the overhead of connecting to a database—or the database server may need more horsepower to handle the increased demand placed on it. Second, database-driven sites are rarely search engine-friendly; most of them in fact put up "Do not enter" signs with the robots.txt file discussed in Chapter 7. Although the information contained in the database is probably well-structured and easily searchable, there's no easy way for a search engine to connect to a database and collect structured data. (It would probably indicate an enormous security hole as well.) Finally, complex database-driven sites usually require a fairly dedicated team of developers to build applications that can manage the database in addition to the usual team of HTML developers, adding considerable expense to a Web project.

Even though database-driven sites have taken advantage of the processing power of the server, the client side has received a boost with the release of version 4.0 of both the Netscape and Microsoft browsers. Both browsers offer significant improvements in interface control and contain enough tools for some data processing (usually in Java, but also in JavaScript or VBScript) to take place on the client. Microsoft's Internet Explorer 4.0 even includes controls that permit the browser to connect directly to back-end databases, although clearing security for this requires getting past many roadblocks.

The slow spread of Cascading Style Sheets and dynamic HTML has also had an impact on site architecture. It's becoming more common for certain aspects of Web design to become centralized. Style sheets in this model can be controlled at one location, allowing the company to provide a basic look for their sites that can then be modified. Dynamic HTML interfaces can be stored as JavaScript code files or as Microsoft's new scriptlets, which combine scripting with HTML to create reusable interface controls.

HTML documents today are far more than text with markup. Currently, the roster of items that can appear in Web pages includes

- HTML
- Images (GIF, JPEG, PNG, XBM, etc.)
- Sounds (AIFF, AU, WAV, etc.)
- Video (QuickTime, MPEG, AVI, etc.)
- Specialized Plug-in Content (Splash, Shockwave, Acrobat, etc.)
- JavaScript
- VBScript (Internet Explorer only)
- Java applets
- ActiveX controls (Internet Explorer only)

The Web is already a rich programming environment, with constantly improving tools for programming and presentation. Many people, including Web developers, would argue that the Web is complex enough as it is without adding another layer of complication. Adding XML (and all its associated standards) to the Web may be, from this perspective, unnecessary.

Transitional Architectures

XML is definitely creeping up on the Web. Although Microsoft's Internet Explorer 4.0 now includes two XML parsers, XML documents can be addressed only through scripts and programming, and aren't presented as part of the regular browser interface. Figure 12.1 shows the latest Microsoft XML demo, a JUMBO-like tree interface to XML documents that is accessible as an applet to Internet Explorer 4.0.) This leaves XML with data-handling duties, not document handling duties.

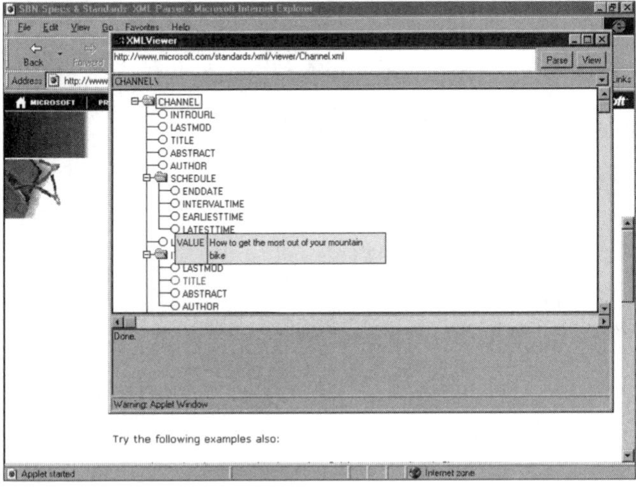

Figure 12.1 Tree interface for MSXML in Internet Explorer 4.0.

Despite the lack of support for XML in the browser window, XML is still useful for a number of tasks in Internet Explorer 4.0. Microsoft has presented several demonstrations (available at http://www.microsoft.com/standards/xml/xmlparse.htm#demos) that use the XML Data Source Object and scripting to create formatted HTML documents based on XML documents. Even though the slow speed and complexity of this process limit its applicability to small projects, Microsoft has taken some first steps toward making XML available in the browser. Figure 12.2 shows one example of the kinds of pages made possible by this combination of scripting and parsing: a weather page that presents forecasts for cities chosen by the user.

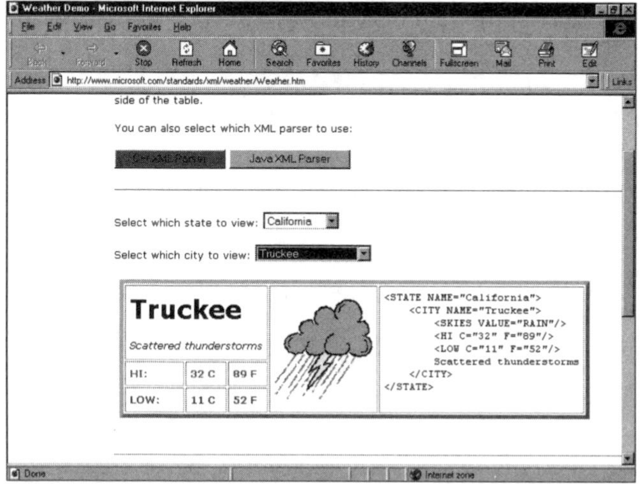

Figure 12.2 XML weather forecasting, scripted into HTML.

In additional to the C++ and Java parsers, Microsoft offers an XML data source object (written in Java) that can be used with Internet Explorer's data binding extensions to HTML. This approach is generally useful only when the XML data represents a table or other similarly structured data se because the original implementations of data binding were targeted at relational databases and their weaker cousins, delimited text files. While the XML data source object may provide enough power for some simple applications, it lacks the flexibility of the parsers. (For more information on the Microsoft XML DSO, visit http://www.microsoft.com/standards/xml/dso/xmldso.htm.)

Even though these transitional tools are useful, they suffer from certain limitations. First of all, even though they are written in Java, successful implementation of these tools is currently possible only with Microsoft's Internet Explorer 4.0 because the supporting technologies (data binding and dynamic HTML) are not yet generally accepted standards. Even if Netscape comes out with similar tools, the odds are excellent that they will have similar limitations. It might be possible to use the same XML files with both browsers, but the surrounding programming that presents the documents will need to be customized for each browser.

Secondly, these tools treat XML documents in an extremely limited context. Although XML documents can now be addressed through an object model, that object model is completely distinct from the document object model the browser uses for HTML, and connecting the two models requires significant scripting effort. This scripting bridge stands in the way of using XML with style sheets (e.g., creating a wide range of viewable XML documents). It also makes using XML to build dynamic interfaces difficult because the document needs to be converted to HTML first and then manipulated again through script. The programming overhead for these translations (even if they work the same in Netscape and Microsoft products, an unlikely scenario) is still dramatic, requiring custom implementations of all but the simplest XML to HTML translations.

This translation also imposes unacceptable performance limitations on XML. Users have become accustomed to quick processing of HTML files. Loading a shell document, loading the XML document(s), parsing the document(s), and using a script to present the XML in HTML takes time, even on my 150 MHz Pentium. (On my 75 MHz Pentium, I can watch the scripts add the HTML almost step-by-step.) Although Java performance is hardly ideal, the performance of interpreted scripting languages is even poorer.

Finally, this implementation blocks the use of many of XML's finest features, notably linking. Using HTML as the interface precludes the application of any links beyond simple in-line links, and even those must be converted so that they can bring up shell HTML files that will in turn load and process the XML. Implementing multitargeted, multidirectional links in this scenario is probably not possible, unless a processor on the server takes over the task of reading in XML documents and spitting out HTML documents that are rough equivalents. Links that have more than one target will still cause some dramatic problems.

This limited architecture may have some promise as an interim solution, however. Microsoft has already applied it to the channels shown in Chapter 9, so many users are processing XML without even realizing it. Simple applications like CDF will continue to use these parsing applications without direct presentation to the screen because they were designed to operate this way from the start. Files that contain only metadata don't need direct presentation, and the issue discussed previously may or may not be applicable. Still, these metadata architectures are only one tiny part of XML's potential.

XML in the Browser: Implications

Whether or not the browser undergoes the dramatic transition I suggested in the previous chapter, the advent of XML document presentation in the browser will likely change the underlying architectures of many sites. The XML syntax itself and the XML-Linking specification will drive these changes in architecture and design, although in different ways. XML syntax promises to bring a Web where content, formatting, and script are separated from each other more distinctly than they have been in HTML, while XML-Linking will distinguish itself by providing richer interfaces and a chunk model for document retrieval.

As we saw at the very beginning of the book, XML's development has been based on a firm belief in the separation of markup and formatting information. The early XML community also continues the SGML tradition of the separation of document content from processing. These two philosophical motivations have concrete implications for the future structuring of Web sites.

The move to separate content from formatting has already gained some impetus in the HTML world from the appearance of the Cascading Style Sheets recommendation and the key role it plays in both Netscape and Microsoft's implementations of dynamic HTML features. The most appealing aspect of Cascading Style Sheets to many designers is its ability to centralize style information, avoiding much of the repetitive work needed to create and update HTML pages. Style sheets are an automated version of the graphic designer's spec book, providing a smooth path for formatting to flow into documents without constant hand tweaking. CSS's advantages for programming are also becoming clear to programmers, providing a basic structure for formatting that can be applied to elements without as much concern for what kind of element the target of an operation is.

Although CSS is not an entirely adequate style sheet standard, lacking tables and a wide variety of structural tools that more advanced style tools will bring, it is an important first step. Its mechanisms are easily implemented with XML, requiring only minor additions to DTDs. Even if designers need to add style information to individual elements, CSS requires only the addition of a CDATA STYLE attribute to the elements that need styling. Even though XSL or another more sophisticated style tool may come and knock CSS off its throne, the CSS model allows developers to begin creating style sheets for XML documents and store formatting information separately from their content.

As this book was going to press, the W3C released a new set of specifications for CSS. This standard still has considerable life in it.

The relationship of XML to scripts is more complex. SGML purists seem puzzled, and occasionally offended, by the common mixture of scripts with markup that is common practice in the HTML world. Because of its use as an interface as well as a document presentation format, HTML has needed stronger, more flexbile tools than are commonly used in SGML environments. The introduction of the SCRIPT tag in Netscape 2.0 opened the floodgates for millions of documents that combine some amount of scripting with document information. The appearance of dynamic HTML has led to the creation of documents that contain complete interface structures (e.g., a program to handle opening and closing headings on an outline) as well as the content they display. More and more of these documents, in fact, are becoming incomprehensible without the scripts needed to make them work. Because of the often-close relationship between a script and the structure of a particular document (and the odd problems that can happen when transmission difficulties prevent the scripting file from loading properly), HTML scripters have tended to combine as much information as possible in a single file. Scripts are sometimes stored in separate files (using the SRC attribute or server-side includes), but usually this degree of separation is reserved for scripts that are used by multiple documents. Library files containing code used by multiple HTML documents are easier to manage than duplicate copies of code stored in 50 different files.

XML's advent will probably push many developers to begin separating code from content. XML's syntax is not friendly to SCRIPT elements, requiring CDATA-marked sections for any code that includes markup characters, as discussed in Chapter 7. Even if developers can cope with these requirements, XML's status as a potential universal file format may further promote the separation of code from content. Probably not all processing applications will be script enabled, and some will need to ignore scripting content anyway. Separating script from content will reduce the load on these applications.

Changing from HTML's integrated model to XML's modularized architecture will cause some problems at first, although HTML developers have certainly had to learn to keep track of all the images, applets, controls, and other content material linked into documents. The change will require close examination of documents and their structures to determine what can profitably be shared across multiple documents. In an ideal case, a set of HTML documents that was stored as shown in Figure 12.3 could be reorganized in XML as shown in Figure 12.4.

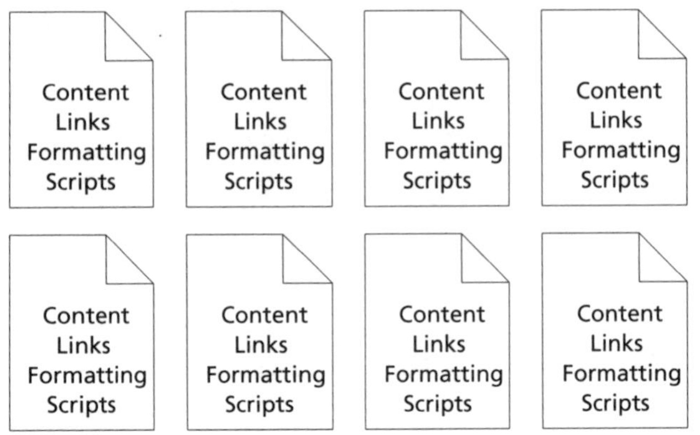

Figure 12.3 HTML's integrated model tends to keep content, links, formatting, and scripting in the same document.

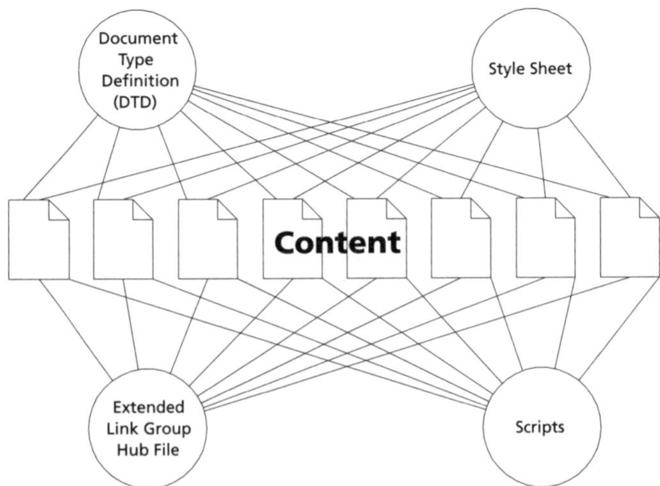

Figure 12.4 XML's linking structures and encouragement of modularity can break documents down into content and a set of shared components.

Keeping track of these relationships and making them work efficiently will require another generation of tools. At present, the Web-building tools available can keep up with HTML documents, graphics, and a few components, but few of them can manage scripts or style sheets this way, and extended linking groups have added an entirely new dimension to the task. Until the tools catch up, it's likely that developers will continue to mix and match content, format, script, and links, if only because it avoids the need for a librarian to keep track of all the parts.

Java applets and ActiveX controls will still play similar roles to the parts they play now, although they may be activated quite differently, as we saw in Chapter 11. Images, sounds, and other data files will also remain separate. The need for site organizers is, as always, on the rise.

XML-Linking's long-term impact on site architectures will probably be even greater. XML-Link makes it possible to split and combine documents in ways that get developers past the limitations of conventional file structures. Although taking full advantage of these abilities will require the server developments outlined in Chapter 11, chunking and linking offer developers a new way of thinking about their documents that makes the file-based systems of HTML seem as quaint as the the terminal interfaces of yesteryear. Because of their grounding in file systems, HTML documents have had to appear as complete units. Half an HTML file might occasionally be readable (as long as it isn't a table), but there's no way to download portions of files. As a result, most developers have leaned toward creating sets of smaller documents, which load more quickly but can become difficult to manage. Anyone who has had to print out documentation that was spread out over hundreds of HTML pages has encountered the limitations of this method first hand.

Chunking and linking make it possible to refer to parts of documents and embed them in other documents to create new documents. Chunking and linking have the potential to unseat many of the database-driven applications currently available, by making it easy for developers to reuse data and include it in multiple documents without needing to write custom applications. A catalog, for example, could store all its information in an enormous document that does nothing but keep track of items. The "pages" of the catalog could reference that catalog with XPointers to retrieve chunks based on attributes and content. As a result, templates could link to all the items on sale, all sporting goods, a particular deck of cards requested by a customer, or even all the items in the catalog by making the appropriate request. If the server was capable of handling chunks, all this information could be transferred appropriately, with only the needed items being sent.

Making chunking and linking work to full effect requires a whole set of enabling technologies: servers than can process XPointers efficiently to return appropriate chunks, browsers that can cope with the XML-Linking specification to allow embedding of linked content, and authoring tools that will help site managers keep track of the data stored in these new document structures. The revolution this can make possible is probably a few years off, if the speed at which HTML tools have been developed is any indication.

Web Structures as Application Architecture

Even though Web browsers have rapidly grown into a popular interface, they haven't yet been able to offer the kinds of services that users expect of their computers. The latest rounds of improvements to Web browsers and servers have beefed up the Web's claim to being a universal interface for all kinds of data. Although Java arrived several years ago, Java development is finally reaching the point where applets and Java applications are capable of competing with full-blown operating system-specific applications. Dynamic HTML and the DOM have made it possible to create polished interfaces inside of a Web browser that offer considerably more functionality than form fields, drop-down boxes, and clickable buttons and images. The scripting languages, particularly JavaScript, have grown up, acquiring object-oriented extensions and other improvements along their path from form validators to interface managers. In the midst of this explosive growth, XML has appeared to clean up the messes created by six years of rapid development and provide a firm foundation for all these technologies.

XML is not likely to make the browser a better interface for creating graphics editors or video games. XML is not the solution for every problem by any means. Still, XML is a better solution for projects from CAD/CAM (where it lets users exchange information) to document management to presentations to possibly even the worlds of word processing, spreadsheets, and databases. XML's structures are flexible enough to store relational database tables, spreadsheet information, and complex documents. Developing interfaces that will make writing XML documents as easy as reading them will take years of development and improvements in other key standards. Moving the Web from presentation engine to workhorse will require many more steps, and probably years of development. XML may find a "killer application" that moves it quickly to the fore, or it may need years of quiet infiltration.

Despite the challenges, however, XML seems likely to succeed. The SGML community has provided an initial base of applications and support, and the interest of key players like Microsoft, Netscape, and Sun promises it a bright future. So far the W3C has provided XML with a strong center, a place where these competitors can participate in discussions leading to common standards and prepare for their implementation. If XML continues to develop as it has, it should quickly find favor as the architecture that allows the Web to finally deliver on its promises of convenient, friendly, cheap, and interactive information access .

GLOSSARY

application Either a program that does something (formats, sorts, imports, etc.) with XML or a set of markup tags created with XML. HTML, for example, is an application of SGML, definable with an SGML DTD.

attribute A source of additional information about an element. Attribute values may be fixed in the DTD or listed as name-value pairs (name="value") in the start-tag of an element.

Cascading Style Sheets (CSS) A standard that provides formatting control over elements using information contained in <STYLE> tags and STYLE attributes. Less powerful than XSL, it nonetheless looks like it has a bright short-term future as the only style mechanism already recommended by the W3C and (partially) implemented in major browsers.

Channel Definition Format (CDF) An XML-based "push" standard that describes documents containing URL information along with descriptions, icons, and information on when the material should be automatically retrieved.

character data (CDATA) Information in a document that should not be parsed at all. This allows the use of the markup characters &, <, and > within the text, even though no elements or entities may appear in the section. CDATA declarations may appear in attributes, and CDATA-marked sections may appear in documents.

child element An element nested inside another element. In <FIRST><SECOND/></FIRST>, the SECOND element is the child element of the FIRST element.

chunk A portion of a document identified by an XPointer. A chunk may refer to one element and all its content (including subelements), a group of elements, or even a selection based on content.

document A "textual object." In HTML, documents (or "pages") were single files containing HTML. In XML, documents may contain content from several files or chunks and should included markup structures that make it valid or well-formed.

document object model (DOM) A means of addressing elements and attributes in a document from a processing application or script. The W3C has a Document Object Model Working Group that is developing a standard model for HTML and XML documents.

document type declaration In valid documents, the declaration that connects a document to its document type definition. The declaration may connect to an external file or include the definition within itself.

document type definition (DTD) A set of rules for document construction that lies at the heart of all SGML development and all valid XML document construction. Processing applications and authoring tools rely on DTDs to inform them of the parts required by a particular document type. A document with a DTD may be validated against the definition.

Document Style Semantics and Specification Language (DSSSL) A transformation and style language for the processing and formatting of valid SGML documents.

element The fundamental logical unit of an XML document. All content in XML documents must be contained within elements.

empty element An element that has no textual content. An empty element may be indicated by a start-tag and end-tag placed next to each other (<EMPTY></EMPTY>) or by a start-tag that ends with /> (<EMPTY/>). Empty elements may contain attributes only.

end-tag A tag that closes an element. An end-tag follows the syntax </Name>, where Name matches the element name declared in the start-tag.

entity A reference to other data that often acts as an abbreviation or a shortcut. By declaring entities, developers can avoid entering the same information in a document or DTD repetitively.

extended link A link that contains locator elements rather than a simple HREF attribute to identify the targets of the link.

extended link group A group of documents whose contents are analyzed for links to help establish two way links without requiring their declaration in every document.

Extensible Markup Language (XML) A standard under development by the W3C that provides a much simpler set of rules for markup than SGML, while offering considerably more flexibility than HTML.

Extensible Style Language (XSL) A style sheet standard submitted by Microsoft, ArborText, and Inso Corporation to the W3C. XSL allows developers to specify formatting far more precisely than Cascading Style Sheets permit. XSL seems promising, but is not yet a W3C working draft or recommendation.

external DTD subset The portion of a document type definition that is stored outside of the document. External DTDs are convenient for storing document type definitions that will be used by multiple documents, allowing them to share a centrally managed definition.

general entity An entity for use in document content. When used in documents, the name of a general entitity must be preceded by an ampersand (&) and should be followed by a semicolon (;).

Generalized Markup Lanugage (GML) The predecessor to SGML, developed in 1969 by IBM in efforts led by Charles Goldfarb. GML originated the use of <, >, and / for markup and is still in use for document applications.

Hypertext Markup Language (HTML) The most popular markup language in use today, HTML is an application of SGML. HTML is one of the foundations of web development, providing formatting and basic structures to documents for presentation via browser applications.

Hypermedia/Time-based Structuring Language (HyTime) A set of multimedia and linking extensions to SGML, formalized as ISO/IEC 10744-1992. HyTime is one of the foundations for XML-LINK.

Hypertext Transfer Protocol (HTTP) The protocol that governs communications between clients and servers on the World Wide Web. HTTP allows clients to send requests to servers, which reply with an appropriate document or an error message.

in-line link A link in which the element making the linking declarations is itself a part of the link.

instance The actual use of an element or document type in a document, as opposed to its definition. An instance may also refer to an entire document; a document may be an instance of a DTD if it can be validated under that DTD.

internal DTD subset The portion of a document type definition that appears inside the document to which it applies. Internal DTD subsets can be hard to manage, but provide developers an easy way to test out new features or develop DTDs without disrupting other documents.

ISO The International Organization for Standardization (the acronym is derived from its French name), which sets industrial standards relating to everything from character sets to quality processes to SGML.

markup Structural information stored in the same file as the content. Traditionally, structural information is separated from the content and isolated in elements (defined with tags) and entities.

markup declaration The contents of document type declarations, which are used to define the elements, attributes, entities, and notations. They specify the kinds of markup that will be legal in a given document.

Meta-Content Framework (MCF) A standard developed by Apple and continued by Netscape that represents metadata as a multidimensional space for user navigation.

name A name must begin with a letter or underscore and may include letters, digits, hyphens, underscores, and full stops. (Full stops in Latin character sets are periods.)

name characters Letters, digits, hyphens, underscores, and full stops. (Full stops in Latin character sets are periods.)

name token Any string composed of name characters.

notation An XML structure that identifies the type of content contained by an element and suggesting a viewer to present it.

out-of-line link A link in which the element definining the link is not itself a member of the set of targets defined by the link. Out-of-line links allow developers to declare links separately from the content of the document; out-of-line links may even appear in separate files.

parameter entity An entity used to represent information within the context of a document type definition. Parameter entities may be used to link the content of additional DTD files to a DTD, or as an abbreviation for frequently repeated declarations. Parameter entitities are distinguished from general entities by their use of a percent sign (%) rather than an ampersand (&).

parent element An element in which another element is nested. In <FIRST><SECOND/></FIRST>, the FIRST element is the parent element of the SECOND element.

parsed character data (#PCDATA) Parsed character data is text that will be examined by the parser for entities and markup. Parsed character data should not contain any &, <, or > characters; these need to be represented by the & <, and > entities, respectively.

parser An application that converts a serial stream of markup (an XML file, for example) into an output structure accessible by a program. Parsers may perform validation or well-formedness checking on the markup as they process it.

processing application An application that takes the output generated by a parser (it may include a parser, or be a parser itself) and does something with it. That something may include presentation, calculation, or anything else that seems appropriate.

processing instruction Directions that allow XML authors to send instructions directly to a processing application that may be outside the native capacities of XML. A processing intruction is differentiated from normal element markup by question marks after the opening < and before the closing > (i.e. <? instruction ?>). The XML declaration is itself a processing instruction.

prolog The opening part of a document, containing the XML declaration and and any document type declarations or markup declarations needed to process the document.

recursion A programming technique in which a function may call itself. Recursive programming is especially well-suited to parsing nested markup structures.

root element The first element in a document. The root element is not contained by any other elements and forms the base of the tree structure created by parsing the nested elements.

simple link A link that includes its target locator in an HREF attribute.

Standard Generalized Markup Language (SGML) The parent language of HTML and XML. SGML provides a complex set of rules for defining document structures. HTML uses structures defined under that set of rules, whereas XML provides a subset of the rules for defining document structures. SGML is formally standardized as ISO/IEC 8879—1986, although a series of later amendments have continued its development.

start-tag The opening tag that begins an element. The general syntax for a start-tag is <Name attributes>, where Name is the name of the element being defined, and attributes is a set of name-value pairs. All start tags in XML must either have end-tags or use the empty element syntax, <Name attributes/>.

style sheet A formatting description for a document. Style sheets may be stored in separate files from the documents they describe.

Unicode A standard for international character encoding. Unicode supports characters that are 2 bytes wide rather than the 1 byte currently supported by most systems, allowing it to include 65,536 characters rather than the 256 available to 1-byte systems. Visit http://www.unicode.org for more information.

valid A document is valid if it conforms to a declared document type definition (DTD) and meets the conditions for well-formedness. All elements, attributes, and entities must be declared in the DTD, and all data types must match their definition's requirements.

W3C The World Wide Web Consortium, the standards body responsible for many of the standards key to the functionality of the World Wide Web, including HTML, XML, HTTP, and Cascading Style Sheets. The W3C site includes the latest public versions of their standards as well as other information about the web and standards processes. Visit http://www.w3.org for more information.

well-formed A well-formed document may or may not have a DTD. Well-formed documents must begin with an XML declaration and contain properly nested and marked-up elements.

XML see eXtensible Markup Language

XML declaration The processing instruction at the top of an XML document. It begins with <?XML, includes a version identifier, required markup declaration, and encoding identifier, and closes with ?>. (The XML declaration may be case-sensitive at some point; the standard at present is unclear on this issue.)

XPointer A reference to a chunk of a document. XPointers use a syntax derived from the Text Encoding Initiative, modified to take into account the needs of the HTTP protocol for encoding URLs.

XSL see eXtensible Style Language

INDEX

E

F

G

H

I

J

K

L

M

N

S

T

U

V

W

X

Y

Remember—for the latest updates to this book, visit http://www.mispress.com/xml/. For the latest updates to the XML standards themselves, visit http://www.w3.org/xml/.